HOW TO READ THE BIBLE

HOW TO READ THE BIBLE

History, Prophecy, Literature—
Why Modern Readers Need to Know the Difference,
and What It Means for Faith Today

STEVEN L. McKENZIE

OXFORD
UNIVERSITY PRESS

2005

OXFORD
UNIVERSITY PRESS

Oxford University Press, Inc., publishes works that
further Oxford University's objective of excellence
in research, scholarship, and education.

Oxford   New York
Auckland   Cape Town   Dar es Salaam   Hong Kong   Karachi
Kuala Lumpur   Madrid   Melbourne   Mexico City   Nairobi
New Delhi   Shanghai   Taipei   Toronto

With offices in
Argentina   Austria   Brazil   Chile   Czech Republic   France   Greece
Guatemala   Hungary   Italy   Japan   Poland   Portugal   Singapore
South Korea   Switzerland   Thailand   Turkey   Ukraine   Vietnam

Published by Oxford University Press, Inc.
198 Madison Avenue, New York, New York 10016
www.oup.com

Oxford is a registered trademark of Oxford University Press

Library of Congress Cataloging-in-Publication Data
McKenzie, Steven L., 1953–
How to Read the Bible : history, prophecy, literature—why modern readers need to know the
difference, and what it means for faith today / Steven L. McKenzie.
p.   cm.
Includes bibliographical references.
ISBN-13: 978-0-19-516149-6   ISBN-10: 0-19-516149-1
1. Bible—Introductions.   2. Bible—Criticism, interpretation, etc.   I. Title.
BS475.3M38 2005   220.6—dc22   2005003875

3 5 7 9 8 6 4 2
Printed in the United States of America
on acid-free paper

ACKNOWLEDGMENTS

This book arises out of more than twenty years of trying to teach undergraduate college students to read the Bible in its historical, cultural, and literary context. My goal is to prod them toward more in-depth reading and analysis of biblical literature and to provoke them to critical evaluation of their preconceived ideas about it. I am grateful to my students for provoking me over the years both in formulating my understanding of the Bible and in expressing my ideas clearly.

John Van Seters first showed me the significance of genre for biblical study in a 1989 seminar on historiography, and I shall always be grateful to him for that and for his friendship. I am also grateful to his student, Kenton Sparks, for sharing portions of a manuscript he is preparing on literary genres in the Bible and the ancient world.

This is the second book I have published with Oxford University Press and I am indebted to their editorial and production staff for consistently efficient and cordial work. In particular, Cynthia Read's detailed critique of the manuscript proved indispensable.

I am especially fortunate to have several superb scholars and teachers in both Hebrew Bible and New Testament as colleagues. Ryan Byrne, Patrick Gray, John Kaltner, and Milton Moreland have been dialogue partners throughout the process of research, writing, and revision of this book. My most supportive dialogue partner has been my wife Aimee. The interest and enthusiasm she displayed in listening to me talk about the progress on each chapter was an enormous encouragement. To these, my dialogue partners, I dedicate this book.

CONTENTS

HOW TO READ THE BIBLE

JONAH AND GENRE

Satire is a sort of glass wherein beholders do generally discover everybody's face
but their own.   —Jonathan Swift, Preface to *The Battle of the Books*

What writing is. Telepathy, of course.   —Stephen King, *On Writing*

The thesis of this book is simple. It is that many—I would even venture to say
"most"—people who read the Bible misunderstand it. This is not exactly a novel
claim. I had a teacher once who was fond of saying that the Bible is bigger than
all of us. No one understands the Bible completely, but most readers of the Bible
fail to appreciate the true nature of its literature. I would add that the consequences of their misunderstanding can be devastating. I don't mean that they
can be spiritually devastating—as in the idea that misunderstanding the Bible can
lead to eternal damnation—but that they can be psychologically devastating—as
when an individual feels torn between abandoning faith because the Bible seems
unreasonable and untrue, or committing to a belief system that affirms the complete accuracy of the Bible in all matters despite reasonable indications to the
contrary. These are extreme reactions, but they illustrate the point that the question of what to do with the Bible is a real one for those people who want to hold
on to a faith that allows for a realistic view of the world.

Jonah: A Fishy Tale

The story of Jonah furnishes a good case in point. It is one of the Bible's best-
known stories. Every Sunday school child has heard about Jonah and the whale.

But Jonah is also one of the least-understood stories in the Bible. Its real message often gets lost amid the debate over whether the story actually happened. How, exactly, is the story to be understood? Is it history or some kind of fairy tale? Could a person really survive for three days and nights inside a whale? Some staunchly defend the possibility, while others ridicule it and dismiss the book—and in some cases the entire Bible—as a ridiculous fable or myth. But if Jonah is not history, what is its point?

A careful reading of the book of Jonah suggests that the misunderstanding arises from attempts to make it something that it is not. The story is full of humor, exaggeration, irony, and ridicule. These features indicate that the book was never intended to be read as history but was written as a kind of satire. No wonder it has been misunderstood! Trying to read the story as history can only lead to a failure to appreciate its true nature and to misconstrue its primary message. The treatment of Jonah that follows points out the many instances of exaggeration and the like and discusses how they work to make a satirical point. The translations of Bible passages in this book are mostly my own and are usually marked AT for "author's translation." Otherwise, they are taken from the New Revised Standard Version of the Bible and marked NRSV.

Outline

Jonah is comprised of two distinct halves, each introduced by the statement, "the word of Yahweh[1] came to Jonah" (1:1; 3:1) with the additional Hebrew word "again" or "a second time" occurring in 3:1. Jonah's prayers further divide each half in two.[2] Thus, the book falls into four principal scenes mostly corresponding to the four chapter divisions.

1. Jonah's call and flight

2. Jonah's psalm

3. Jonah's mission to Nineveh

4. Yahweh's lesson to Jonah

The symmetry between the two halves of the book shows Jonah to be a well-organized work of narrative literature. The symmetry is even clearer in the Hebrew numbering[3] The outline also shows that Jonah is the central character of the book and suggests that its contents revolve around the interactions between him and the other characters. An examination of the book's content by its four scenes will help to answer the questions raised earlier about its main point and how the details of the story relate to that point.

Jonah's Call and Flight

The book of Jonah begins, "The word of Yahweh came to Jonah, the son of Amittai." Jonah is one of the writings within the division of the Hebrew Bible known as the Prophets (Hebrew *Nevi'im*). More specifically, it is one of the works in the Book of the Twelve, also known as the Minor Prophets. Its beginning is both similar to and different from other prophetic books. The opening sentence is not like those found at the beginnings of most prophetic writings. It does not say "the word of Yahweh *that* came to Jonah." Rather, it launches right into the story: "The word of Yahweh came to Jonah, *saying . . .*"

This beginning already signals something unusual about the book of Jonah: it is a narrative, a story about the prophet rather than a collection of his sayings. It is not unusual for prophetic books to contain some biographical narrative. The first three chapters of Hosea, for example, relate intimate details of the prophet's marriage and family life. But prophetic books are generally collections of the oracles or speeches of the prophets. Jonah is the opposite, being nearly all narrative. There is only one oracle in Jonah (3:4), and it is very brief.

Some other prophetic books, such as Haggai and Zechariah, begin kind of like Jonah by launching directly into a narrative. Haggai and Zechariah both begin their narratives with a dating formula: "In the X year of such-and-such ruler," but Jonah does not begin with such a formula. The author does not explain when Jonah lived or worked or give any additional details about his life. The book never even calls him a prophet. The only additional information about Jonah comes from 2 Kings 14:25. In 2 Kings we learn that Jonah, the son of Amittai, was a prophet who lived during the time of King Jeroboam II of Israel (approx. 786–746 BCE). He was from a town called Gath-Hepher in Israel, and he prophesied the enlargement of a portion of Israel's northern border under Jeroboam. The absence of such details, especially the lack of chronological information, from the book of Jonah suggests that the author deemed the specifics about the historical setting of the story as unimportant.

One other significant feature of the story of Jonah related to its first verse has to do with the meanings of his name and that of his father. "Jonah" means "dove" in Hebrew. Perhaps this suggests something about Jonah's character in the story— that he was flighty and unstable like a dove. The dove is also sometimes used in the Bible as a symbol for Israel (Hos 7:11). So it may be that Jonah, the "dove," is meant to symbolize Israel or an attitude or characteristic prevalent in Israel. His father's name, Amittai, derives from the Hebrew root meaning "truth" or "faithfulness." Here is the first irony in the book. Jonah, the "son of truth," is hardly a model of faithfulness in the story. The meanings of his and his father's names may be at least part of the reason that Jonah was chosen as the "hero" of this satirical tale.

Continuing the story, Yahweh commands Jonah to go to "the great city" of Nineveh and to "cry out" against it because of its wickedness. If reading Jonah as history, the reference to Nineveh raises a chronological problem. Nineveh came to prominence as the capital of the Assyrian empire in the seventh century (the 600s) BCE, long after the Jonah of 2 Kings 14:25. In fact, by the time Nineveh became the capital, the nation of Israel had ceased to exist. The Assyrians themselves brought an end to the kingdom of Israel by destroying its capital, Samaria, in 721 BCE and taking many of its citizens into captivity from which they would never return (see 2 Kings 17). Thus, the role of Nineveh in the book of Jonah appears to be an anachronism.

The occurrence of an anachronism in Jonah is a problem only if the story of Jonah is history or if one assumes that it is. It is not a problem, though, if Jonah is some kind of story, such as a satirical parable, in which the characters represent an attitude or even a larger class of people. Nineveh might have been chosen by the author of Jonah as the embodiment of the evil foreign city precisely because it once served as the Assyrian capital. Assyria, in turn, had likely come to symbolize the foreign "evil empire" ever since it destroyed Israel in 722 BCE. This is the role that Nineveh and the Ninevites play in the story of Jonah, in order to make the point that if God cares for them, God cares for everyone.

The Ninevites and Jonah complement each other in their respective roles in the book of Jonah. Jonah the prophet lived in Israel in the eighth century at the time the Assyrian empire was on the ascent and before its destruction of Israel. Nineveh was not yet the Assyrian capital at the time Jonah lived and would become so only in the following century. The author of Jonah, writing several centuries later, may not have known that it was not actually the capital during Jonah's lifetime. But this did not matter, since the author was not trying to write history.

Jonah's response to God's command is surprising on several levels. He boards a ship in order to flee toward Tarshish. Nineveh lay northeast of Israel in the modern country of Iraq. Tarshish, on the southern coast of Spain (modern Tartessos), represented the westernmost extreme of the known world for the writer of Jonah and his audience. In essence, therefore, Jonah heads in the opposite direction from where God tells him to go.

This part of the story again presents some historical problems that indicate that the author lived long after Jonah's time. The reference to Joppa as Jonah's port of embarkation is odd, since Joppa was in Philistine hands, not Israelite, in the eighth century. Also, the Phoenician port of Tyre was closer to Jonah's northern Israelite hometown of Gath-hepher than was Joppa. These problems of detail do not impede the point of the story and are not of much consequence unless one insists on trying to read it as history.

More surprising for the reader is Jonah's response in the first place. Prophets are messengers from God, and "Crying out" is what prophets do. They are privy to special divine revelation and go where the divine word sends them. Then they utter God's judgments against people in hopes of bringing them to repentance. Not Jonah. He does just the opposite, blatantly disobeying a direct order from God. To anticipate the story, Jonah, the prophet, whom the reader expects to be Yahweh's closest servant, is the only one of all the characters in the story—human and nonhuman—who fails to obey God. Jonah is a very unusual prophet indeed!

The narrative twice uses the expression "from the presence of Yahweh," making it clear that Jonah is trying to *run away* from God. The statement that he paid the *ship's* hire, rather than *his* hire or fare, may even mean that he was in such a hurry that he chartered the ship. (This also makes his choice of Joppa all the more strange since it was not the closest port.) Why exactly does Jonah flee? What is he running away from? What does he fear? The writer will have Jonah explain his actions later on in the story when he sees the people of Nineveh repent.

Whatever the motive for Jonah's response, his attempted flight makes no sense in his own belief system. On board, he boasts to the sailors that he worships (lit. "fears") Yahweh "who made the sea and the dry land" (1:9). If he really believes that Yahweh is the Lord of land and sea, how can he hope to run away? His actions are nonsensical. His deeds do not correspond either to his expressed beliefs or to the expectations for his vocation as a prophet. Jonah is a contradictory character, who does not act in accordance with what he claims to believe. The author paints him as foolish, even deluded—a ridiculous character. The story gradually reveals what it is that makes Jonah a ridiculous figure and that blinds him to the foolishness of his deeds.

Yahweh reacts to Jonah's flight by hurling a "great wind" and a "great storm" against the ship where Jonah is a passenger. This is part of a rather unusual view of God in Jonah. Yahweh is depicted as a real micromanager, personally involved in every facet of the story. These are the second and third uses (in addition to the reference to Nineveh as a great city) of the word "great" in Jonah. There will be other "greats" in Jonah, notably the famous "great fish." The frequent use of "great" is a mark of the book's penchant for hyperbole. The storm is so severe that the ship is on the verge of breaking up. The Hebrew literally says that the ship "thought about" breaking up. The idea is silly; inanimate objects don't think. But images like this one occur repeatedly in Jonah and are a sure sign that the book was not written as history.

Another laughable image follows immediately. With the ship in grave danger, everyone on board prays fervently. Everyone, that is, except Jonah. He is asleep in the hold, completely oblivious to the weather and the peril of the ship. The Hebrew verb (נרדם, *nirdam*) means to sleep soundly or deeply; the Greek translation even adds the detail that he is snoring! Though humorous, the scene also suggests how far out of touch with God's activity Jonah has become.

The sailors contrast with Jonah—they are more in tune with God, more righteous than Jonah, and they immediately sense the hand of the divine in the storm. They are not monotheists or worshippers of Yahweh; they have different gods but are religious men, who turn immediately to prayer. They throw the ship's cargo overboard and thus do away with any economic gain they might have hoped for from the voyage; in doing so they exhibit their respect for human life over material gain. Even after the ship's captain awakens Jonah with a request that he pray for deliverance from the storm, there is no mention of any prayer on Jonah's lips. Ironically, the man of God is the only person on board the ship who does not pray.

The sailors perceive that the sudden storm is no coincidence but is a divine response to something someone on the ship has done. They cast lots in order to discern who the responsible party is. Lot casting was something like drawing straws and occurs elsewhere in the Bible as a way for Yahweh to designate a person who is guilty of breaking a commandment (Achan in Josh 7:10–21) or an oath (Saul in 1 Sam 14:24–46). The sailors believe that the lot will be divinely guided to pick out the culprit whose disobedience caused the storm to be sent. The lot falls on Jonah, and it is understood that Yahweh has guided its outcome. In response to the sailors' questioning, Jonah arrogantly boasts about his national origin and his religion, "I am a Hebrew. I worship (lit. "fear") Yahweh, the God of heaven, who made the sea and the dry land."

This response seems calculated to enhance the sailors' estimation of Jonah's importance as well as their fears. They do indeed become more afraid—literally, they "feared with *great* fear." Jonah's confession comes as a revelation to the sailors; he has already told them that he is fleeing from Yahweh, but apparently they did not know who Yahweh was. Now that Jonah reveals that Yahweh is the supreme God, the sailors are terrified. The confession, however, also makes clear just how ridiculous Jonah's attempt to run away from Yahweh is. How can he possibly hope to escape the presence of the Maker of both land and sea? The sailors' question, "What is this that you have done?" shows their recognition of the foolishness and irrationality of Jonah's actions. Jonah claims to *fear* Yahweh but disobeys and tries to run away, and it is the non-Israelite mariners who are the true *fearers* of God.

The sailors ask what they should do to Jonah in order to quiet the increasingly tempestuous sea. Jonah tells them to pick him up and throw him overboard. One might expect hardened men like sailors to do just that—with pleasure—especially since their own lives are in peril. Besides, Jonah clearly thinks that he is superior to them and no doubt has as little regard for their lives as he does for all the other people in the book. Yet the sailors, as moral men, are reluctant to harm Jonah. Instead, they do everything possible to save him. They have already thrown the cargo overboard, and now they try hard to row the ship back to shore. It is only as a last resort and with great regret that they toss Jonah into the sea. Even then, they first pray to Yahweh (instead of their gods) asking him not to hold them accountable for Jonah's life.

The sea halts its fury at the moment it engulfs Jonah. The word here (זעף, zā'af) typically refers to raging anger or vexation, so that the story again ascribes a human attribute to an inanimate object. Also, for a second time "great fear" is attributed to the sailors. This time the text explicitly states that they fear Yahweh, to whom they now sacrifice and make vows. In other words, they are instantly "converted" into worshippers of Yahweh. The "pagan" sailors, in short, have a greater regard for human life than does Jonah and are also more pious.

Jonah's Psalm

Next comes the best known and most controversial part of the story. Yahweh, the micromanager, has appointed a "great fish" to swallow Jonah and keep him in its belly for three days and nights. The text never actually identifies the fish as a whale, though most readers have assumed that a whale is what the writer had in mind, since it would have been the only "fish" large enough to swallow a human. Some have pointed out that a whale is not a fish, but that in itself well illustrates the point of this book—the tendency of modern readers to try to read the Bible on their terms instead of those of the Bible's authors and original audience. The latter were unaware of the scientific differences between mammals and fish, so those kinds of modern, technical issues are irrelevant as far as the story of Jonah is concerned.

There is another detail in the text, however, that suggests the deliberately farcical nature of the story: It uses two slightly different words for "fish."[4] Both words stem from the same Hebrew root, but the word in Jonah 2:1 is masculine, while the one in 2:2 is feminine. In 2:11 it is again masculine. There is no explanation for these changes from a historical or biological standpoint that makes any sense. The best explanation lies in the nature of the story as a satire with its many deliberately exaggerated and nonsensical features. Considering the nature of the Jonah story, the idea of someone being inside a large fish for three days is just as ridiculous as the idea that the fish changes gender. Whether such a thing is actually possible is irrelevant. The whole story is intended to be preposterous because its very purpose is to make fun of Jonah and his attitude.

The entire scene now becomes even more comical. Trapped inside of the fish, Jonah finally prays. Jonah's prayer is actually a hymn of thanksgiving and as such is not entirely appropriate to his situation.[5] Here is the wayward prophet, who is not exactly the grateful type, intoning a rousing hymn of thanks inside of a large fish. The humorous image that this chapter conjures up may be precisely the reason that the psalm was included.

The original setting of the psalm was apparently its author's survival of a "near death" experience. The psalmist says that he cried out to Yahweh from the belly of Sheol. "Sheol" is the Hebrew name for the underworld or place of the dead, also called the "Pit" later in the poem. The Hebrew term for "belly" here is different from the word used for the belly of the fish, though they are both translated the same in the New Revised Standard Version (NRSV). Even so, the reference to Jonah being in the "belly" of Sheol easily brings to mind his predicament in the recesses of the fish. Another image for death used in the poem is that of drowning, and it also reminds one of Jonah's situation. Still, even though Jonah has not drowned in the sea, he does not yet know that he will survive his ordeal in the fish. Thus, the psalm of thanksgiving is inappropriate because it is premature.

There are other differences between Jonah's situation and that reflected in the psalm. It is Yahweh in the psalm, rather than the sailors, who throws the psalmist into the sea. There is no mention of the fish or any of the circumstances that landed Jonah there in the psalm. The references to Yahweh's "house" or "temple" are also inappropriate to Jonah's situation; the temple was in Jerusalem, the capital of Judah, while Jonah was from the kingdom of Israel. The condemnation of idol worshippers as forsaking their loyalty fits ill with the story in Jonah, since the foreigners, who presumably worship idols, are more faithful and obedient to Yahweh than Jonah. The mention of sacrifice at the temple also presupposes a setting on land rather than in the fish's interior. The vow mentioned at the end of the poem ("and what I have vowed I will pay") is presumably occasioned by the psalmist's restoration . . . of which there is no mention yet in the story of Jonah.

Despite the inappropriateness of the psalm to Jonah's situation, the scene in the belly of the fish furthers the story and the characterization of Jonah by what it does *not* say. There is no indication on Jonah's part of any regret for his disobedience and failure to carry out God's order. In spite of his experience in the fish, he remains obstinate and unrepentant. The humor of this scene continues. In what must be intended as a wry twist, after three days Yahweh speaks to the fish. The idea of the Almighty personally addressing a fish is comical enough, and adding to the comedy is what Yahweh tells the fish to do. We have a saying that "Fish and guests stink after three days." Both Jonah and the great fish agree, though for different reasons. Following Yahweh's command, the fish spews (lit. "vomits") up the distasteful prophet.

Jonah's Mission to Nineveh

Yahweh tells Jonah a second time to go to Nineveh, and this time he goes. He has at least learned that he cannot run away from the Maker of sea and dry land—something that was already quite obvious to the non-Israelite sailors. Nineveh is called an exceedingly large city, literally, "a great city to God." The further specification, "a three days' walk across," (NRSV) indicates an enormous city indeed. Although the expression alone is ambiguous, its reference to diameter is evident from the statement that Jonah walks a day's journey into the city. Figuring twenty miles as the approximate distance that one can walk in a day, this would mean that Nineveh was sixty miles across—huge even by modern standards! In fact, the figure is exaggerated beyond any semblance of reality and can only be considered hyperbole. This is another problem for a historical reading of the book. The location of ancient Nineveh was identified and excavated well over a century ago. At its height, the city had a circumference of only about 7.75 miles; at its widest point it was about three miles across—nowhere near the size that Jonah attributes to it.[6] Again, the discrepancy is only a problem if one attempts to read Jonah as history. This kind of exaggeration is to be expected, however, in satire.

Entering a day's walk into the heart of Nineveh, Jonah utters a terse oracle consisting of only five words in Hebrew: "Forty days from now Nineveh will be overturned" (עוד ארבעים יום ונינוה נהפכת, 3:4). There is no indication in the text that he repeats the message. Rather, he apparently turns abruptly and leaves. Again, his behavior is out of character for a prophet (remember that prophets "cry out") and reflects his stubbornness. Other prophets deliver extended oracles full of colorful language and vivid metaphors. Jonah does the bare minimum, nothing more. The reason for this terseness is simple. Unlike every other prophet in the Bible, Jonah does not want his audience to listen. He refuses to prolong his message or his visit because he does not want them to be effective; he does not want his audience to repent. As he soon makes clear in the story, he hopes that the Ninevites will ignore his message and that God will destroy them.

Jonah's oracle is less straightforward than it initially appears to be. He apparently means to say that Nineveh's "overturning" is coming soon. But "forty days" is typically a round-number metaphor for a long time in the Bible. One expects a period more like three days for such an ultimatum. As a result, Jonah seems confused. Is he calling the Ninevites to immediate action or assuring them that they have adequate time to change their ways? The point of the oracle is also ambiguous. The verb for "overturned" (נהפכת, *nehfàket*) may mean "destroyed" or "changed." Thus, Jonah's prediction will prove true regardless of how the Ninevites react. If they fail to listen and respond, the city will be destroyed. On the other hand, if they repent, the city will not be destroyed, but it will be changed. This means that, counter to an interpretation that has sometimes been offered, Jonah's subsequent anger is not occasioned by his concern over his "prophetic record" (i.e., the accuracy of his predictions). His record remains intact however the Ninevites respond. There is some other reason that Jonah gets angry—a reason that gets at the heart of the book's message.

In spite of the curtness of Jonah's oracle, it is enormously successful—to a ridiculous extreme. All the people of Nineveh believe in God, making Jonah the most effective prophet in the Bible by far. The Ninevites are amazingly perceptive. Not only do they discern the implicit threat in Jonah's oracle, they also perceive that the threat comes from God, even though the oracle did not mention God. What is more, they intuit how they should respond in order to avoid destruction. The entire citizenry of Nineveh, from the greatest or most important to the smallest or least important (4:6), fasts and dresses in sackcloth—conventional signs of mourning. The king of Nineveh himself comes down from his throne to sit in the dust dressed in sackcloth. Incidentally, the title, "king of Nineveh," is not attested in the voluminous literature recovered from ancient Nineveh and Assyria, and again suggests the unhistorical nature of the story.

The king issues a decree requiring all the people *and the animals* in the city to fast, dress in sackcloth, pray, and repent of evil deeds and violence. Like his people, the king is incredibly perceptive. He makes this decree without any certainty of the abatement of divine punishment but only in the mere hope that Yahweh may relent and decide not to destroy the city. The decree appears at first glance to be superfluous, since it follows the notice that the people repented. However, the royal decree highlights the ridiculousness of the extent of effectiveness of Jonah's oracle in the story. Imagine sheep, cattle, and other animals dressed in sackcloth refusing to eat or drink, preferring instead to lament their evil deeds and pray for mercy! The idea is ludicrous. No other scene in the book quite so clearly illustrates the satirical nature of the story with its ridiculous images and hyperbole.

The repentance of the Ninevites—humans and animals alike—is effective. Yahweh is moved by it to change his mind about the disaster he had intended for the city. Ironically, Nineveh is not destroyed, because it *is* changed. One might expect Jonah to be gratified at the effectiveness of his proclamation. He is not. Instead, he is displeased. The Hebrew literally says that he perceived it as a "great evil," and he became angry—angry at God for being merciful. Yet, the very mercy of God that infuriates Jonah and upon which the Ninevites rely is also the mercy that has kept Jonah himself alive. This is another of the book's great ironies.

Yahweh's Lesson to Jonah

In the final scene of the story Jonah at last explains why he so foolishly tried to run away when Yahweh first ordered him to go to Nineveh. The explanation, or the reasoning behind it, is even more startling than Jonah's flight.

> Oh Yahweh, is this not what I said when I was still in my own country? This is why I preemptively fled towards Tarshish. For I knew that you are a gracious and merciful God—slow to become angry, great in kindness, and who changes his mind about bringing disaster. (4:2, AT)

He ran away, he says, because he knew God to be merciful and gracious, patient and forgiving. Jonah, it seems, wanted Nineveh to be destroyed, and he was afraid that God would relent if his preaching caused the city's residents to repent. That is precisely what happened, and now Jonah is angry—angry with God for being merciful.

Jonah is so angry that he asks God to take his life. "It is better for me to die than to live," he says. Yahweh responds with a question, "Do you do well to be angry?" (AT) But Jonah does not answer. Instead, he takes a position overlooking Nineveh, apparently hopeful that God will change his mind again and destroy the city with its inhabitants.

But Yahweh decides to try yet once more to teach Jonah a lesson. He appoints a bush to grow up and give Jonah shade. Jonah finds "great joy" in the bush—in contrast to the "great evil" that he felt at Yahweh's decision not to destroy Nineveh. Then, the Almighty, who previously spoke to a fish, now appoints a worm. Following divine command, the worm attacks the bush so that it withers. Finally, God appoints a dry, eastern wind that, together with the hot sun, bears down oppressively on Jonah. The prophet is miserable and for the second time asks God to take his life. He repeats his earlier lament: "It is better for me to die than to live." So Yahweh also repeats his rejoinder question: "Do you do well to be angry?" this time adding "about the bush?" And this time Jonah answers—defiantly: "I do well to be angry enough to die." Yahweh's speech concludes the book with a question:

> You cared about[7] the bush, which you did not work or grow, which came to be in a day and perished in a night. And should I not care about Nineveh, the great city, in which there are more than 120,000 people who do not know their right hand from their left, as well as many animals? (AT)

Like its beginning, the ending of Jonah is unusual and points to the book's uniqueness. Only one other book of the Hebrew Bible concludes with a question.

It is the book of Nahum, which, interestingly, is also a prophetic book dealing with Nineveh. Both questions are rhetorical. The difference is that the question in Jonah is transparently didactic. That is, it is designed to teach a theological lesson—that God cares for all people and indeed all creation. The question is directed to Jonah, but the lesson is meant for the book's readers.

The Message and Purpose of Jonah

It is obvious from the foregoing examination of its content that the book of Jonah was not written as biography or history. There is an almost total lack of the sort of specific information that one expects of such works. Thus, no date or time frame is supplied for the story. One assumes that Jonah is an eighth-century Israelite prophet because of the mention of him in 2 Kings 14:25. But Jonah's location when he is called is not specified. Indeed, no biographical details about Jonah are given. We are also not told at what place on dry land the fish vomits Jonah up, nor is the name of the king of Nineveh provided. There are historical inaccuracies, such as the title "king of Nineveh" and the description of Nineveh's size, not to mention the prominence of Nineveh in the eighth century. Even more important for recognizing the story's unhistorical nature is its penchant for exaggeration—the "great" wind, "great" storm, "great" city, and "great" fish, to name a few examples. Some of these go beyond mere hyperbole to ridiculousness— especially the claim that it is sixty miles across the city of Nineveh and the idea that the entire city, including the animals, repents at Jonah's one-sentence utterance.

The characters in Jonah are also exaggerations, or better, stereotypes, that at least border on the ridiculous. The two main characters are God and Jonah. The other people and the animals provide contrasts to Jonah as well as comic relief. The comedy is not merely for purposes of entertainment; it is used to make serious points about the nature of God and human attitudes.

Yahweh is an omnipotent micromanager who controls not only the forces of nature but also personally appoints and commands fish, insects, and plants. The God of Israel is also the God of the entire universe, the creator of sea and land. The idea of the Almighty speaking to individual fish, plants, and worms, and sending them on special missions is comical, but it makes the point that God is concerned for and involved in all creation. God's concern for the lowliest of creatures also contrasts with Jonah's callousness toward his fellow human beings in wanting to see Nineveh destroyed.

God's purposes throughout the story are unfailingly redemptive and merciful. The reason for Jonah's mission in the first place is to bring the Ninevites to repentance so that they may avert destruction. Yahweh's power teaches the sailors to revere him but does not destroy them. God is especially merciful to Jonah and does not punish him despite his disobedience and his selfish and arrogant attitude. Even in the face of Jonah's pleas for death, Yahweh remains patient and tries to instruct Jonah. The greatest irony of the story may be that the divine mercy that so angers Jonah is what keeps him from being the target of divine wrath.

Jonah is by far the most ridiculous character in the story. Everything Jonah does is comical—his attempt to flee the creator of the universe, his nap during a raging storm at sea, his intonation of a hymn of praise in the fish's belly, his exit by regurgitation, and his deep affection for a plant. This Jonah is an unreal figure—a satirical imitation of a prophet rather than the historical prophet of the same name. His flagrant rebellion against God's command contrasts with the piety and obedience of the "pagan" sailors and the evil Ninevites, not to mention the dumb animals, plants, and forces of nature.

Jonah is full of contradictions. Even more than an imitation of a prophet, he is an "antiprophet," who does not want to prophesy and whose behavior and attitude are the opposite of what the reader expects in a man of God. He is deluded; his actions do not match his beliefs, for he confesses the Creator and then tries to run away from him. He is a self-centered bigot whose reasoning is clouded by prejudice and hatred. As a result, his priorities are dreadfully mixed up. Yahweh's mercy toward other people only frustrates him—to the point that he decides life is no longer worth living, to the point that he harbors deeper feelings for a plant that shades him than for myriads of people and animals.

The interview between the two principal characters, Yahweh and Jonah, in the final scene of the book is where its message through satirical characterization is clearest. Jonah would rather die than have God be merciful to other people. His attitude of prejudice and hatred toward non-Israelites is what the book satirizes. The ludicrous features of the story ridicule this attitude of bigotry. Ideally, the humor and exaggeration help the audience to perceive in Jonah the silliness of their own attitudes and the ridiculous lengths to which arrogance and prejudice can lead them. The concluding question points to the story's didactic purpose, for Jonah's character is a mirror for the book's audience. He embodies an attitude present or at least perceived by the author to exist in Israel. Again, the story about him is not history but satire or parody, a ridiculous story that makes a serious point.

Genre and Expectation

The key to understanding the message of Jonah is recognizing its genre. "Genre," borrowed from French, is a term used to refer to the type or category of a piece of literature. Broadly, there are fiction and nonfiction genres, and within each of those genres there are other genres or subgenres. Novel, short story, and science fiction, for instance, are subgenres of fiction. Biography, instruction manual, and catalogue are subgenres of nonfiction. Each of these subgenres in turn may have its own subgenres. Autobiography, for example, is a subgenre of biography.

Genre categories are not firm or fixed but are fluid and flexible, so a literary work can incorporate different genres, just as the book of Jonah incorporates the psalm in chapter 2.

Discernment of genre is an essential part of the process of communication between author and readers. It provides a literary "frame of reference" within which the reader interprets and makes use of a text. Misconstruing the genre of a piece of literature, therefore, can be disastrous. This is nicely illustrated by the movie *Galaxy Quest*.[8] In it, a science fiction television series about the crew of a space ship is mistaken by aliens for real history or journalism. The aliens draft the cast members to help them fight a real interplanetary war. The film illustrates how confused someone who reads science fiction as history could become. Similarly, imagine the disaster that might ensue if a surgeon took an instruction manual as fiction, or a work of fiction as a medical guidebook. Such scenarios may seem far-fetched. Someone as educated as a surgeon would not likely mistake a work of fiction for an instruction manual or vice versa, at least as long as that surgeon is reading literature from his or her own culture and time period. The potential for confusion increases when a reader, any reader, confronts literature from an entirely different culture and time—such as the Bible.

Despite the importance of determining a work's genre, there are no firm rules for doing so. Rarely does a literary work expressly identify its own genre. In fact, the idea of identifying genre as an important step in the study of texts is a relatively recent phenomenon, though ancient readers and authors were certainly aware that they were using or producing different kinds of texts and documents.

Discernment of genre is something readers do subconsciously. It has been compared to speaking a language. It is an interpretive tool engrained within culture. People typically "absorb" language as they grow up in a culture. They can tell if someone makes a grammatical error or is not a native speaker even though they may not be able to describe the grammatical rule that has been broken. People learn to speak their native language first, and then they learn the grammar.

Similarly, people automatically recognize the genre of a work produced within their culture even if they cannot explain the process or rules by which recognition has occurred. It is an interpretive tool we possess for documents produced within our culture simply by virtue of having been raised in it. We apply it without thinking, without even being aware of what we are doing. Only when we encounter texts from a new genre or a culture with which we are unfamiliar do we become cognizant of the issue.

Genre recognition, like learning a foreign language, is always harder for people outside of the culture of a work. But, just as a language has grammatical rules, so there are guidelines or clues for determining genre. Sometimes those clues come in the physical form of a literary work. Newspapers, magazines, and books are easily distinguished from one another, even when they are in an unfamiliar language. In the ancient world there were inscriptions, royal decrees, letters, and other documents that might be distinguished by the way in which they were presented. Unfortunately, such physical differences disappeared in the formation of collected works like the Bible, and readers must now rely on clues within the texts themselves in order to discern genres.

Such clues typically come in the form of features in a text that signal its genre through the use of conventions established within a particular culture or readership. These clues often occur at the beginning or end of the text and lead the reader to certain expectations about its content. For modern American readers, the words, "Dateline New York," indicate that they are reading a newspaper article, even if it does not appear in newsprint. The greeting "Dear Sir/Madam" is the typical beginning of a business letter, and we expect it to end with "Sincerely," or the like, followed by a signature of some sort. Fairy tales commonly begin "Once upon a time" and end "They lived happily ever after."

The creation of literature has always been, to at least some extent, a creative activity. Theoretically, an author could create a new genre that was unlike any work previously in existence. But if that were to happen, no reader would be able to recognize or understand it. Hence, authors vary or mix genres to creative ends, playing upon the knowledge and expectations of their readers. A business letter that begins "Dear Sir/Madam" would hardly end with "All my love," unless it was part of some kind of publicity or advertising campaign. By the same token, a personal letter between (former) lovers that is written on letterhead rather than personal stationery and that ends, "Sincerely," instead of "Love," may be making a not-too-subtle point about the relationship. Similarly, a fairy tale that begins "Once upon a time" but ends without "They lived happily ever after" does not bode well for the relationship of the couple who are the subject of the story.

These examples illustrate how a text's genre in and of itself may convey a message. The features of the texts just described do not match conventions that readers in those cultures would expect, or they mix features from different genres, or they mix genres in such a way as to make a point. The message is subtle to the extent that only readers who are intimately familiar with the usual genres and their features are able to pick up the changes.

Authors can use genre just as effectively and creatively as they can word choice, sentence structure, allusion, and a host of other features of language and writing. In so doing an author plays upon the reader's expectations. This means that there is, by necessity, circularity or give-and-take between a text's genre and its content, to which readers must be sensitive. Just as one must properly discern a text's genre in order to understand it, at least in the way intended by its author, so it is also up to readers to recognize subtle variations in genre employed by an author if they are to profit fully from a text.

Our treatment of Jonah illustrates the importance of the discernment of genre for interpretation of the Bible. Jonah, like many literary works, does not identify its genre but leaves it to the reader to discern. Still, the book gives significant clues about how it was meant to be read. Readers who have misconstrued the genre of Jonah as history have therefore approached it with an erroneous set of expectations and have often tried to force it to fit their expectations. When it is discovered that the book does not fit those expectations, the tendency is often to blame the book, declaring it "untrue" and implying that it is somehow of less significance because it does not describe historical events. It is important to recognize, therefore, that the problem in the interpretation of Jonah does not lie with the book itself but with its readers—readers who fail to discern its genre from internal clues and thereby to appreciate its true nature and purpose. The problem is only exacerbated by the fact that Jonah is an ancient piece of literature from a foreign culture and written in a foreign language.

This problem of failing to discern a book's genre goes beyond Jonah to much of the literature in the Bible. Fortunately, biblical scholarship has long been aware of the importance of properly discerning a work's genre and has recently made crucial insights about various genres present in the Bible, which allows for a more precise understanding of their nature.

Form Criticism

Because the literature of the Bible is so far removed in time and culture, modern readers, unlike their ancient Israelite counterparts, do not automatically recognize the genres it contains. Genre can be discerned only through detailed study and analysis. The approach that biblical scholars use to help discern the genres represented in different parts of the Bible is called "form criticism." Basically, form criticism attempts to determine what is typical and what is unique about a given piece of literature in order to understand what its author wished to communicate.

There are four parts to a form-critical analysis. It begins by plotting the structure or shape of the passage in question. The scholars who initially came up with the approach of form criticism were Germans, and *Form* is the German word for shape or structure. Discerning a text's shape or structure means determining first of all its extent. Where does the unit of text begin and end? Initially, form criticism focused on small literary units and was sometimes defined as a treatment of the smallest possible unit. However, in more recent years biblical scholars have recognized the value and indeed the need for form-critical analysis of larger units, including entire biblical books and even units that transcend books. This shift is very important for our work in this present book. What I hope to do is to show how recent advances in our understanding of the main genres contained in the Bible help to counter broadly held misconceptions of what the Bible is and what it is trying to say.

A second phase of form-critical investigation entails determining the genre of the passage under examination. As we have seen, genre refers to the category of literature to which one assigns a text, be it a specific passage, an entire book, or a collection of books. A leading biblical scholar has defined genre this way: "a group of written texts marked by distinctive recurring characteristics which constitute a recognizable and coherent type of writing."[9] There are two components to this definition, one internal and the other external. The internal component consists of the characteristics of a given text that can be discerned by careful reading and analysis. The external component is the comparison of the text with other similar texts inside and outside of the Bible. Careful comparison reveals which characteristics of a text are "recurring" enough within "a group of written texts" to allow one to recognize a "coherent type of writing," and which are "distinctive" to the particular text in question.

The third and fourth steps of form criticism represent the attempt to trace the history of the text being analyzed and its genre. The third is the positing of a setting in the actual, daily life in which the genre would have arisen. Potential settings include temple worship, legal proceedings, a wedding, a funeral, a classroom, or any other of the myriad of activities that human beings engage in. Form criticism was initially conceived particularly as a means of uncovering the oral components that were assumed to underlie biblical literature. This was the reason it focused on the smallest possible units—because it was assumed that only they could be retained in memory and recited orally. For example, the prophets sometimes expressed God's grievances against Israel by means of the genre of a legal complaint for the violation of a contract. Thus, a prophet might describe Yahweh as "filing suit" against Israel for breaking the covenant. The original setting of this genre was the law court of ancient Israel. The principal genres and large literary works of the Bible also had settings in life, often in scribal circles responding to specific historical events and crises, but sometimes more specific in nature.

The fourth part of a form-critical treatment is the discernment of the intended purpose of the genre in the passage under scrutiny. This is the most important phase of form-critical analysis because it gets at the very reason for the passage's existence—the author's intention in writing it—and this is the ultimate goal of form criticism. Continuing with the example above, the form critic is just as interested, if not more so, in the setting of the prophets who adapted the genre of an indictment in their oracles against Israel as in the legal setting of the original genre. Form critics should also be interested in the setting of the scribes who then transcribed and arranged the prophetic oracles into written books. There are no rules for uncovering the intent behind a text's use of a given genre. The intent must simply be inferred or deduced from the features and content of the text. Of special importance in this respect are the distinctive characteristics of the text in comparison to others of its genre.

The treatment of Jonah earlier in this introduction was basically a form-critical one. We began with matters of structure. Because we were interested in discerning the genre and purpose of the book as a whole, there was no question about its extent—where it began and where it ended. We did have to consider the question of whether the psalm in Jonah 2 was an original part of the book, and this involved the form-critical issues, specifically having to do with the original setting of the psalm, which appeared to be a poem of thanksgiving for rescue from near death that was adopted—not entirely appropriately—for Jonah's predicament.

While the extent of the book was not an issue, its beginning and ending proved to be extremely important because of the uniqueness of Jonah among the prophetic books. A careful look at the book's content further confirmed its uniqueness among the prophets as a narrative with a plot rather than a collection of oracles. The outline of the book alone led to the recognition that its plot revolves around the interaction between Jonah and the other characters in the story. Further examination of its contents showed that the interaction of God with Jonah is the focus of the book.

On the basis of these form-critical observations, we were able to make a determination about Jonah's genre. Again, determination of the book's genre is the key to its interpretation. It is not historical narrative but a fictional story. Biblical scholars generally characterize Jonah as a "novella," a kind of short story in which a series of episodes involving the same set of characters leads to a conclusion or resolution of a problem that has arisen. Other examples of novellas in the Bible, to which Jonah might be compared, include the books of Esther and Ruth, and the story of Joseph in Genesis 37–50.

The unhistorical nature of certain details in Jonah, such as those concerning Nineveh, suggests that its setting was considerably removed from the eighth century when the story is set. A number of late linguistic features in the book indicate a date in the postexilic period (around 400 BCE). This date fits well with the themes of Yahweh's universal dominion and concern for all people, which surface in Jonah and which became especially pointed issues of debate in the postexilic period. These matters loom large in other biblical books from this period, such as Chronicles and Ezra-Nehemiah. Jonah was likely written to contribute to this theological debate.

Determining that Jonah's genre is not history frees us to examine the question of the story's intent and purpose, which is the main objective of interpretation and the focus of our form-critical analysis of Jonah. Jonah's intent must be inferred from the book's content, as there is no statement in it articulating the author's purpose in writing. The many exaggerations and absurd elements in the story are good indications that the story was not intended to be read as a historical novel or biography. Rather, these features, along with the caricatural or stereotypical nature of its characters, lead to the reasonable deduction that the story was intended as a satire or parody. The concluding interview between God and Jonah, especially the question with which the book ends, further indicates that its purpose was didactic—Jonah was intended to serve as an object lesson, illustrating in bold relief the stupidity of the attitude that the author perceived in the book's intended readership.

The book of Jonah furnishes a paradigmatic example of the importance of identifying the genre of a piece of biblical literature for properly appreciating its intent and of form criticism as a tool for genre identification. Each reader of a given text makes an assumption about the genre of that text. The reader then adjusts that assumption in the course of reading according to the signals in the text and the reader's familiarity with literary and cultural conventions. Since the book of Jonah does not expressly identify its genre, the assumption that it is history has no special claim to correctness or legitimacy at the outset. Its genre must be adduced from its content.

The attempt to read Jonah as history gives priority to an assumption about its genre over its actual content. A historical reading ignores or struggles to explain the clear exaggerations, caricatures, and absurd features that are essential to the nature of the story as satirical fiction. Worst of all, the historical reading of Jonah is monolithic and runs the risk of missing the book's richness. It misleads the reader into focusing on relatively insignificant details—such as whether a man could live in a whale for three days—and missing its main point—the stupidity of bigotry. Ironically, religiously conservative commentators who advocate the historical veracity of the story may actually cause problems for the faith of readers who observe features in the story that conflict with what they expect

from a historical account.[10] Recognition that the story is satirical allows the reader
to perceive truth in its message about prejudice apart from the question of historical accuracy.

The Purpose of This Book

The thesis behind this book is that the Bible at large, like the book of Jonah within
it, has been and continues to be widely misunderstood because its principal genres
are misconstrued. Readers of the Bible have long recognized the diversity of its
literature and the importance of being sensitive to the kind of literature one is
reading. The Bible is an anthology containing law, history, biography, hymns,
letters, contracts, and a host of other genres. Most people recognize this and do
not want to read everything in the Bible as a law or commandment. Those who
do attempt to read it all as law fail to see how dangerous this move is, since there
are plenty of stories in which the actions of characters—even "good" ones—are
not meant to be emulated. The example of Jonah shows that correct discernment of genre is crucial for proper interpretation.

In Jonah's case, the genre was misconstrued as history and then the satirical
intention of the story was missed. More commonly in the Bible, the genre of a
book or section of literature is misconstrued in a different, less dramatic way—
not by improper classification or identification of its genre —but by improper
definition of the *ancient* genre. To put it another way, a genre is correctly identified, but the nature and meaning of the genre in its ancient setting, what it
entailed for its ancient Israelite authors and readers, is misunderstood. As a result, the intent is misinterpreted.

The Bible, quite naturally, reflects the culture of the ancient Israelite and Greco-
Roman societies that produced it. It was written in Hebrew and Greek, not English. We do not expect to find references to modern Western clothing styles or
modes of transportation within its pages. Neither should we expect it to use modern literary genres. Misconstrual of genre leads modern readers to unrealistic and
sometimes unreasonable expectations about the contents and message of the Bible.

An ancient genre is not always, in fact almost never, identical to a modern
one. For instance, law in the Bible includes "secular" and "religious" legislation
and is therefore quite different from modern, American law. The separation of
church and state is not even imagined. Indeed, the very word "law" (*tôrāh*) actually means "instruction," so that biblical law is really primarily religious instruction. It is closer to what we might call "catechism" than it is to our secular law.
To think of the Law of Moses, therefore, in terms of modern law codes, like the
Constitution of the United States, is to misdefine it and to misinterpret its intent.

The same is true of each of the five genres treated in this book: historiography, prophecy, wisdom, apocalyptic, and letters. In each case, the genre is more or less familiar to modern readers; but in each case, as well, there are significant differences between the ancient genre in the Bible and the modern one or the way people usually define it. The problem, as in the case of Jonah, is not with the Bible but with the way people try to interpret the Bible, without properly understanding its genres and their intents.

The purpose of this book is to help readers of the Bible understand the major genres of literature in the Bible—to identify its genres, define them properly, and correctly characterize their intents. As we saw in our discussion of Jonah, all readers make assumptions about the genres of texts as they read them. Yet biblical books, like Jonah, do not usually explicitly identify or define their respective genres. Biblical writings do provide clues to their genres—in such things as their structures and internal features, such as the litany of ridiculous ideas and images in Jonah. That is where form criticism comes in: It seeks to highlight those internal clues, in comparison with features of similar texts in and outside of the Bible, in order to determine a work's genre and intent.

Each of the following chapters discusses a distinct genre of biblical literature. The chapters typically begin with an attempt to define the genre in its ancient setting. The definitions are based on internal and external considerations. In almost every case, the definitions represent advances of recent comparative scholarship. Then, each chapter contains close readings of specific texts, focusing on the four major concerns of form criticism (structure, genre, setting, intent). These concerns will not be dealt with mechanically or systematically for each passage, nor will equal space always be given to each one. Our main objectives will be to highlight the characteristics of the principal genre under discussion and to show its intent in its historical and cultural setting.

These readings will pay close attention both to what is typical of a particular genre and to what is distinctive in a given text that represents the genre. The better we understand what is typical of a genre, the easier it is to pick out what is unique in a specific text. Familiarity with the history and culture behind the Bible, as well as the languages in which it was originally written, can be important for discerning the setting of a genre, and I make use of such items where appropriate. I also draw on other ancient sources outside of the Bible for evidence about the nature of the ancient genres. But I hope to show that many of the clues to proper understanding of the Bible's literature are available to non-specialists through careful reading of specific texts. For it is often in the uniqueness of a text, as we saw in Jonah, that its intent surfaces most clearly.

Chapter One

NOT EXACTLY AS IT HAPPENED
Historiography in the Bible

The Misconception:
Biblical historians relate what happened in the past.

> You wouldn't know it from attending a church or synagogue, or from reading the annual Christmastime articles in *Time* magazine, but for the past half-century scholars have steadily chipped away at the Old Testament's credibility as a historical document. The big story in Near Eastern archaeology has been how many biblical narratives have been moved from the category of accepted fact to the misty realm of fable.
>
> First to go was the Creation story, in Genesis—what evidence could ever be found to support it? Then Noah and the Flood, a catastrophic event for which there should be clear geological marks. There are none. Abraham, Isaac, and Jacob, who once fit into secular histories of the second millennium B.C., left behind no evidence of their existence. If they were historical figures, we have to take the word of the biblical scribes, who wrote centuries after the patriarchs died.
>
> The story of the Israelites' conquest of Canaan, blaring trumpets and all, has given way to a rather mundane vision of peaceful infiltration and a social revolt among indigenous peasants. There was no walled city at Jericho when Joshua was supposed to have destroyed it.[1]

This quotation comes from the leading publication on higher education in America. It shows how biblical scholars have been forced by new evidence to retrench or revise their positions about the point at which the Bible begins to relate actual historical events. People who hear about these deliberations in the field of biblical scholarship typically have one of two reactions. The first may be characterized as "blind faith." It is illustrated by a conversation I had a few years ago with a man who was doing some work on my house. This man was college educated, a business owner, honest, reliable, and a good worker. He was also a devout Christian. When he found out that I was a professor of Bible and had visited the Middle East, he began asking me about the archaeological evidence for certain events narrated in the Bible. He was especially interested in the exodus from Egypt under Moses and the conquest of Canaan under Joshua. I told him that archaeological evidence, or the lack of it, had led most biblical scholars to question whether those events had actually taken place, at least in the way the Bible describes them. He replied that the archaeological evidence did not matter to him. "No matter what they find, I will always believe that it happened just the way the Bible says it did."

As admirable as the strength of this man's convictions may be, his faith was "blind." He refused to consider any factual evidence that might challenge or force him to revise his faith. Biblical scholars encounter this kind of response all the time in the classroom. There are students who "just 'shut down' and refuse to engage biblical scholarship in a creative way at all."[2] They react this way because they believe critical study of the Bible to be a threat to their faith.[3] Yet a faith that cannot stand up to challenges or cope with empirical evidence hardly seems worth having. This is another common reaction of students and other people who encounter biblical scholarship for the first time—they reject faith altogether and adopt a negative view of the Bible.

The fact that so much of the Bible's early history appears, in the light of scientific analysis and historical investigation, not to have happened in the way that the Bible claims raises a question about the Bible's nature. But as with Jonah, the problem may lie not with the Bible but with the way readers have approached it.

The traditional assumption has been that the Bible relates or purports to relate what happened in the past. Recent biblical scholarship, however, has shown that this assumption is misleading, that the typical understanding of the genre of the Bible's historical literature is incorrect. This means that, as in the case of the book of Jonah, a new way of reading this literature is warranted. Moreover, this new way of reading may be especially beneficial for people of faith, and a clearer understanding of the genre of historiography in ancient Israel may help to resolve the tension between the Bible's account and the historical investigations of biblical scholars and archaeologists. It may permit a faith that is not forced to blind itself by ignoring modern scholarly analyses.

In the first part of the chapter, we look at the nature of ancient history writing as recent biblical scholars have defined it and illustrate the nature of ancient history writing with examples from the book of Genesis relating to the events raised in the quotation that began this chapter. In the second part of the chapter, I discuss how history in the Bible was written by exploring the work of various history writers preserved in the Bible.

Ancient History Writing

History to most modern Westerners is what happened in the past, and as a genre of literature it is an account of what happened in the past. We judge written history by how accurately and objectively it recounts past events. In other words, we tend to apply to history the same standards that we apply to journalism. We recognize, of course, that like journalists, historians may have their own biases. After all, no one is completely objective, so we know that writing history often involves interpretation. If pressed, most of us would probably admit that it may be impossible to know for certain exactly what happened in the past. But relating exactly what happened remains the goal and the essential definition of the genre as we envision it.

We assume that ancient historians, and the biblical writers in particular, had the same definition of history. This assumption has been and continues to be the source of problems. If readers of Jonah sometimes feel compelled to choose between believing that the story happened exactly as described and dismissing the book as worthless nonsense, the same choice can be even more pointed for other portions of the Bible, especially the early chapters of Genesis. Must one, in the face of scientific evidence to the contrary, believe that the world came into existence in seven days, or that there was a universal flood that wiped out all of the earth's species except those preserved aboard a single vessel, or that people before that flood had life spans of nearly one thousand years? Is the alternative to dismiss the Bible as work of sheer mythology with little or no contemporary value? This is the choice that some people have faced. This choice is occasioned at least in part by a failure to understand the genre of ancient historiography, especially as it appears in the Bible. As for Jonah, the problem is not with the Bible but with the way it is (mis)understood.

In Search of History

The title "historical books" has long been applied to a large number of writings in the Bible from Genesis through 2 Kings. Sometimes, 1 and 2 Chronicles and Ezra-Nehemiah are included in the list as well. However, the question of the definition of history writing in the Bible remained largely unexplored until quite recently. In 1983 a leading biblical scholar, John Van Seters, published a groundbreaking study of historiography in the ancient world and the Bible titled *In Search of History.*[4] Van Seters sought to describe the nature and origin of history writing as a literary genre, especially as it appears in the Bible. He did this by comparing the Bible's historical books with historiographical works from other cultures, notably Greece, Mesopotamia, the Hittites, and Egypt. Van Seters adopted the definition of history coined by a Dutch historian, Johan Huizinga: "History is the intellectual form in which a civilization renders account to itself of its past."[5] This definition has three important parts whose implications were pursued by Van Seters in his comparison of historiographical materials from Greece and the ancient Near East. These three parts are: the word "history," the expression "intellectual form," and the phrase "a civilization renders account to itself of its past."

History

Following Huizinga's definition, Van Seters distinguished between the terms *historiography* and *history writing*. Historiography is a general term for all historical texts. History writing, on the other hand, refers to the specific literary genre in which a civilization or nation tries to render an account of its collective past. Historiographical materials have been preserved from Egypt, Mesopotamia, and the Hittites, but Van Seters concluded that true history writing developed first in Israel and then in Greece, where the closest analogs to biblical history writing are found.

Intellectual Form

Van Seters discerned a number of features of history writing in ancient Greece, especially in the work of Herodotus, the so-called father of history, that shed light on the nature of history writing in the Bible. There are two facets of Herodotus's work that constitute it as an intellectual form. First, Herodotus engaged in personal research or investigation. The word "history" is actually derived from a Greek term (*historiē*) meaning "investigations" or "researches." Herodotus titled his work "Researches" because he gathered information in his travels and then wrote about the things he learned: geography and social customs, as well as traditions, legends, and even myths of local peoples. Whether the events he recorded actually happened was of secondary importance to Herodotus, as he stated, "For my part I am not going to say about these matters that they happened thus or thus. . . ."[6] Hence, about Egypt he wrote,

> As for the stories told by the Egyptians, let whoever finds them credible use them. Throughout the entire history it is my underlying principle that it is what people severally have said to me, and what I have heard, that I must write down.[7]

This leads to the second facet of Herodotus's work as a historian—his recording in writing of the traditions he received. History writing, as the name implies, was a deliberate literary product—the product of a literate society—and not the result of gradual accumulation of traditions. Herodotus gathered stories and other materials in his travels and investigations that were in both oral and written forms. He then crafted these materials into a unified, written whole, which is what made his work different from that of the individual storytellers who preceded him and from whom he got some of his stories. Recognizing this literary aspect of the work of Herodotus and other historians who followed him is important for a proper understanding of history writing. "Consequently, historiography is not the same thing as objective, detached reporting. It is a type of literature, and as such, it has a literary intent. The writer of history seeks to make the past alive for the reader by telling a story."[8]

Herodotus's techniques in writing down his histories are intriguing for the similarities they bear to biblical history writing. Herodotus and his successors generally organized their histories "paratactically." That is, they strung together different stories and episodes, often with their own introductions and conclusions but with little or no verbal connection between them. Some Greek historians also used genealogies to form a framework for their works, just as biblical writers did.

Ancient Greek historians also used speeches and narrative formulas as structuring devices. Such speeches were typically invented by the historian according to what was deemed appropriate to the occasion because the historian was usually not present at the occasions when speeches were delivered, especially those in the distant past. Yet, Herodotus records not only private conversations between individuals but the thoughts of individuals as well. The later Greek historian, Thucydides, admits that he composed speeches in a well-known passage from his *History of the Peloponnesian War*:

> As to the speeches that were made by different men . . . it has been difficult to recall with strict accuracy the words actually spoken , both for me as regards that which I myself heard, and for those who from various other sources have brought me reports. Therefore, the speeches are given in the language in which, as it seemed to me, the several speakers would express, on the subjects under consideration, the sentiments most befitting the occasion, though at the same time I have adhered as closely as possible to the general sense of what was actually said.[9]

As one renowned classicist puts it, "We have no good reason for taking the speeches to be anything but inventions by the historians, not only in their precise wording but also in their substance."[10] The ancient readers understood this. The composition of speeches was such an accepted convention among ancient historians that they even criticized each other's speech-writing abilities.[11]

Ancient historians may have occasionally invented stories and other materials for inclusion in their histories. Inevitably, their sources were incomplete and left gaps in the coverage of history. "But ancient writers, like historians ever since, could not tolerate a void, and they filled it in one way or another, ultimately by pure invention. The ability of the ancients to invent and their capacity to believe are persistently underestimated."[12]

While this may be something of an overstatement, the ancient Greek historians at least appear to fill such gaps by borrowing stories from other contexts or by repeating a particular storyline or motif.[13] The point is that Herodotus and other ancient Greek historians exercised considerable freedom in their literary creations, especially in the arrangement of materials, but also sometimes in the basic content.

A Civilization Renders Account to Itself of Its Past

History writing in ancient Greece was not primarily concerned with relating past events "as they really happened." This is surprising to modern readers, because it is how we now tend to define history. But telling exactly what happened in the past was "neither an important consideration nor a claim one could substantiate."[14] Rather, the primary objective of ancient history writing was to "render an account" of the past that explained the present.

This "rendering an account" carried two connotations. First, it entailed assessing responsibility for and passing judgment on a nation's past actions as a way of explaining consequences for the present. Herodotus says as much in 1.5, partially quoted earlier:

> For my part I am not going to say about these matters that they happened thus or thus, but I will set my mark upon that man that I myself know began unjust acts against the Greeks, and, having so marked him, I will go forward in my account, covering alike the small and great cities of mankind. For of those that were great in earlier times most have now become small, and those that were great in my time were small in the time before. Since, then, I know that man's good fortune never abides in the same place, I will make mention of both alike.

Herodotus says, in short, that he is writing to explain changes that have taken place for better and worse and thus introduces here the concept of transition, which has implications for his theme of happiness. The point is that ancient historians wrote in order to make theological or political points. They were not objective reporters; they had axes to grind. And grinding axes was not incidental to their project of writing history; it was the reason they wrote. "The study and writing of history, in short, is a form of ideology."[15]

Second, a civilization rendering an account of its past also entailed an expression of the corporate identity of the nation—what it was and what principles it stood for. Again, the ancient historian's primary concern was not with detailing exactly what happened in the past. Rather, it was with interpreting the meaning of the past for the present, with showing how the "causes" of the past brought about the "effects" of the present. Thus, the quotation above shows both Herodotus's interest in the Greeks as a corporate entity and in the causes of what happened to them.

These cause-effect explanations were not scientific in nature; they often had to do with moral and religious matters. Greek historians used what we would classify as myth or legend as causes of the past leading to the present. Indeed, myth and legend were the only sources available for the distant past, which had not produced written records. Even those historians who did not believe the myths were compelled to use them because they had no other sources. These historians often rationalized the myths they incorporated by offering more scientific interpretations for them. Historians would sometimes include variant explanations or "causes"—one mythological and one scientific—for the same event or phenomenon, especially if they found both explanations in their sources.[16]

History as Etiology in the Bible

Van Seters applied his observations from Huizinga's definition and from Greek history writing to the Bible. He isolated the following five criteria for identifying history writing in ancient Israel:[17]

1. History writing was a specific form of tradition in its own right rather than the accidental accumulation of traditional material.
2. History writing considered the reason for recalling the past and the significance of past events and was not primarily the accurate reporting of the past.
3. History writing examined the (primarily moral) causes in the past of present conditions and circumstances.
4. History writing was national or corporate in nature.
5. History writing was literary and an important part of a people's corporate tradition.

These criteria are important for identifying the genre of "history writing" in the Bible and for understanding the nature of the genre of ancient history writing as opposed to other genres such as epic or legend. Of particular interest for our present purposes are items 2 and 3. The Greek word for "cause" is *aitia*, which lends itself to the word "etiology." An etiology is a story that explains the *cause* or origin of a given phenomenon—a cultural practice or social custom, a biological circumstance, even a geological formation. An etiology of this nature is not a scientific explanation. It is not historical in the modern sense of an event that actually took place in the past. It is, rather, a story that "renders an account" by offering some explanation of present conditions and circumstances based on past causes. Ancient history writing, which sought to "render an account" of the past was, in effect, *etiology*.

An excellent illustration of the nature of etiologies is found in a group of stories by Rudyard Kipling called the *Just So Stories*.[18] They bear such titles as "How the Camel Got His Hump," "How the Leopard Got His Spots," "How the Alphabet Was Made." These stories provide imaginative explanations for children about the origins of a variety of natural and cultural phenomena. In "How the Camel Got His Hump," for instance, the horse, ox, and dog each attempt to get the camel to work and are rebuffed in turn by the same reply: "Humph!" When a Djinn or genie is similarly rebuffed, he turns the camel's back into a humph (= hump). The hump allows the camel to live for three days without eating so that it can make up the three days that it remained idle at the beginning. The story not only provides a fanciful explanation of the camel's distinctive anatomy but it also includes a false etymology of the word "hump."

The etiologies from ancient Israel and Greece, though based on tradition, can be just as imaginative as Kipling's stories. They are equally unscientific and just as unhistorical in the sense of actually having taken place. Yet they function within the genre of history writing because they have been collected as the result of research into traditional materials and because they provide an explanation for the existence of some circumstance or condition in the historian's day. This does not mean that all of the traditions recorded as part of Israel's history writing are fictional and unhistorical in the modern sense. Some are no doubt based on actual events of the past, but to attempt to read the account of Israel's history in the Bible strictly as a record of actual events is to misconstrue its genre and to force it to do something it was not intended to do. To make this literature history in a modern sense is to misunderstand it every bit as much as the book of Jonah is misunderstood if one attempts to read it as a record of actual events.

There are plenty of individual etiologies in the Bible. Our purpose is not to examine them all but to show how they function within the larger genre of history writing to provide explanations and causes from the past for prime elements of Israel's self-understanding. Key to that self-understanding is Israel's perception of its relationship to its God, Yahweh. As with the story of Jonah, the theology (or theologies) of the various examples of history writing from ancient Israel is not dependent on the actual historicity of the episodes they describe. Ancient Israelite historians, who sought to render an account of their nation, found the ultimate explanation for its origin and its present state in Yahweh. As for ancient Greek historians, so in the Bible, history was written for an ideological purpose. History *was* theology.

Etiology in Genesis: Prime Example (Gen 1–3)

Creation (Gen 1:1–2:3)

The account of creation in Genesis 1 is an etiology in the sense that it relates the *origin* of the world. But the impulse to regard it as historical fact often leads readers to overlook its literary sophistication. Careful attention to its structure and content indicates that the chapter's intent is to account not only for the origins of the world but also, and perhaps primarily, for social and religious phenomena of the author's day. Following a form-critical approach, we begin with an analysis of the text's structure.

To begin with some general observations related to structure, there are several places where the description in this chapter is at odds with science, so that it is hard to see it as historical reality. Thus, while the sun and moon are not created until the fourth day, there is already light, day and night, and thriving vegetation—all of which we know to be impossible without the sun. The sky is called the "dome" (NRSV). The word used here properly refers to a bowl-shaped vessel that is beaten out and therefore implies that the earth beneath it is flat. Day five sees the creation of "sea monsters" or "dragons," which are mythological creatures.[19] The sequence "evening and morning" (rather than "morning and evening") reflects the ancient Israelite calendar, which marked the beginning of a new day at sunset. (The same calendar continues today in the start of the Jewish Sabbath at sundown on Friday.) This feature of the document indicates that it embodies a particular cultural outlook that was different from a modern, scientific one.

The account of creation in Genesis 1 is obviously organized by days. This is the strongest indication that this account continues into chapter 2, since 2:1–3 continues this organizational scheme by telling about the seventh day.[20] The account for each day is highly formulaic with the repetition of the same basic set of expressions:

God said, "Let there be X."
And there was X / So God made X / And it was so.
God saw that X was good.
God called X "X."
There was evening and morning, day Y.

The set of expressions is not rigid but accommodates variation. For instance, on the fifth and sixth days, there is the statement that God blessed animals, including birds and fish, and humans with the command, "Be fruitful and multiply." Still, there is enough consistency to discern a basic pattern or formula upon which each day's account of creation is built. Remarkably, this basic formula occurs twice for days three and six. For the third day the account reads:

> And God said, "Let the waters under the sky be gathered together into
>   one place, and let the dry land appear."
> And it was so.
> God called the dry land Earth, and the waters that were gathered
>   together he called Seas.
> And God saw that it was good. (NRSV, Gen 1:9–10)

At this point, following the formula established in the other verses, one expects the text to say, "And there was evening and there was morning, the third day." Instead, the formula begins again:

> And[21] God said, "Let the earth put forth vegetation . . ."
> And it was so . . .
> And God saw that it was good.

Only then does the time reference, "There was evening and there was morning, the third day," occur. Similarly, for the sixth day, one finds the basic formula:

> And God said, "Let the earth bring forth living creatures of every kind . . ."
> And it was so . . .
> God made the wild animals of the earth of every kind.

Then one expects to read, "And it was evening and it was morning, the sixth day." Instead, the formula restarts and is expanded through the end of the chapter:

> And[22] God said, "Let us make humankind in our image . . ."
> So God created humankind in his image . . .
> And it was so.
> God saw everything that he had made, and indeed, it was very good.
> And there was evening and there was morning, the sixth day.

The result of this repetition of the standard formula for days three and six is that the narrative describes the creation of two categories of things, two creative acts for each of those days. The first act on day three is the gathering of the waters to form seas and dry land. This is followed by the creation of vegetation on the dry land. On day six, land animals and humans are created in separate acts. Only one creative act is detailed for every other day.

The structure of the entire account may thus be sketched as follows:

Day 1:	light	Day 4:	sun, moon, stars
Day 2:	dome (sky) in the midst of waters	Day 5:	birds, fish
Day 3:	seas and dry land	Day 6:	land animals
	vegetation		humans

Day 7: Sabbath

This structure suggests that a version of creation in eight installments under-lies this account of creation. The biblical author kept the eight installments, as indicated by the repetition of the daily pattern on days three and six. But instead of having creation take place over eight days, the author compacted it into six days by placing two installments on days three and six, that is, having two cat egories of things created on those days. The reason for doing this was appar-ently to leave the seventh day, the Sabbath, as a day of rest for God.

The foregoing observations about the structure of Genesis 1:1–2:3 permit us to make inferences about the other form-critical concerns of genre, intent, and setting. This text is a creation story—an explanation for the origin of the world. But it is also an etiology for the Sabbath. Its intent seems to be to make two very powerful theological points: (1) that God, specifically Israel's God Yahweh, is the creator of the world, and (2) that the Sabbath is so important that it is engrained in the very order of the universe; even God at creation kept the Sabbath.

The second theological point has implications for the setting of this text, at least the social and political aspects of its setting. Ensuring the observation of the Sabbath and other ritual practices was the function of the priestly class in ancient Israel. By locating the Sabbath at creation and giving it such an exalted role, Genesis 1:1–2:3 was also promoting the function of priests as essential to ancient Israel. This is one of the reasons that biblical scholars typically speak of this creation account as a document probably written by a priest. It is etiology, theology, and sociopolitical ideology all at once.

Adam and Eve (Gen 2:4b–3:24)

The famous story of Adam and Eve and the Garden of Eden is one of the best examples of etiology in the Bible. It contains a number of etiologies, which might be given titles resembling Kipling's *Just So Stories*, such as "How the Snake Lost Its Legs." Like Kipling's stories, the Genesis story does not report history, at least not in the modern sense of actual events.

Again, we may begin our analysis with matters of structure. It is fairly obvious that the story of Adam and Eve is a story of creation. But it is an independent story and not a continuation of the account we have just treated in Genesis 1:1–2:3. This is evident from the fact that the Adam and Eve story has a distinctive beginning. In fact, both stories begin with the same grammatical structure. Both have a temporal clause, interrupted by a parenthetical description of conditions at the time of God's act, followed by God's first creative deed in each story.

	Gen 1:1–3 (AT)	Gen 2:4b–7 (AT)
Temporal clause	When God began to create[23] the heavens and the earth	When ("in the day") Yahweh God made earth and heavens
Parenthetical description	(the earth being formless and empty with darkness on the surface of the deep and the divine wind/spirit sweeping over the surface of the water)	(before there was any shrub or grass on the earth, since Yahweh God had not brought rain on the earth, nor was there any human to work the ground but a mist came up from the earth and watered the ground's surface)
First deed of creation	God said, "Let there be light," and light came into existence.	Yahweh God formed the human of dust from the ground and breathed into his nostrils the breath of life so that the human became a living being.

Although they begin the same way grammatically, the two stories differ markedly in significant details, especially concerning the order of creation, and this is revealed by close attention to structure. In Genesis 1, human beings are the last item of creation, following plants and animals. There is also no reason to assume that the creation of humankind in Genesis 1 refers to a single pair. It is not the case that only one pair of the other animals was created. A reader would make that assumption only if he or she already knew the subsequent story about Adam and Eve. In the Adam and Eve story, in contrast, one man is created, followed by the garden for him to inhabit, then the animals in search of a suitable companion, and finally a woman is made from the man, as we see from this comparative list:

Gen 1:1–2:3	Gen 2:4b–3:24
Day 1 – light	the man
Day 2 – dome (sky)	the garden
Day 3 – seas and dry land + vegetation	the animals
Day 4 – sun, moon, stars	the woman
Day 5 – birds, fish	
Day 6 – land animals + humans	
Day 7 – Sabbath	

Thus, two versions of the same event—creation—have been juxtaposed or placed together, one right after the other. This kind of juxtaposing of variant traditions is also found in Herodotus and other Greek history writing.

Turning to genre and intent, which may be treated together, it is unlikely that the story in Genesis 2–3 was ever intended to be understood as an actual set of events. The symbolic nature of the story would have been clear to its original audience from the names of its characters. Adam and Eve were not proper names in ancient Israel. They do not occur elsewhere in the Bible for any other characters (ʾādām is the Hebrew word for "man" or "human"; Eve (Hebrew: ḥawwāh) is related to the word for "life.") The names are a signal to the reader that ʾādām is a symbolic character for humans in general or for all men and that Eve represents all women or womankind—the wellsprings of life.[24]

The Adam and Eve story is a story of origins. It mentions the creation of the world, but that is not its real focus. It refers to Yahweh's creation of "the earth and the heavens," and describes this in detail. The description that follows indicates that the earth in some form is already in existence. The story focuses, rather, on the creation of human beings—first the man, then the woman as his companion, after the animals created in the meantime fail to satisfy that need. The story, therefore, offers explanations for the origin of the genders and their respective roles in society. It also accounts for the attraction of men and women to one another: They are of the same substance, the same "bone" and "flesh," in contrast to the animals. This attraction lies behind the origin of marriage: "*For this reason* a man leaves his father and his mother and stays with his wife and they become one flesh"(AT). The story accounts for why the two genders are embarrassed to be naked in one another's presence and why humans, alone of creation, wear clothing. On a deeper level, the story suggests a connection between sexuality and knowledge that brings to mind the experience of puberty. Just as, in the biblical story, the man and woman become aware of their nakedness when they eat from the tree of knowledge, so in adolescence the development of conscience and a sense of moral responsibility coincides with the maturation of the sexual organs and the libido.

The curses at the end of the story both account for and presuppose different social roles in its ancient Israelite setting. The subordination of women in this story seems pervasive, despite "politically correct" attempts to downplay it.[25] The woman is created second, out of the man, as his companion. It is she who is deceived by the snake and who then leads the man astray. Ultimately, her husband "rules over" her. But the woman's pains in childbirth do not begin with the curses; they are "greatly increased" at that point. Similarly, the man's cultivation of the earth starts before the curses; it is just that the ground is cursed so as to make his labor more difficult. The social hierarchy was already in place before the forbidden fruit was eaten.

The blatant sexism of the story pointedly illustrates the crucial role discernment of genre plays in interpretation. If the story is read as an actual event as has typically been the case in the past and continues as an influential perspective today, then the subordination of women becomes normative—the divinely sanctioned order of the universe. If, however, the story is understood as etiology, then its setting in the ancient Israelite cultural and societal context is obvious. It is simply a tradition borrowed by the ancient Israelite historian in an effort to account for the domestic status quo of that particular society. Universality and particularity coalesce, because the historian writes with the pen of national theology. Just as each nation would view its deity as the creator, so for the Israelite historian Yahweh is the originator of the cosmos.

Above all, this story's etiologies are theological. It explains separation from God and human mortality as the result of sin. Perhaps more to the point, the hardships of daily survival find their causes in human disobedience. The story is scripture not because it contains a divine mandate ordering human society but because it reflects Israel's struggle to understand its life theologically.

In sum, the story in Genesis 2–3 functions within the genre of ancient history writing partly as an account of the creation of the world, but that is not its primary intent. Rather, it serves to explain the reasons or *causes* for the difficulty of human life within the setting of ancient Israel's domestic structure. Implicit in the account is the recognition by the historian that the characters are symbols and not actual persons or the episodes actual events of the past.

Etiology in Genesis: Other Examples

Repopulating the Earth (Gen 9:18–10:32)

Just as one of Kipling's *Just So Stories* dealt with the origin of the alphabet, so one of the items ancient Greek and Israelite history writers sought to explain in creation stories was the beginning of human inventions and crafts. The genealogy in Genesis 4:17–22, for example, describes various individuals in it as the builder of the first city, the founder of pastoral nomadism, the inventor of musical instruments, and the fashioner of metal tools.

Perhaps the most famous such inventor in the Bible is Noah, whose accomplishment is usually overlooked because of his reputation as the hero of the flood. Noah's father, Lamech, gave him the name "Noah" because he would "bring relief" or "comfort"[26] people from the "grievous labor" (lit. "work and hardship") that Yahweh's curses in Eden had brought upon them (Gen 5:29). After the flood, Noah became the first person to plant a vineyard and make wine, thus bringing relief out of the ground, as his father had foreseen. Unfortunately, on this same occasion, Noah also overindulged and became the world's first drunk in one of the Bible's strangest stories (Gen 9:20–27). To outline the story briefly, a drunken Noah falls asleep naked in his tent. His son Ham sees his father naked and reports it to his two brothers, Shem and Japheth, who then cover their father, being careful to avert their view. When Noah revives and finds out what has transpired, he invokes a curse of slavery on Ham's son Canaan.

This story presents a host of interpretive difficulties.[27] What is relatively transparent is its intent to justify the traditions of Israel's later subjugation of the Canaanites. The story does this by means of an eponymous story or tradition. An eponym is defined as a real or imaginary person for whom some group of people, such as a tribe or nation, is believed to be named. An eponymous ancestor does more than bear the name of a group of people. He or she actually represents and even embodies them. In the present story, Canaan is the eponymous ancestor of the Canaanites, the individual after whom the Canaanites were supposedly named. Since there were different groups of Canaanites, it is unlikely that they actually all descended from a single individual. But that is irrelevant to the story. Canaan stands for the Canaanite people. The point of the story is to show that Israel's conquest of the land of Canaan and subjugation of its inhabitants was justified because of the curse of slavery that Noah imposed upon Ham's son Canaan.

The use of eponymous figures continues in Genesis 10, which is closely linked to the story of the curse on Canaan. The genre of this text is purportedly a genealogy of the descendants of Noah's three sons. But closer inspection reveals that it is actually a list of peoples and geographic locations. In fact, it is often dubbed the "table of nations." Its intent is to account for the repopulation of the earth following the flood, and it accomplishes this by the clever use of eponyms.

The names in the chapter correspond to three basic geographic divisions. The descendants of Japheth were places in Anatolia (modern Turkey) and the western Mediterranean. For example, Gomer, Tubal, and Meshech were regions in Anatolia. Javan was the name for Greece in the Hebrew Bible. Its descendants include Tarshish, Kittim, and Rodanim. Tarshish was the site in southern Spain, on the Mediterranean coast, that was mentioned in Jonah as the place to which he tried to flee. Kittim and Rodanim were the islands of Cypress and Rhodes in the Mediterranean.

The descendants of Ham were areas in the Egyptian sphere of influence: Cush was the African region south of Egypt, Nubia or Ethiopia; Put was west of Egypt, Libya. Egypt (Hebrew: miṣrayim) and Canaan were the eponymous ancestors of those countries. Shem incorporated the eastern area of the fertile crescent, including Elam (= Persia), Asshur (= Assyria or northern Mesopotamia), and Aram (= Syria).[28]

The ancient Israelite historian composed or adapted this list of place names in the form of a genealogy in order to account for the repopulation of the earth through Noah's three sons. It is obvious that the historian did not have the entire planet in view. Most of Europe and Africa are unaccounted for, and there is no mention of India, Asia, the Americas, or other parts of the globe. The "genealogy" in Genesis 10 accounts for the world known or of primary interest to the writer and his audience. The writer hereby renders an account of how the world of his readers was repopulated after the flood from the offspring of one man, Noah, through his three sons.

As in the case of the Adam and Eve story, the history of interpretation behind the story of Noah's sons pointedly illustrates the danger of misconstruing the genre of a biblical text. Read as history, this text became the most widely used biblical passage in favor of slavery before the Civil War and was then used to promote segregation following the War.[29] The view of the flood story and subsequent materials, including the genealogy in Genesis 10, as historical fact was combined with the pseudoscientific notion of three great races of humankind: Ham was identified as the progenitor of Negroids (since Cush was recognized as Ethiopia), Japheth of Asians, and Shem of Caucasians. The subjugation of people of African origin was justified as the proper fulfillment of Noah's curse on Ham's descendants. There were glaring problems with this interpretation, of course. Most obvious was the fact that Noah's curse was directed not against all Ham's descendants but only against Canaan, the brother of Cush. But such problems were ignored or explained away. The point for our purposes is that proper recognition of the etiological nature of this episode within the genre of ancient history writing makes its genre as etiology and its intent clear. Failure to recognize its etiological nature has had a pernicious effect on Western, especially American, society.

The Tower of Babel (Gen 11:1–9)

The story of the tower of Babel is set in southern Mesopotamia (ancient Iraq)— the location of the plain of Shinar and of the city of Babylon, here called Babel.

The tower, made of brick and reaching to heaven, alludes to a ziggurat, a temple in the form of a stepped pyramid, characteristic of Mesopotamian religion. Thus, the author had some acquaintance with Mesopotamian culture. The author may be poking fun at Mesopotamian religion, ridiculing its temples as failed attempts to build towers to heaven. The etiological nature of the story is again relatively apparent. Its intent is to provide an explanation for the origins of the different human languages and cultures associated with them.

Abraham and Lot (Genesis 18:16–19:38)

Beginning with chapter 12, the focus of the history in Genesis narrows from the origins of the entire world and all its peoples to those of Israel and the neighboring countries. The stories are of national and ethnic significance as they deal with traditions about Israel's ancestors. The historian typically adopts kinship relationships between eponymous ancestors as the way of accounting for the proximity and rivalry of Israel with the surrounding countries.

The story of the destruction of Sodom and Gomorrah in Genesis 18:16–19:38 is the culmination of the relationship between Abraham (Abram) and Lot. The historian apparently had traditions that identified Lot as Abram's nephew who journeyed with him to Canaan.[30] The story of Sodom and Gomorrah is set up by one in Genesis 13, in which Lot and Abram separated from each other because they had become too wealthy to remain together. Abram generously gave Lot his choice of location in the separation, and Lot chose the lower Jordan Valley, now the site of the Dead Sea. The story explains that at that time it was fertile and well watered. Lot moved to the region, eventually settling in Sodom.

Lot's presence in Sodom is apparently what induces Yahweh to reveal to Abraham his intention to destroy Sodom and Gomorrah.[31] Abraham persuades Yahweh to leave Sodom untouched if as few as ten righteous people are in it. The utter wickedness of the city, illustrated by the story in Genesis 19:1–11, leads Yahweh to proceed with the destruction. The account of the destruction of Sodom and Gomorrah and its aftermath is full of etiologies that account for the terrain around the Dead Sea. Lot escapes to a small city nearby named Zoar ("small"). Yahweh destroys the cities of Sodom and Gomorrah by raining "fire and brimstone (sulfur)" upon them. This accounts for the sulfur odor and high mineral content of the Dead Sea, which is, scientifically speaking, the result of evaporation of a body of water without outlet. The destruction also accounts for the dryness and barrenness of the region, which the story envisions as formerly lush and fertile.

At the end of the story are two eponymous etiologies, which explain the origin of the Ammonites and Moabites, the peoples on the other side of the Dead Sea from Israel, by recounting a tale about their eponymous ancestors.

This story is a colorful one. Afraid to stay in Zoar, Lot moves with his two daughters to a cave. Believing that their father is the only chance for them to reproduce, the daughters, on consecutive nights, intoxicate their father and engage in sexual relations with him. The resulting sons are the eponymous ancestors of the Moabites and Ammonites. The name Moab resembles the Hebrew word for "from father" (*mēʾāb*). Ben-ammi is Hebrew for "son of my people." These contrived etymologies may have inspired the incestuous content of the story, which in turn reflects disdain for the Ammonites and Moabites. At the same time, the story recognizes Israel's proximity to them. Their description as kin to the Israelites through Abraham's nephew Lot may be a way of alluding to a treaty between them, or it may simply express geographical and cultural proximity.

Ishmael and Isaac (Gen 16:1–16; 21:1–21)

The principal theme in the Abraham story is that of the divine promise that Abraham would become the father of a great nation. This promise is the historian's way of accounting for the origin and existence of the nation of Israel. It also bears theological messages: Yahweh has chosen Israel as his people through their ancestors, and Yahweh keeps his promises, albeit in his own time and way.

The major obstacle to the fulfillment of the promise of a great nation is the barrenness of Abraham's wife, Sarah (Sarai). The couple, at Sarah's insistence, seek to circumvent this obstacle by utilizing Sarah's handmaid, Hagar, as a surrogate mother. This practice is attested in marriage contracts from Mesopotamia, which stipulate that it is the wife's responsibility to provide an heir, if not on her own accord then by supplying a female slave for the purpose. The servant's son then becomes the heir as though he were the wife's natural son. The servant is not to flaunt her new status, and the wife may not expel the servant.[32] The relevance of these contracts for the biblical story is obvious. In the story, Hagar bears Abraham a son. But God promises that the heir to the promise will come from Sarah, despite her and Abraham's advanced age. True to the promise, Sarah bears a son, who then replaces Hagar's son as heir. Contrary to custom, but according to divine mandate, Sarah sends Hagar and Ishmael away.

The two passages about the births of these two sons each contain an account of Hagar's departure from Abraham and Sarah and an encounter she has with God in the wilderness. In the Genesis 16 story, Sarah presents her slave, Hagar, to Abraham to serve as a surrogate mother. When Hagar becomes pregnant, she looks down on her mistress, who in turn mistreats her. As a result, the expectant Hagar runs away, apparently heading back to her home in Egypt. An angel or messenger (the same Hebrew word can mean both) from Yahweh meets her by a spring in the wilderness. The angel tells her to return to Sarah and submit to her. The angel blesses her with the same promise given to Abraham: "I will significantly multiply your descendants, so that they cannot be counted because they are so numerous" (AT). The angel tells her that she will bear a son and name him Ishmael. "He will be a wild ass of a man, with his hand against everyone and everyone's hand against him, and he will dwell over against all his kin" (AT). Hagar returns, as ordered.

In the story in chapter 21, Hagar and Ishmael are sent away by Abraham at Sarah's insistence and God's command. Ishmael is portrayed as an infant.[33] They run out of water in the wilderness. Certain that they are going to die, Hagar weeps. God hears her and speaks to her, showing her a well, so that she and her son are saved. The text then says that God was with the boy, Ishmael, as he grew up in the wilderness. He became an expert with a bow and married an Egyptian woman.

The two stories of Hagar's departure, then, are quite similar. In both, Hagar and her either unborn or infant son leave Abraham and Sarah and find themselves alone in the wilderness, where an angel appears to her at a water source and reveals to her the future of her son. The similarities are enough to suggest that the two are variants of the same story. However, the ending of the version in chapter 16 has been changed so that the two may be read sequentially.

The structure or form of the original story is still evident in the version in Genesis 21. A crisis arises when Hagar runs out of water. The crisis is resolved by divine intervention—an angel shows Hagar a water source. As the version of the story in chapter 16 now stands, there is no crisis. The story still takes place at a spring, but the spring no longer plays a role in the plot; it is simply a remnant of the original story. Another indication that the story in Genesis 16 has been altered is that the text repeats the identical expression, "the angel of Yahweh said to her," three times in a row (16:9, 10, and 11). The insertion of the angel's order to return changed the original purpose of the story. The reason for the angel's appearance originally was to save Hagar's life and to reassure her by promising that God would make her son the father of a nation. The promise is preserved in some form in both versions. Following the promise, though, one expects to find a notice of its fulfillment, telling how Hagar and her son thrived in the wilderness because of God's blessing. The version in Genesis 21 has such a notice, but the one in chapter 16 does not. The latter simply has Hagar return to Abraham. The story of Hagar's flight in chapter 16, therefore, seems a literary adaptation of the story in chapter 21 for a new purpose.

The precise intent behind this literary composition is uncertain, but it may have been simply for dramatic artistry—to prolong the suspense of the narrative in its explanation of how Isaac became Abraham's heir through whom the nation of Israel came into being. As the story unfolds, Abraham becomes the father of not just one, but two nations—the Israelites and the Ishmaelites.

As with previous narratives that we have surveyed, these two contain numerous etiologies. There is constant play in these stories on the name Isaac, which ostensibly means "he laughs."[34] Both Abraham and Sarah laugh when they hear the prediction that they, in their old age, will produce a son. Sarah remarks on the laughter that Isaac's birth has brought her. Then the very sight of Ishmael laughing reminds her that he is the heir and motivates her to demand that Hagar and Ishmael be sent away.[35]

The etiologies surrounding Ishmael are more interesting. Ishmael's name means "God hears" and is occasioned by Yahweh's hearing Ishmael's "affliction" at the hands of Sarah. The characterization of Ishmael is really that of the Ishmaelites, whose eponymous ancestor he is. "Ishmaelites" is a term for several clans who inhabited the northern Sinai and Arabian peninsula.[36] The characterization of Ishmael as a "wild ass of a man" who lives at odds with his neighbors suggests a view of the Ishmaelites as a rough and rugged people who carve out a living in hostile terrain, frequently warring with those around them. They also seem to have had a reputation as archers.[37]

In sum, the pair of narratives about Hagar's departure render an account to readers of the origin of the Ishmaelites. They also further the story of Israel's origins through the figures of Abraham and Isaac. Comparison of the two texts illustrates the extent of creativity sometimes exercised by ancient history writers in formulating their accounts of the past. The historian either composed the first version, the one in chapter 16, in its entirety or significantly revised its ending to have Hagar return to Abraham and Sarah. We will consider the creativity of biblical historians in greater detail in the second half of this chapter.

Esau/Edom and Jacob/Israel (Gen 25:19–34)

There is no clearer instance in Genesis of an eponymous etiology than the story of the birth of the twin sons, Jacob and Esau, to Isaac and Rebekah. When Rebekah is pregnant with them, she feels them literally struggling inside her within her womb. She asks Yahweh what is happening to her. The answer she receives in form of an oracle states that the twins are two nations or peoples. They are, in other words, eponymous figures. They bear the names of the nations they embody.

Both "Jacob" and "Israel" are used in the Bible as names for the nation. "Israel" is much more common, but "Jacob" is also occurs a number of times for the entire nation and people. A good example is Deuteronomy 32:9:

Yahweh's portion is his people;
Jacob is the share of his heritage. (AT)[38]

The Genesis narrative incorporates both names in reference to the same epony-mous ancestor by explaining that Jacob's name is later changed to Israel (Gen 32:22–28). Similarly, Esau is more commonly known as Edom (Gen 25:29). Both names refer to the country south and east of the Dead Sea. The prediction in the oracle given to Rebekah when she was pregnant with the twins shows how the narrative identifies the nations of Israel and Edom with their eponymous ances-tors. The oracle states: "the one *people* shall be stronger than the other *people* [so the Hebrew] and the elder shall serve the younger (AT)." Thus, the stories of the individuals, Jacob and Esau, are really the stories of the nations, Israel and Edom. Even the characterization of twins as they grow may really be of the peoples they represent. The Edomites, embodied in Esau, were hunters living in the rugged wilderness, while the Israelites, in Jacob, were more settled, tent dwellers.

The stories about Jacob and Esau and their depictions have been shaped by plays on their names and by traits that the historian ascribes to the peoples they represent. "Jacob" in Hebrew sounds like the noun for "heel" and like the verb for holding or taking by the heel or supplanting.[39] Because this root has nuances of assailing from the rear by stealth, Jacob is portrayed throughout the stories about him as a trickster who gains by deceit. Hence, in the stories about his birth, Jacob comes into the world grasping his brother's heel, and he later sup-plants his brother in the role of oldest son by acquiring first his birthright and then his blessing by deception. Esau is described as red and hairy because the Hebrew word for "red" (*'admônî*) resembles "Edom," and the word for "hair" (*śē'ār*) sounds like "Seir," another name for Edom. Similarly, in the subsequent story, Esau exchanges his birthright for "red stuff," and this is the reason, the author asserts, that he was called Edom.[40]

By means of these eponymous stories about the births of Jacob and Esau, the historian in Genesis accounts for the origin of the peoples of Israel and Edom. Their description as twin brothers explains their geographical proximity, and the stories about their rivalry accounts for the friction between the two nations as well as Edom's eventual subordination to Israel. Esau/Edom is older and stron-ger than Jacob/Israel but loses his/its superiority to the latter's trickery.

The Sons/Tribes of Jacob/Israel (Gen 29:21–30:24)

As the Jacob story continues, the historian begins to focus less on Israel's place among and relationship to its neighbors and more on the identity and makeup of Israel itself. A key text is the story of the births of Jacob's children. Jacob's deceitful acquisition (with his mother's help) of his father's blessing occasions threats on his life from Esau, so that Jacob flees for safety to his mother's family. There he falls in love with his cousin Rachel and arranges to work seven years for

Laban, his uncle, in exchange for marrying her. On the wedding night, however, Laban substitutes his older daughter Leah for Rachel, thus forcing Jacob to continue his servitude for another seven years.

The story is then structured around the two wives, Leah and Rachel, their two handmaids, and the children that all four women bear. God blesses Leah with children because she is unloved by her husband. As a result, Leah bears four sons: Reuben, Simeon, Levi, and Judah. Since Rachel cannot bear children, she provides her handmaid, Bilhah, as a surrogate, and Bilhah bears Dan and Naphtali. Leah, who has ceased bearing, also provides her handmaid, Zilpah, who bears Gad and Asher. Then, after eating mandrakes, a plant considered to endow fertility, Leah bears two more sons, Issachar and Zebulon, and a daughter, Dinah. Rachel, perhaps because she too consumed mandrakes but also because God remembered her, bears Joseph. Later on, Rachel will bear a second son, Benjamin, but lose her own life in the process (Gen 35:16–20).

The etiological nature of this birth narrative becomes evident when it is compared with the earlier story of Sarah providing her handmaid, Hagar, as a surrogate mother. As we saw in the discussion of that story, the practice of a wife furnishing a female slave for the production of an heir is attested in ancient Near Eastern sources. It fits perfectly in the Abraham and Sarah story, where the primary theme is the production of an heir in fulfillment of the divine promise to make Abraham into a nation. The situation with Leah and Rachel, however, is entirely different and completely unattested in ancient Near Eastern practice. There is no need for Rachel or Leah to give their handmaids to Jacob, because Leah herself bears four male heirs at the beginning of the story. Here the handmaid motif serves a different function on a purely literary level. It accounts etiologically for the twelve sons of Jacob, who are the eponymous ancestors of the twelve tribes of Israel. The author might have achieved the same purpose without the handmaids—by having Leah and Rachel bear all twelve sons. But the handmaids also add to the drama of the story by highlighting the competition between the wives.

The story of the births of Jacob's sons, then, is a literary creation intended to account for the origins of the twelve tribes that comprised the nation of Israel in the historian's day. The birth story is not history in the sense of actually having transpired, but it is an example of ancient history writing in that it provides an explanation for the origin of the tribes of Israel as they were in the author's day.

Israel's Relationship to God (Gen 32:22–32)

Having fled from his father-in-law, Jacob escapes reprisal as a result of divine warning to Laban. His gesture of reconciliation to Esau brings him news that Esau is on his way with four hundred men. Uncertain of Esau's intentions, Jacob divides his company in two, with his wives and children in the rear so that they can escape in the event of an attack. That night he is attacked by a man, with whom he wrestles until dawn. That the man is divine is indicated by the etiologies for the names "Peniel/Penuel" (face of God) and "Israel," which the man explains by saying, "You have wrestled with God and with humans and have prevailed (AT)."[41]

This story is another piece of creative writing. It is full of word plays and popular etymologies. Besides Peniel and Israel, there is "Mahanaim" (two camps) and "Jabbok" (like Jacob and similar to one of the verbs for "wrestle" in the story). It also contains a series of folkloric motifs familiar to modern readers who are acquainted with the genre of fairy tales. The attack upon Jacob after he fords the Jabbok reminds one of tales of river demons and trolls (as in "The Three Billy Goat's Gruff"). The apparent need of the man to disappear before dawn also recalls tales of demons and spirits, and is most familiar to moderns in the Dracula story. The being's refusal to share his name reflects superstition about the power of knowing someone's name and is familiar from the story of Rumplestiltskin.

The focus of this collection of plays and motifs is the change of Jacob's name to Israel. The new name is obviously an eponym. The explanation captures Israel's identity as a people who have prevailed over adversaries by the help of their God, with whom they nonetheless continue to struggle. The intent of the story, then, appears to be to explain Israel's corporate identity in relation to its God. This identity is well illustrated by Israel's history throughout the Bible, which is one of continuous struggle with God, who constantly blesses. The story is theological as well as etiological in nature.

The stories about Jacob, therefore, not only account for Israel's relationship with Edom and the origin of Israel's twelve tribes but also for the character of the nation and people of Israel. The eponymous nature of the Jacob stories is not limited to Genesis. Consider the following quotation from the book of Hosea:

Yahweh has a dispute with Israel
To punish Jacob according to his ways
According to his deeds he will requite him.
In the womb he seized his brother's heel
In his manhood he wrestled with God.
He wrestled with God and prevailed.
He wept and entreated him.
At Bethel he found him/finds us.
There he spoke with him/speaks with us. (AT)[42]

Hosea cites an older poem about Jacob/Israel that was popular because of its eponymous nature. Hosea gives the poem a negative interpretation, accusing the people of Israel of trading in deceit like their forebear and namesake. Here we see that the eponymous nature of the stories of Jacob and others in Genesis was widely recognized by ancient historians and their audiences alike. To attempt to read these stories as actual events and deeds of historical individuals is to misconstrue their genre and their intent.

Writing Biblical History

Some of the texts treated above, especially the creation account in Genesis 1:1–2:3 and the two stories about Hagar and Ishmael in Genesis 16 and 21, hint at the creativity that the biblical historians sometimes exhibit. One might expect the authors of other histories in the Bible to be less creative, because they probably had more available sources and hence less room to invent. We will see, however, that authors of other biblical histories continued to exercise a great deal of freedom in the organization, revision, and invention of materials to render an account of their national past.

Prime Example: Chronicles

The books of 1 and 2 Chronicles are some of the least known writings of the Bible. Yet, they provide an opportunity for unique insights into how biblical historians worked because we possess not only Chronicles but also the principal sources that the author used. Written probably in the fourth century BCE, Chronicles is among the later books of the Hebrew Bible. Its main source was the books of 1 and 2 Samuel and 1 and 2 Kings, which had been completed around 560 BCE. The Chronicler (the name given to the author of Chronicles) also made frequent use of many other books in the Hebrew Bible because Chronicles is essentially a rewritten version of the history of Israel presented earlier in the Hebrew Bible. In the following table, an overview of the structure of 1 and 2 Chronicles compared with Samuel and Kings indicates some of the Chronicler's revisions.

The changes introduced by the Chronicler are mostly theological in nature or intent. Chronicles attests four main theological interests that shaped its account of history: (1) the idealization of the reigns of David and Solomon as the "golden age" of Israel and the presentation of the two men, especially Solomon, as model kings; (2) the central importance of the temple, its worship, and its personnel to the faith and life of Israel; (3) the unity of "all Israel" as Yahweh's

Genealogies	1 Chron 1–9	—
Saul's death on Mt. Gilboa	1 Chron 10	1 Sam 31
Civil war	—	2 Sam 1–4
David anointed, conquers Jerusalem, transfers ark	1 Chron 11–16	2 Sam 5–6; 23:8–39
Promise of a dynasty	1 Chron 17	2 Sam 7
David's wars	1 Chron 18–20	2 Sam 8–10; 11:1; 12:26–31
Affair with Bathsheba	—	2 Sam 11:2–12:25
Rape of Tamar, Absalom's revolt	—	2 Sam 13-20
Census	1 Chron 21	2 Sam 24
David commissions Solomon	1 Chron 22–29	—
Struggle to succeed David	—	1 Kings 1–2
Reign of Solomon	2 Chron 1–9	1 Kings 3–11
History of Judah	2 Chron 10–36	—
History of Israel and Judah		1 Kings 12–2 Kings 25

chosen people; and (4) the idea of immediate reward for righteousness or retribution for evildoing. In revising his (the Chronicler was probably a male from the priestly tribe of Levi) sources according to these theological interests, the Chronicler was not attempting to rewrite history for its own sake but to provide instruction and a model for the present and future restoration of Israel. Closer analysis shows how radically and creatively the Chronicler altered his sources in order to render a very different account of the past.

The first nine chapters of 1 Chronicles are genealogies. These are poorly understood by modern readers, who often skip them. In the ancient world, however, genealogies were a powerful tool for supporting a nation's or people's identity and traditions.[43] The Chronicler's use of genealogies as a prologue to his history is comparable to the use of genealogies by Greek historians.[44] The Chronicler borrowed most of his genealogies from other parts of Bible. He used them first of all to make the point about who Israel is and to promote the unity of "all Israel."[45]

Ancient genealogies were not static but were constantly shifting to reflect changes in social relationships. Such changes might be signaled in a genealogy by the order of names or the space devoted to a given individual or family. In 1 Chronicles 1–9, the genealogies of Judah, Levi, and Benjamin are much longer than those for other tribes. The entire genealogy, moreover, is structured around these three tribes with Judah first, Benjamin last, and Levi in the middle. This is because these tribes comprised the Israel of the Chronicler's day, and Levi was the priestly tribe.

The Chronicler also introduced smaller changes into his genealogy for theological or ideological purposes. A good example is the insertion of Samuel's name in the genealogy of the Levites, while in Samuel he is from the tribe of Ephraim.[46] The change was made in order to legitimize Samuel's exercise of priestly functions, such as offering sacrifices, which in the Chronicler's day were the exclusive prerogative of the Levites.

The Chronicler begins his narrative with the death of Saul, which he has essentially taken from the last chapter of 1 Samuel. He omits the rest of 1 Samuel, which recounts Samuel's rule as judge and Saul's reign. Saul's death may seem like a strange starting point for a history of Israel. But the Chronicler's reason for starting here is to focus on David, showing how Yahweh removed Saul and "turned the kingdom over to David the son of Jesse" (1 Chron 10:14, AT).

Not surprisingly, the next event reported in Chronicles is David's becoming king over Israel. In Samuel at this point, David had ruled for seven and a half years as king over Judah alone. The Samuel narrative is preoccupied with the civil war between David and Saul's heir, which occurred during that seven-and-a-half-year period. Hence, when Samuel mentions "all the tribes of Israel" crowning David, it means only the northern tribes. The Chronicler, however, omits any reference to the civil war and moves directly from Saul's death to David's coronation over "all Israel." The language is similar, but the meaning the Chronicler gives to it is entirely different. "All Israel" in Chronicles means not just the northern tribes, but all tribes united as a nation.

David's coronation is combined in 1 Chronicles 11–16 with the conquest of Jerusalem and his transfer of the ark of the covenant there. These are separate events in Samuel. But in Chronicles they are described as one enormous, joyful celebration involving all Israel. These events turn the reader's focus to Jerusalem and the project of building the temple. David offers to build the temple (1 Chron 17) but is told that this task will belong to his son. The Chronicler here borrows the text of 2 Samuel 7, and the Chronicler will later interpret and clarify the reason David was not allowed to build the temple. David's role was to do away with Israel's enemies in order to create a state of peace for Solomon to build the temple. Hence, David shed too much blood to be permitted to build the temple.[47]

The Chronicler rewrites history not just by what he includes but also by what he omits. In recounting David's wars (1 Chron 18–20), the Chronicler borrows from 2 Samuel 8–12 but omits the story of David and Bathsheba as unbefitting the model king that he presents in David. He also omits the stories about the rape of Tamar and Absalom's revolt, since these troubles in the royal family again were inappropriate for the model he was building in David.

It is, therefore, somewhat unexpected to find in 1 Chronicles 21 the story about David's sin in ordering a census borrowed from 2 Samuel 24. The Chronicler includes this story because God's acceptance of David's offering at the end of it gave divine legitimation to the site upon which the temple, and particularly its sacrificial altar, were to stand. Still, the Chronicler has made a minor, but significant, change in the story. He could not accept the statement at the beginning of the Samuel version that Yahweh incited David to take the census, changing it instead to read that one of Israel's enemies provided the incitement.[48]

The remainder of 1 Chronicles deals with the transition from David's reign to Solomon's. Again, the Chronicles version differs remarkably from that of Samuel-Kings. The latter (1 Kings 1–2) describes a rivalry between Adonijah, who, as David's oldest surviving son is the natural choice for his replacement, and Solomon. The rivalry is resolved when the aged David, who is feeble and probably senile, is persuaded by Bathsheba and Nathan into naming Bathsheba's son, Solomon, as his successor. Chronicles never mentions the rivalry or Adonijah. Its focus is on David commissioning Solomon to replace him and, more important, to build the temple.

In a series of speeches in 1 Chronicles 22, 28, and 29, David states that Solomon was chosen by Yahweh to build the temple because, in contrast to David, he is a man of peace (*shālôm*, a play on Solomon's name, *shĕlōmōh*). The speeches are unique to Chronicles, and the ideology reflected in them—the focus on the temple and the respective roles of David and Solomon—is exactly that expressed elsewhere by the Chronicler. These speeches, therefore, are almost certainly the author's composition, according to the practice common among ancient historians, and did not really emanate from David's mouth. In further contrast to the divided loyalties in Kings, the description in Chronicles is one of joy and generosity on the part of *all* Israel as they contribute funds for the temple.

Of the nine chapters concerning Solomon's reign at the beginning of 2 Chronicles, six deal with the temple. In preparing to build the temple, Solomon writes to Hiram (Huram), king of the Phoenician city-state of Tyre, requesting his assistance with lumber and expertise. Huram writes back to assure Solomon of his cooperation. The Chronicles version of Huram's letter coalesces what appear to be two communiqués from Hiram.[49] It also elaborates Hiram's message theologically. In Chronicles, Huram, appearing as something of a convert to Israelite religion, confesses Yahweh as the maker of heaven and earth. His observation that Solomon has been "endowed with discretion and understanding" in order to build the temple is identical to the Chronicler's view, expressed as David's wish (1 Chron 22:12), that Solomon's wisdom is manifested in the temple. Like David's speeches, this letter is the Chronicler's composition. Remarkably, it is here attributed to a foreign king, making him well versed in Israelite theology and politics.

Two further examples from 2 Chronicles may suffice to show the Chronicler's continued use of these historiographical techniques in his account of the divided kingdom. The division of united Israel into the separate kingdoms of Israel and Judah was blamed (in Kings) on Solomon, which could not happen in Chronicles, since the Chronicler presented Solomon as a model king. Instead, the Chronicler placed the bulk of the blame on Jeroboam and the people of the North (Israel) for rejecting the divinely chosen Davidic dynasty and proper worship in Jerusalem. The Chronicler regarded the kingdom of Israel as illegitimate and did not recount its history in the rest of 2 Chronicles, except when it overlapped with the history of Judah.

Such is the point of the speech of King Abijah (Abijam) of Judah in 2 Chronicles 13. In the brief account about him in Kings (1 Kings 15:1–8) Abijam is judged evil, but the Chronicler turns him into a good king and invents a speech. Abijah, chiding the army of Israel for rebelling against Judah and the Davidic dynasty, says that God is on the side of Judah because they have the temple in Jerusalem and worship God properly there. It is clear not only from its theology but also from the circumstances in which the speech is set that the Chronicler has invented Abijah's speech. It is hardly possible that Abijah could have addressed all 1,200,000 soldiers said to be present on the occasion. The Chronicler further displays Abijah's righteousness in his response to the ambush that follows his speech. Abijah and his men cry out to Yahweh, which is the appropriate response according to the Chronicler's theology. Yahweh, in turn, rescues them and gives them victory.

A second example is the Chronicler's account of the boy king, Joash (2 Chron 24). The account of J(eh)oash's reign in 2 Kings 12 depicts a good king who, despite restoring the temple, suffered disasters in the form of a foreign invasion and assassination. The Chronicler's theology would not allow him to retain this account unchanged. Disaster, in his view, was the inevitable retribution for sin. This meant that the calamities that befell Joash were necessarily brought on by his sin. Hence, the Chronicler adopts what is for him a common technique—"periodization"—in which he divides a king's reign into different parts or periods. Joash in Chronicles is righteous only in the first half of his reign while his mentor, the priest Jehoiada, is living. During that time, Joash's reign prospers. Later, however, Joash allows his advisors to lead him into idolatry. He even executes Jehoiada's son Zechariah, who has prophesied against him. These misdeeds bring about the invasion and Joash's assassination.

These examples from Chronicles illustrate key features of history writing in the Bible. The striking differences between the accounts in Chronicles and Samuel-Kings show that the recounting of exactly what happened in the past was not the chief objective of biblical historiographers. Rather, history served ideological purposes. The Chronicler used history to draw theological lessons and to illustrate them. The composition of speeches was a principal tool of the Chronicler's for drawing out the lessons he wished to illustrate. Chronicles also serves to illustrate the inventiveness of biblical historians. The Chronicler exercised great freedom in altering his sources and filling in gaps left by them. No other work of the Bible illustrates these qualities as clearly as Chronicles, for which we have both the historian's final product and his main sources. Still, we can discern other instances of history writing in the Bible where similar techniques and principles of composition are operative.

How Biblical History Was Written: Other Examples

The Flood Story (Gen 6–9)

In 1872 George Smith, a bank clerk who had been hired by the British Museum to collate inscribed tablets from ancient Mesopotamia and who had taught himself to read their cuneiform script, made an amazing discovery—a fragment of a version of the flood story similar to the one in the Bible. Smith was sent on an expedition to Iraq to look for more fragments of the story, and remarkably, he found them.

Since Smith's initial discovery scholars have learned a great deal more about the Mesopotamian flood story and its relationship to the Bible.[50] The Mesopotamian story is much older than the biblical version. The Old Babylonian version of the story (ca. 1750 BCE) was part of a creation myth. Humans had been created to do the work of the gods but proved to be so noisy that they disturbed the sleep of the chief god, Enlil, who determined that they had to be destroyed. The hero, Atrahasis, was warned by a friendly god and told to build a boat in which to preserve human and animal life. The story was adapted for the Gilgamesh Epic, and it was a fragment of that version of the story that Smith found.

There is little doubt in the minds of most biblical scholars that the biblical story was borrowed from the Mesopotamian one. They are, in effect, the same story. One man receives divine warning about the impending flood and detailed instructions about building a boat in which to save his family and to preserve the varieties of animals. Seven days later the flood comes; there is rain, and the waters, which are understood to surround the earth, are loosed. All life not on board the boat is lost. As the waters abate, the boat comes to rest on a mountain.

Birds are sent out to determine when it is safe to disembark. The occupants of the boat leave and offer sacrifices. The deity / deities are gratified by the pleasing odor and promise not to destroy the world by flood again.

Like other portions of the "primeval history" of Genesis 1–11, the flood story was a part of the biblical writers' effort to account for the origins of the world and its civilizations using materials that were available to them—including myths and legends. As with other portions of Genesis 1–11, such as the tower of Babel story, the Bible's flood story was influenced by Mesopotamian tradition.

What distinguishes the flood story from other parts of the primeval history is that it is composite. We have already seen how the historian responsible for Genesis 1–3 juxtaposed two versions of creation. The two creation stories were too different to combine but in some respects complemented one another. The first dealt with the creation of the world and provided an etiology for Sabbath; the second focused on the nature of human beings and their social roles. In the flood story, however, the historian faced two versions that were basically the same except for certain details. The historian simply combined them, leaving in certain tensions and duplications that scholars have long noticed and that are obvious to the careful reader. For instance, there are two distinct explanations for the cause of the flood.

Gen 6:5–7 (AT)	Gen 6:11–13 (AT)
Yahweh saw that human evil was great on the earth such that every form of their minds' thoughts was continuously and exclusively evil. Yahweh was sorry that he had made humanity on the earth and it troubled him. Yahweh said, "I will wipe out humanity whom I have created from upon the ground's surface—humans, animals, reptiles, and even birds, because I am sorry that I made them."	The earth had become corrupt before God, and the earth was full of violence. God saw that the earth had become corrupt in that all flesh had corrupted its way upon the earth. God said to Noah, "I have decided to bring an end to all flesh because the earth is full of violence because of them. So I am about to destroy them with the earth."

Both versions in Genesis tell of God's decision to destroy the world because of the wickedness of humanity. They agree in seeing the flood as the response of a moral God to human wickedness rather than the reaction of a sleep-deprived anthropomorphic deity, as in the Mesopotamian version. Note that they use different terminology in their explanations, including different names for God.

As the story of the flood progresses, other tensions arise in the narrative. One of the more obvious relates to the number and kind of animals that Noah is to load onto the ark. God tells him to take one pair—male and female—of each kind of living creature (6:19). Later, however, Yahweh commands him to take seven pairs of clean animals and one pair of unclean animals (7:2–3). The difference becomes crucial at the end of the story when Noah offers sacrifices to Yahweh of every species of clean animal. This version of the story presupposes Israelite law (Lev 11), according to which only clean animals may be sacrificed and eaten. More than one pair of clean animals was necessary or else this version would have had Noah obliterating all clean animals!

Other differences between the two versions include the length of the flood: forty days according to the "Yahweh" version (7:12, 17; 8:6), but nearly a year according to the "God" version (7:11; 8:1–5, 13). Also, the birds used by Noah at the end of the flood are different. In the "Yahweh" version, a raven is sent out repeatedly until the water has dried up (8:6–7). In the "God" version, it is a dove, and the process is described in more detail (8:8–12).

These differences make it possible to trace the continuation of the two versions throughout the story with relative ease[51] and thus to discern the historian's compositional technique. In the case of the flood story, the historian combined two similar versions by interweaving them. This was a different technique from that of juxtaposing the creation stories in Genesis 1–3. Nevertheless, it provides another illustration of the freedom and versatility exhibited by biblical historians with the sources they inherited.

Abram and Sarai in Egypt (Gen 12:10–20)

This story is the first of three in Genesis in which the patriarch claims that his wife is his sister out of fear for his life in a foreign land. (The relationship between the three stories is complicated, and attempting to resolve it is not our present concern.) The story illustrates two points about history writing in the Bible. First, the presence of the three versions of this story in itself shows the deliberateness and craft of the historian who incorporated them. In each case, the characters or location of the story differ from the other two versions, thus allowing the historian to include all three versions without overly stretching the reader's credulity.

12:10–20   Abram and Sarai with the Pharaoh in Egypt
20:1–17   Abraham and Sarah with King Abimelech in Gerar
26:6–11   Isaac and Rebekah with King Abimelech in Gerar

The second point focuses specifically on the version in 12:10–20. The contours of this story bear a striking resemblance to the larger story of Israel's sojourn in and exodus from Egypt. Abram and Sarai are forced to travel to Egypt because of famine, just as Jacob and his family will move to Egypt as the result of a famine in the Joseph story. As Yahweh afflicts Pharaoh's house with plagues because of Abraham until Pharaoh orders him to leave, so Yahweh will bring plagues upon the Egyptians under Moses until Pharaoh drives them out. Moreover, as Abraham becomes wealthy at the hands of Pharaoh, so the Hebrews in the Exodus will despoil the Egyptians (Exod 3:21–22; 11:2–3; 12:35–36).

The story in Genesis 12:10–20, in other words, was composed on the pattern of the Exodus story. Though they are not exactly eponymous ancestors, Abram and Sarai embody their descendants in this episode, and their time in Egypt foreshadows what the Hebrews will experience there. The writer who composed this story appears to have been familiar with a tradition about the patriarch and his wife—the same basic story shared by Genesis 20:1–17; 26:6–11—and elaborated it with the motifs borrowed from the Exodus.

The Period of the Judges (Judg 1–16)

An outline of key features of the accounts of the judges will help us to discern how the historian has (re)constructed this period of Israel's history.

Judge	Tribe	Enemy	Years oppression	Years judged
Othniel (3:7–11)	Judah	Cushan-rishathaim of Aram-naharaim	8	40
Ehud (3:12–30)	Benjamin	Eglon of Moab	18	80
Shamgar (3:31)	?	Philistines	?	?
Deborah (4–5)	Ephraim	Jabin of Canaan & Sisera his general	20	40
Gideon (6–8) [Interlude: Gideon's son, Abimelech (9)]	Manasseh	Midian	7	40
Tola (10:1–2)	Issachar	—	—	23
Jair (10:3–5)	Gilead	—	—	22
Jephthah (10:6–12:5)	Gilead	Philistines & Ammonites	18	6
Ibzan (12:8–10)	Judah	—	—	7
Elon (12:11–12)	Zebulun	—	—	10
Abdon (12:13–15)	Ephraim	—	—	8
Samson (13–16)	Dan	Philistines	40	20

The book of Judges presents two kinds of figures bearing that title. The so-called major judges are military deliverers who lead Israel in breaking free from a foreign oppressor. The book recounts in detail the stories associated with their liberation of Israel. There are six major judges: Othniel, Ehud, Deborah, Gideon, Jephthah, and Samson. The first four of these come together, and their stories represent effectively the first half of the account about the judges.

The minor judges are more localized administrators whose exact function is unclear. They include Tola, Jair, Ibzan, Elon, and Abdon. They do not overthrow enemies. Consequently, there are no stories associated with them or figures for years of oppression. Another difference between these two groups is the numbers given for years of judgeship. The numbers for the major judges, except for Jephthah, are all multiples of forty: forty for Othniel, Deborah, and Gideon; eighty for Ehud; twenty for Samson. The number forty in the Hebrew Bible is often a round number for a generation. The prime example is the wilderness wandering, which lasted forty years, until the Exodus generation had died off. The tenures of the major judges, then, represent a generation, two generations, or half of a generation. The numbers of years attributed to the tenures of the minor judges are more specific and do not appear to be round numbers.

Jephthah's case is unique in that it includes elements of both the major and minor judges. He resembles a major judge because there is a story about him in which he leads Israel against a foreign oppressor, but the figures for the length of oppression and judgeship associated with Jephthah are not multiples of forty but resemble those for the minor judges.

Drawing on these features, biblical scholars have extrapolated a theory about the composition of the book of Judges.[52] The historian who wrote Judges, as well as the books of 1 and 2 Samuel and 1 and 2 Kings, is usually referred to by scholars as Dtr (Deuteronomistic historian). Dtr likely had two main sources or kinds of sources for Judges: stories, either independent or already collected, about the victories of military leaders (Ehud, Deborah, Gideon, Jephthah) and a list of local officials with their administrative centers and lengths of judgeship (Tola, Jair, Jephthah, Ibzan, Elon, Abdon). The Samson stories may have been part of the first collection or they may have been added later by someone else. The materials about Shamgar and Abimelech were independent and were either incorporated by the historian or interpolated later.[53] The occurrence of Jephthah's name in both sources led Dtr to combine them by placing the list of local officials immediately after the collection of war stories and incorporating Jephthah's story into the list at the point where he was mentioned as a local official.

Dtr imposed a theological pattern upon these sources. It is a cyclical pattern of sin, punishment, repentance, and deliverance that is articulated in Judges 2:11–19. The Israelites sin by worshipping other gods. This provokes Yahweh's anger so that he sends a foreign plunderer to oppress them. Their distress under oppression leads them to "cry out" to Yahweh for relief and to repent. Yahweh responds by raising up a judge to save them from oppression, but the people inevitably backslide into their old ways and the cycle begins all over again. This cycle is then illustrated by the story of Othniel, which Dtr probably invented as a model since it contains few details apart from the theological pattern. What details it does have appear artificial and contrived. For instance, the name of Othniel's foe, Cushan-rishathaim, means "dark, double wicked" and rhymes with Aram-naharaim, where he supposedly comes from.

The imposition of the theological pattern entailed other changes as well. Since the stories of the judges were meant to convey a lesson to the nation as a whole, they were treated by the historian as national figures. However, the fact that they originate from different tribes and deal with a variety of adversaries suggests that the stories Dtr inherited were local stories about contemporary local heroes. But Dtr's theological pattern required them to be sequential so he imposed a chronological pattern upon the military leaders, using forty, the round number for a generation, as the base. The casting of Othniel, a Judahite, as a model suggests that Dtr was from Judah.

The Death of Sisera (Judg 4–5)

A different kind of creativity is exhibited in the account of the demise of the Canaanite general Sisera, Deborah's enemy. The "Song of Deborah" in Judges 5 is widely recognized as one of the oldest passages in the Hebrew Bible. There are various indications of its antiquity, most having to do with technical matters of Hebrew vocabulary and syntax, but one such hint accessible to the English reader is the list of tribes of Israel that the poem describes Deborah calling out to war.

The number and names of the tribes may strike the reader familiar with the Bible as somewhat surprising. There are, first of all, only ten tribes mentioned, not twelve as in "standard" lists (cf. Num 26). The tribes of Judah, Simeon, and Levi are not included. This could be because these tribes, Judah and Simeon in particular, were southern and did not take part in the war. The list in Deborah's poem is not limited to tribes that participated, since Reuben, Gilead, Dan, and Asher are all mentioned as not joining in the battle. The exclusion of Judah, Simeon, and Levi may indicate that they were not considered a part of the confederation of tribes making up Israel at the time the poem was written.

Other standard tribal names that are missing are Manasseh and Gad. They are replaced by Machir and Gilead, clans that are mentioned elsewhere as making up the part of Manasseh east of the Jordan (Num 26:28–29), where Gad was also located. Their presence indicates that the poem was written at a time before the list of tribes had become standardized, when Machir and Gilead were still independent tribes that had not yet been subsumed within Manasseh and Gad.

Recognizing the antiquity of the poem in Judges 5 is important for understanding the work of the Israelite historian in chapter 4. These two chapters represent, in effect, two versions of the same battle. The writer, Dtr, has made use of the poem in chapter 5 to formulate the prose account in chapter 4. This becomes clear from a comparison of their respective accounts of the death of the opposing general, Sisera.

As is typical of biblical poetry, the poem in chapter 5 uses parallelism—saying similar things with different words in separate lines—to create an image or convey a message. Like poetry in general, it does not supply precise detail. Thus, when the poem reads,

> Water he requested
> Milk she gave (AT)

it is not a contradiction. The point is that Jael gave him refreshment. Similarly, in the colon

> Her hand to the tent peg she put
> Her right hand to a hammer of laborers (AT)

Jael took some common tool associated with tent dwellers, which she then wielded as a weapon, striking Sisera on the head and killing him. The threefold occurrence of the verbs "sank" and "fell" that follow makes it clear that the poem envisions Sisera as standing, enjoying his drink when Jael dealt him the fatal blow, rather than nailing his head to the tent floor with the peg in one hand and the hammer in the other, as the prose story has it.

The prose version, in fact, differs significantly from the poem. According to the prose, Jael gave Sisera milk to drink after he had requested water. The function of the drink in the poem was to distract Sisera while Jael approached him with her weapon. But this function is lost in prose, where Sisera requests a drink because he is thirsty. This is somewhat awkward because he has already lain down to sleep, and Jael had covered him with a rug (4:18). The awkwardness results from the prose writer retaining the motif of Sisera drinking but altering the circumstances. As he slept, Jael took a tent peg and a hammer and drove the tent peg into the ground through his skull, killing him. The prose version thus interprets and elaborates the poem. Ignoring the poetic device of parallelism, Dtr fashioned a prose account of Sisera's death that incorporated all the details of the poem—water, milk, tent peg, hammer. The other facets of the prose story leading up to Sisera's assassination can all be attributed to logical deductions arising from its interpretation of the means of his death.[54]

The Election of Saul (1 Sam 9–11)

Scholars have long perceived that 1 Samuel 9–11 contains three different versions about how Saul became Israel's first king.[55] In the first version Saul goes searching for some lost donkeys of his father and instead finds kingship. In the second he is chosen in a lottery, and in the third he is acclaimed king after a military victory. The story exhibits clear signs of revision. The most obvious of these is in the donkey version at 9:9: "Previously in Israel, when going to inquire of God one would say, 'Come, let's go to the seer,' for one who is now called a prophet was previously called a seer" (AT). The author of the story, Dtr, here defines the term "seer," thus making clear to the reader that he is relating an older story.

Other revisions of the story are more subtle but surface upon reflection. It is odd that Samuel, who appears in the previous two chapters as the national leader of Israel, is unknown by name to Saul's servant. One would expect that instead of noting that there was an anonymous "man of God" in the town, he would recognize it as the home of the nationally known prophet Samuel. This suggests that the seer or man of God in the older story was only secondarily identified as Samuel by the same author (Dtr) who updated its terminology.

Another clear example of revision appears in Saul's encounter with Samuel inside the city gate. Samuel identifies himself as the seer and invites Saul to accompany him to the city sacrifice to eat and then to his home to spend the night. "I will let you go in the morning," he continues, "and will tell you all that is on your mind" (1 Sam 9:19). The lost donkeys are what Saul has on his mind. They are the reason he has come to visit the seer in the first place. Yet Samuel goes on in the very next verse to tell Saul that he need not worry about the donkeys any more because they have been found. This revision is very telling, because it indicates a change in the story's focus. The original story was about Saul's search for lost donkeys, but Dtr has revised it into a story about how Saul was anointed king. Saul's overnight stay in the older story allowed the seer time to consult the deity in anticipation of a dream revelation that would reveal the location of the lost animals.

These two revisions provide the criteria by which one may separate the older story from its revised version. Those portions of the story that identify the seer as Samuel are part of the revision. Similarly, any part of the story that presumes Samuel's foreknowledge about Saul's coming or future as king—including his favored status at the banquet—is revision. The story of Saul's anointing is the focus of the revision. What is important for our present purposes is the recognition that the reviser of this story is actually its author. That is, Dtr has here taken an older story from his sources about Saul's search for lost donkeys and has revised and rewritten it in order to relate the anointing of Saul as king.

Of particular significance is the ending Dtr gave to this story. Upon his return, Saul is interrogated by his uncle. That the uncle is nameless and plays no role in the previous story suggests that this scene was added to the older story. The interview makes the single point that Saul's anointing was a private affair between him and Samuel, to which no one else, including Saul's servant, was witness. Dtr added this scene to the story in order to pave the way for the second account of Saul's designation as king, which follows immediately.

In this second version of Saul's election to kingship, he is chosen by lot (1 Sam 9:20). There is no contradiction between the two as they now stand, precisely because the first is described as taking place in private while the second occasion was public. Scholars disagree about whether the second story is based on an older source or is simply Dtr's invention. In either case, the ending is once more significant for its literary function. Here certain individuals question Saul's military leadership ("How can this man save us?"), which paves the way for yet a third story about how Saul was chosen king—one in which he demonstrates his military capability and silences his critics.

The third story begins with a crisis—the Israelite city of Jabesh-Gilead east of the Jordan was being assailed by the Ammonite king, Nahash.[56] The elders of the city send messengers throughout Israel looking for someone to rescue them. The messengers go through all Israel rather than directly to Saul, indicating that the story did not presuppose that Saul was king. The messengers happen to come to Gibeah, Saul's hometown. Saul is engaged not in the affairs of state but in the task of plowing his field. He learns of the crisis only when he hears the people of Gibeah weeping at the news from Jabesh. He is then impelled by the divine spirit to lead Israel in victory. Afterward, there is a cry to have those who doubted his prowess executed. These latter two verses constitute another editorial addition by Dtr. He uses this notice to bind this story with the previous one. Saul's victory has answered all doubts about his capability as a military leader. Dtr's hand is also apparent in the way this story ends. Originally, it concluded with the people making Saul king for the first time in Gilgal. By inserting Samuel's call to *renew* the kingship in Gilgal, Dtr connected this third story of Saul's designation as king with the previous two (1 Sam 11:15). This story, then, was once independent of the previous two, because it did not originally presuppose that Saul was king.

In composing the account of Saul's election to kingship, then, Dtr made use of at least two older sources. One story recounted Saul's encounter of a nameless seer during a search for his father's lost donkeys; the other told of Saul's being made king as the result of leading a military victory. Between these two, Dtr inserted a third account, whether based on source material or his own composition. Dtr adapted the three stories with changes and additions to make them function together as an account of Saul's accession in stages: private anointing, public designation by lot, and proof of himself militarily followed by kingship renewal.

The Royal Houses of Israel in 1 and 2 Kings

One of the best examples of the work of biblical historians being shaped by theological interests is the account of Omri's reign in the book of Kings (1 Kings 16:23–28). From a strictly historical and political perspective, Omri was a very important king. He was so important that Assyrian annals began to call Israel "the house of Omri" and continued to use that designation long after Omri's death. Despite his international fame, however, Omri receives very little attention in the Bible. The account of his reign covers only six verses in Kings, and most of these are the standard formulas used for every king of Israel.

In contrast, the book of Kings spends six chapters on the reign of Omri's son Ahab. The reason for this difference is theological. Dtr portrayed Ahab as the worst king of Israel, primarily because he was married to the Phoenician princess Jezebel. In addition, Ahab was opposed by the prophet Elijah. The wickedness of his wife and the religious significance of his enemy led to the prominence of Ahab's reign in this historian's treatment. By contrast, Omri, for all his genuine historical importance, was all but ignored.

The interplay between prophets and kings that helps to make Ahab's reign so prominent also furnishes the structure for the account of the Israelite monarchy in the book of Kings. Following the division of the united kingdom after Solomon, Kings traces a series of royal houses or dynasties, each overthrown in a military coup. Each coup is predicted by a prophet, who also predicts the slaughter of all the males in the household.

Royal house	Prophecy of downfall	Fulfillment
Jeroboam	by Ahijah: 1 Kings 14:7–11	1 Kings 15:27–30
Baasha	by Jehu: 1 Kings 16:1–4	1 Kings 16:11–13
Omri	by Elijah: 1 Kings 21:20–24 and by a disciple of Elisha: 2 Kings 9:7–10a	2 Kings 9:25–26, 36–37; 10:9–11
Jehu	by Yahweh: 2 Kings 10:30	2 Kings 15:12

The series of prophecies and fulfillments begins with the oracle of Ahijah to Jeroboam awarding him ten shares (= 10 tribes) of Solomon's kingdom (1 Kings 11:29–39). Ahijah explains that this is punishment for Solomon's sin of idolatry. He adds that the kingdom will not be removed entirely from Solomon; the dynasty will continue to rule from Jerusalem (the kingdom of Judah) because of God's promise to David. Nor will the division take place during Solomon's lifetime for the same reason. Thus, the division of the kingdom occurs in fulfillment of Nathan's prophecy to David (2 Sam 7) and of Ahijah's to Jeroboam (1 Kings 11:29–39). Both of these prophecies share similar language and themes that have led scholars to attribute them to the same author—namely, the historian Dtr.

The other instances of prophecy/fulfillment relating to the succession of royal houses also show clear evidence of Dtr's intervention. The prophecies and their fulfillments share certain expressions. They typically refer to Yahweh cutting off every male, "bond or free," within the royal house. They use an expression for "male" that literally means "one who urinates on the wall."[57] They also threaten nonburial, making use of a curse probably derived from ancient treaties ("the dogs will eat those who die in the city; the birds will eat those who die in the open country").[58] These similarities in language are a good indication that the same author—Dtr—wrote these prophecies as well as their fulfillment notices and simply attributed them to different prophets.

In composing the narrative about the prophecies, Dtr again makes use of older stories. The oracle against the house of Jeroboam, for instance, is set within a story in which Jeroboam sends his wife to inquire of the prophet Ahijah about his son's recovery from illness (1 Kings 14:1–18). The prophet's message about the boy's death, which was the focus of the original story, has been preempted by the prophecy about the annihilation of Jeroboam's royal house.

An even clearer example is the prophecy of the end of the house of Omri in the mouth of Elisha's disciple (2 Kings 9:1–10a). Elisha tells the young prophet to go to the army commander, Jehu, to anoint him king privately and then to flee without lingering. In the original story, the disciple must have followed these instructions to the letter. In the present version of the story, however, the young prophet actually disobeys his master by continuing to deliver a prophecy against the reigning house. This prophecy is the work of Dtr and is essentially the same as the other prophecies against the Israelite dynasties. Dtr used the older story legitimating Jehu's revolt as a forum to insert the prophecy against the house of Omri.

The most important aspect of this prophecy/fulfillment scheme is the way in which Dtr has used it to account theologically for Israel's national history. It was common practice in the ancient Near East and beyond for a usurper to kill all the males of the royal family that he overthrew in order to prevent any of them from leading a future uprising against him. Baasha, Omri, and Jehu each followed this practice. Dtr explained the practice theologically as the fulfillment of a series of prophecies against sinful dynasties. He composed the prophecies himself, tailoring them to fit the historical circumstances that he narrated. In the same way, Dtr accounted theologically for Jehu's being the longest lasting of the royal dynasties. It survived through four complete generations following Jehu because of his faithfulness in getting rid of the wicked Omride dynasty with Jezebel and her legacy of Baal worship (2 Kings 10:30; 15:12).

Conclusion

My purpose in this chapter has been to show that history writing in the Bible is less concerned with what actually happened in the past and is more of a creative activity than modern readers typically assume. This does not mean that the Bible never describes what actually took place in the past, but that was not the main objective of the ancient Israelite history writers.

I have not dealt with all of the instances of history writing in the Bible but only with ones that illustrate its nature as etiology and the creativity of its authors. Nor have I mentioned the Exodus from Egypt or conquest of Canaan, which many people would consider to be the heart of the issue of the historical reliability of the Hebrew Bible. In the following sections we will briefly consider these episodes as well as the historiograpical literature in the New Testament in the light of what we have learned about the genre of ancient history writing.

The Joseph-Exodus-Conquest Complex

There are serious and widely known difficulties with trying to understand the episodes about Joseph, the Exodus, and the Conquest as actual historical events. There is no mention of Joseph, either by his Hebrew name or his Egyptian name (Zaphenath-Paneah) in any extant Egyptian records, nor is there any unambiguous reference to any of the events in the Joseph story, such as the seven-year famine or the appointment of Joseph as second in power. The biblical story does not name the king of Egypt but uses the title "pharaoh" as though it were a proper name. The Bible does not give any other information that permits a definitive correlation with Egyptian history.

Much the same is true for the Exodus. The reference to the city of Raamses (Exod 1:11) seems to indicate a setting in the reign of Ramesses the Great (1279–

1213 BCE). Again, however, the biblical text does not name the pharaohs, and it is difficult to match the transition from the pharaoh of the oppression to the pharaoh of the Exodus with Egyptian records. Moreover, the Bible's chronological references to the Exodus are not in agreement. In Genesis 15:13, for example, the period of Egyptian oppression is supposed to last four hundred years. Three verses later, the Exodus is presumed to take place in the fourth generation—just one hundred sixty years by the biblical reckoning of forty years per generation. Solomon's completion of the temple is dated in the four hundred and eightieth year after the Exodus (1 Kings 6:1), placing it around 1436 BCE, some two hundred years earlier than the reign of Ramesses.

As with the Joseph story, none of the events surrounding the Exodus in the Bible's narrative, including the plagues and the Red Sea event with the drowning of the Egyptian army, have any real reflex in Egyptian records. Some aspects of the story, such as the escape of something like two million people (600,000 men + women and children, Exod 12:37; Num 1:46), strain credulity. Could such a large group—one-third to one-half of Egypt's population at the time—have left Egypt at once without any trace in its historical records, to say nothing of the problems surrounding the survival of such a multitude for forty years in the Sinai wilderness?[59]

Archaeology has also raised doubts about the historical veracity of the conquest story. Cities such as Jericho and Ai, which are at the heart of the biblical account of the conquest, attest little or no occupation at the time that they were supposedly conquered by the invading Israelites. Furthermore, Israelite culture seems to have its origins in central highland villages that were native to Canaan rather than being introduced from the outside.[60]

The difficulties involved in reconstructing actual events behind these episodes suggest that the narratives about them are ripe for a different kind of interpretation. As with the story of Jonah, the problem lies not with the Bible but with the way it is interpreted. We have seen that there is plenty of precedent for a different understanding of history writing in the Bible. The texts we have analyzed are not primarily intended to relate exactly what happened in the past, even when actual events of the past underlie them.

The Joseph-Exodus-Conquest complex makes perfect sense when one recognizes the nature and techniques of ancient history writing. The story of the flight of the Hebrews from Egypt and their defeat of Canaanite cities may contain genuine historical elements.[61] But to focus on these is to miss the intent of the story, which is to account for how Israel gained possession of the land of Canaan. Its explanation is theological: God chose Israel, rescued the people, and gave them the land of Canaan.

The etiological nature of these stories is most apparent in the case of Ai, which means "ruin." It is hard to escape the impression that the story of Ai's conquest is an etiology explaining how the site came to be a ruin.

Jericho was one of the oldest cities in the world, dating back to 7000 BCE, and a legendary symbol of Canaanite might. That such a city had come to belong to Israel could only be understood by biblical historians as representative of God's gift of the land to them.

The Joseph story, in contrast to preceding sections of Genesis, is a flowing narrative with a single set of characters and consistent character and plot development (a novella). It was probably written to connect the patriarchal traditions with the Exodus traditions by explaining how the Israelites got from Canaan to Egypt.

New Testament Historiography:
The Gospels and Acts

The understanding of ancient history writing also has important implications for the New Testament, especially the Gospels (Matthew, Mark, Luke, and John) and the book of Acts.[62] New Testament scholars debate the genre of the Gospels. The tendency was to see them as a unique genre founded in popular traditions and stories about Jesus that had become the core beliefs of the early church. More recently, scholars have begun to explore other genres and have pointed increasingly to ancient biography, a subgenre of ancient history writing, for analogies.

Even so, the Gospels are not biographies in a modern sense. They do not present a comprehensive account of Jesus's life. For instance, they relate virtually nothing about Jesus's childhood. Rather, they use the story of Jesus to bring theological instruction to their respective audiences—to persuade them about Jesus's identity and nature, and to hold up Jesus's character and teachings as models to be emulated and followed.

Thus, something as presumably straightforward as a genealogy becomes a vehicle for theological instruction. Matthew (Matt 1:1–17), targeting Jews or Jewish Christians, begins Jesus's genealogy with Abraham in order to stress Jesus's Jewish identity. The writer includes the list of kings of Judah, showing that Jesus is qualified to be the Messiah or "anointed" in the line David. Luke's genealogy for Jesus (Luke 3:23–38) differs because his audience is different. He traces Jesus's line all the way back to Adam, making the point for his primarily Greek readers that Jesus's ministry was for all people.

Mark and John do not include a genealogy, perhaps because of their stress on Jesus as the son of God. John, whose work differs entirely from the other three

Gospels, is explicit about his purpose in writing. It is not to recount exactly what happened during Jesus's lifetime but to convert the reader to faith in Christ (John 20:31). To be sure, there is genuine historical and biological information behind the Gospels. But like other ancient works of history, their main purpose relates to theological instruction rather than historical accuracy or detail. And like other ancient works of history, including ancient biography, the Gospels may contain materials that are fictional or based on plausibility rather than actual fact.

Much the same is true of the book of Acts.[63] Acts is a continuation—volume two, so to speak—of Luke's Gospel. In the prologue to the Gospel (Luke 1:1–4), Luke notes that he conducted the kind of *research* that was the essence and root meaning of ancient history. He drew on examples of history writing and biography in the Hebrew Bible, the Gospel of Mark, and the Greco-Roman world in general in composing his two-volume work. Acts relates the history of the early church. But it is ancient history writing and does not meet the standards of modern historiography. Following the conventions of other ancient historians, Luke composed the speeches and letters in the book of Acts according to what he deemed appropriate to the occasion. He may also have invented some of the stories in the book, again according to what seemed appropriate.

Continuing the primary interest established in his Gospel, Luke is concerned to show the spread of Christianity beyond its Jewish origins. In particular, Luke traces the growth of the new faith, in the work of Paul, to Rome. Thus, he does not follow up on the spread of Christianity in Ethiopia in the wake of the conversion of the Ethiopian official (Acts 8:26–4). Instead, he focuses on the controversy following the conversion of the centurion Cornelius (Acts 10–15) as part of his attempt to show that Christianity is not a threat to the Roman Empire. The historical accuracy of the book of Acts is a matter of ongoing debate. However, it is important to recognize that historical inaccuracy and invention would not disqualify Acts as a useful and significant example of ancient history writing—indeed, the first church history.

Chapter Two

FORTHTELLING, NOT FORETELLING
Biblical Prophecy

The Misconception:
Biblical prophets foretell the future.

Prophecy in the Bible has more to do with forthtelling the word of God in the present than it does with foretelling the future. —Anonymous

They said one to another, "Behold here cometh the dreamer. Let us slay him and we shall see what will become of his dreams."

—Gen 37:19–20 (King James Version),
inscribed on a plaque outside of the
National Civil Rights Museum in
Memphis, Tennessee, the site of the
assassination of Dr. Martin Luther King Jr.

The first quotation above expresses the main point of this chapter. Christian readers typically misunderstand prophecy in the Bible because they assume that its primary intent is to foretell the future. This chapter will show that the intent of the genre of prophecy in the Hebrew Bible was not primarily to predict the future—certainly not hundreds of years in advance—but rather to address specific social, political, and religious circumstances in ancient Israel and Judah. This means that there is no prediction of Christ in the Hebrew Bible. The writers of the New Testament and later Christian literature reinterpreted or reapplied the Hebrew prophecies, something along the lines of the way that the words from the Joseph story in Genesis are reapplied to Martin Luther King Jr. in the second quotation above. This is not to disparage these later Christian authors, however, for they were participating in a long-standing process of reinterpretation that goes back to the prophetic books themselves.

The Genre and Intent of
Prophecy in the Hebrew Bible

The Role of Prophets

The assumption that Hebrew prophecy was intended to predict the future is natural. The main dictionary definition of the English verb "prophesy" is "to foretell or predict."[1] Similarly, the primary definition of the noun "prophecy" is "the foretelling or prediction of what is to come." However, the dictionary also defines "prophet" not as someone who foretells the future but as "a person who speaks for God." Indeed, the Greek root of the word "prophet," *prophētēs* comes from two words, *pro*, meaning "before" and *phētēs*, meaning "speaker." In ancient Greece a prophet was a person who spoke for another, usually a god, and interpreted the god's will.

The Hebrew word translated "prophet," *nāvi'*, refers to one who is called to be a spokesperson for Yahweh. Israelite prophets typically began their oracles with "Thus says Yahweh," which was a messenger formula in the ancient Near East. Before postal systems, kings sent messengers, who prefaced their messages with, "Thus says X," giving the name of the king who had sent them. In the same way, Israelite prophets typically delivered their oracles in the first person, speaking on Yahweh's behalf. Prophets in the Bible, in short, were primarily forthtellers rather than foretellers, proclaimers, messengers, or "preachers" rather than predictors.

Prophets in the Bible do talk about the future. One of the sources of the institution of prophecy was seers like the one whom Saul consulted about the location of his lost donkeys. Similarly, King Jeroboam sent his wife to inquire of the prophet Ahijah whether his son would recover from disease. Kings also consulted prophets before going to war in hopes of knowing the outcome beforehand (see 1 Kings 22). We also saw how the Deuteronomistic historian (Dtr) used prophecies about the future of the royal houses in Israel to structure the account in the book of Kings. In all of these instances the prophet was still a spokesperson for God.

The prophets who lent their names and oracles to the prophetic books in the Hebrew Bible also dealt with the future. But it was always the *immediate* future that was their primary concern rather than the future hundreds of years down the road. Their pronouncements about the future were not so much predictions as threats. Theirs was a "turn or burn" message: "This is what will happen to you if you do not change your ways." They were often very creative in the language and images they used to describe the disaster they envisioned in the future. The prophets were critics of their societies, condemning religious and social practices and institutions of their times. They cannot, therefore, be understood apart from their individual historical and cultural settings.

A good example of a kind of modern-day prophet is Dr. Martin Luther King Jr. Like the prophets in the Bible, he critiqued the society in which he lived. Like them, he issued these critiques on the grounds of religious principles. He was first and foremost a preacher, not a foreteller of the future. He spoke of the distant future only in vague, idealistic terms ("I have a dream"). But he also threatened disaster in the immediate future if America did not alter its course. In addition, like certain biblical prophets, his message was not popular in government circles. And, like those particular prophets, he was arrested and eventually killed.

Prime Example: Jeremiah's "Temple Sermon" (Jer 7:1–15; 26:1–19)

The basic essence of biblical prophecy is critique. This is well illustrated by Jeremiah's Temple Sermon, so named because it recounts an oracle that Jeremiah directed against the temple in Jerusalem and delivered within its precincts. The account in chapter 7 details the content of the oracle; chapter 26 describes the fallout from it.

The Temple Sermon makes two basic points. The first is that the people of Judah are guilty of social and religious offenses. Jeremiah lists injustice, oppression of the disadvantaged (resident aliens, widows, and orphans), murder of innocent people, and the worship of other gods as examples of their "ways and deeds" that they need to improve. He accuses them of stealing, murder, adultery, swearing falsely, burning incense to Baal, and worshipping other gods—all violations of the Ten Commandments.

Jeremiah's second point is that the people of Judah and Jerusalem have misplaced their faith. They have come to trust, he says, in "deceptive words," identified as "this is the temple of Yahweh." The phrase is repeated three times as though it were a kind of mindless, rote recitation: "This is the temple of Yahweh, the temple of Yahweh, the temple of Yahweh," indicating that the people trusted in the temple itself rather than in God. They believed, at least in Jeremiah's caricature of them, that inside of the temple precincts they were immune from prosecution for their deeds no matter how they behaved outside of it. Jeremiah characterizes their attitude toward the temple as that of a band of robbers or "den of thieves" toward their hideout. They commit all manner of crimes and then flee to the temple for refuge.

The intent of the Temple Sermon was to counter this attitude toward the temple. He called upon the people of Judah to improve their behavior, and only then would Yahweh stay with them in his "house."[2] Otherwise, Yahweh would abandon the temple to destruction. As proof that Yahweh would allow Jerusalem to fall and the temple be destroyed, Jeremiah pointed to the site of Shiloh. Shiloh had once been the principal shrine in Israel, the place where Samuel trained, but it had been destroyed by the Philistines.[3]

The account in chapter 26 shows just how radical Jeremiah's declaration of the temple's destruction was for his time. "You must die," the priests, prophets, and people who heard him told him. They took him to the leaders ("princes") of Judah and told them that Jeremiah deserved to be sentenced to death for prophesying against the city of Jerusalem, which housed the temple. They obviously considered his words blasphemy.

What is fascinating about this episode is how Jeremiah's life was spared. Some of the elders of Judah recalled a prophecy very similar to Jeremiah's from the prophet Micah, who lived a little more than one hundred years earlier. (Micah's work is also preserved in the Bible, in the book that bears his name.)[4] The elders quoted Micah 3:12, which prophesied that Jerusalem would become a pile of ruins and be plowed like an empty field. "Did Hezekiah king of Judah and all of Judah have [Micah] executed?" they asked. "Did he not fear Yahweh and ask for Yahweh's mercy so that Yahweh changed his mind about the disaster he had intended for them? We are about to do great harm to ourselves!" (Jer 26:19, AT).

The elders' interpretation of Micah's words reveals two crucial points about prophetic literature. First, they understood Micah's prophecy as relating to Judah of his day and not as a prediction of the distant future. That is how King Hezekiah understood it as well. He and his servants took immediate steps to repent and change their ways in order to avoid the destruction that Micah threatened. Second, both Hezekiah and the elders of Jeremiah's day also understood Micah's prophecy to be conditional. Jerusalem's fate was not sealed but depended on the response of Hezekiah and the city's inhabitants to the prophetic threats. Jerusalem was not destroyed during the two centuries between Micah and Jeremiah. The elders of Judah in Jeremiah's day saw this not as a failed or false prophecy but as the result of Hezekiah's repentance and religious reforms.

The Temple Sermon episode demonstrates that the people of ancient Israel and Judah understood prophecy as we have characterized it—as social and religious critique of the prophet's own society—and not concerned with the future hundreds of years in advance. This characterization of prophecy is not a modern invention of scholars; it was, however, the understanding of the prophets' ancient audiences, such as the elders of Judah in Jeremiah's day.

Other Examples: The Book of Amos

The book of Amos furnishes a number of excellent illustrations of the intent of Hebrew prophecy as social and religious critique. Amos lived and worked in the middle of the eighth century CE, a very prosperous period for the nation of Israel. He was from the village of Tekoa, but he prophesied in Israel. Amos himself was likely a well-to-do herdsman, but he criticized the upper class of Israel for their unjust and oppressive treatment of the poor. The following texts from Amos illustrate his social and religious critiques and the way in which a prophet's threats of future destruction are intimately tied with their present.

"For three transgressions and for four" (Amos 1–2)

The book of Amos begins with a set of oracles against other nations. It is not unusual to find a section of oracles against foreign nations, since other prophetic books also contain such a section (Isa 13–23; Jer. 46–51; Ezek 25–32; see also Obad and Nah). Some prophetic books (Obadiah, Nahum) even consist essentially of one or more oracles against a foreign nation.

The oracles against other nations represent a literary strategy. They open the book of Amos and lure the reader's attention to the prophet's message—all the more so since these oracles condemn hated enemies—but then focus Amos's message on the real target of his prophecy, that of Israel. They do this by including an oracle against Israel itself as the last of the condemned nations—the climax of the series of oracles.

The nations mentioned in Amos's oracles are all neighbors of Israel: Syria, the Philistines, Phoenicia, Edom, Ammon, Moab, Tyre, and Judah.[5] Each of these nations is condemned in turn for such matters as war crimes and treaty violations. The Israelite readers or hearers would be pleased by the condemnations of these other nations, who were Israel's rivals and enemies. But those same readers/hearers would then be caught off guard and dismayed to find that the last and longest of the oracles was reserved for themselves.

The oracles against the nations illustrate the motif of the "day of Yahweh" that comes later in Amos. The Israelites look forward to the "day of Yahweh" as a time when God will take vengeance for them against their enemies, as promised in the oracles against the nations. But then Israel turns out to be Yahweh's prime target. The oracles against the other nations thus serve as a prelude to the real focus of Amos's condemnations—Israel. Amos alters the motif of the "day of Yahweh" from hope to threat. He says that the time is coming when Yahweh will indeed act, not only against Israel's enemies but also against Israel itself. The Israelites, says Amos, should not be looking forward to the coming of the "day of Yahweh" but should be dreading it.

Amos criticizes the Israelites not for treaty violations but for social offenses against their own people. Specifically, the upper class is accused of selling the righteous and the needy, and trampling on the poor and oppressed. There is sexual immorality ("a man and his father go into the same young woman," 2:7,

AT) and exploitation of the poor, since they lie down upon "pledged garments" (2:8). A pledged garment was one that had been taken from a poor person as collateral for a loan. Poor people had nothing but their clothing to offer as collateral. The law forbade taking a garment in pledge from a widow (Deut 24:17) or keeping such a garment overnight, since the poor person would have no other cover for sleeping (Exod 22:26–27 [Heb 22:25–26]). Hence, lying down on pledged garments is a social injustice, taking advantage of the poor.

"Wine extorted by fines" (2:8) also alludes to an oppressive and socially unjust activity. It was, in effect, wine stolen from the peasants. The altars and temple mentioned in this verse may refer to religious apostasy ("God" could be translated "gods"). But it is more likely that they are intended to show the hypocrisy of the Israelite wealthy whom Amos condemns. These people pretend to be religious by keeping all the rituals. But their treatment of others shows that their religion is a sham.

"The cows of Bashan" (Amos 4:1–3)

The beginning of chapter 4 is addressed to the upper-class women of Samaria, the capital of Israel, and "cows of Bashan" is a reference to their prosperity. Bashan was a region east of the Jordan known for its choice grazing land. The noble women of Samaria led the most luxurious lifestyle in the country, but it came at the expense of the poor and was, therefore, oppressive. The Samarian women were concerned only with their own comfort, callously ignoring the repercussions of their lifestyle for the poor, as their words to their husbands suggest: "Bring us something to drink."

Amos graphically describes the punishment awaiting these women: They will be taken away into captivity. Amos does not say when this will happen or who the captors will be. In fact, it is not a prediction at all but a threat. Captivity was a common fate in the ancient Near East, particularly for women; it accompanied defeat at the hands of an invading army. Amos sketches these experiences in broad terms. The city of Samaria will be conquered by an army that breaches its walls and leads its inhabitants away. No specifics are forthcoming. Near the end of the chapter Amos summons Israel to prepare to meet its God, who is coming in judgment. Again, though, he does not predict the exact form that this judgment will take or when it will happen. His oracle is a threat intended to move Israel to repentance, which would, in turn, avert the threatened disaster.

"Set justice in the gate" (Amos 5:10–17)

In ancient Israel the city gateway was, in effect, the courthouse, the place where legal proceedings occurred. Thus, the references to "the gate" in this passage are references to Israel's legal system.[6] In Amos's view, that system had become corrupt. He says that the upper-class Israelites had come to hate righteous judges who reproved and spoke truth. Instead, the Israelites used the legal system to oppress the poor; bribery was rampant.

Ironically, Amos used literary genres that originated in legal settings to condemn this behavior. He follows the preceding indictment with a pronouncement of sentence: "You have built houses of dressed stone, but you will not live in them. You have planted desirable vineyards, but you will not drink their wine" (5:11, AT). Again, these are threats rather than predictions. They are actually known as "futility curses" and were common in ancient treaties. They cursed treaty violators with doing all the work for a particular project, like building a house or planting a vineyard, but being killed or captured before getting to reap the benefits.[7] Amos provides no details about when and how these things will happen because his words are not a prediction. He simply borrows curses from treaties or elsewhere as a means to threaten Israel.

Amos's purpose in articulating such threats is to move the Israelites to repentance. He admonishes his audience to "set justice in the gate," to seek good rather than evil, indeed to love good and hate evil. Integrated with these admonitions are the expressions of hope for change and a positive outcome: "that you may live," "that Yahweh may be with you," and "perhaps Yahweh will show mercy to the remnant of Joseph." These possibilities indicate that the disaster Amos threatens is not a forgone conclusion. They exhibit the conditionality that is characteristic of prophecy. Amos's threats are not predictions because they are not determined to take place. Whether the threats will be realized depends on the people's response to the prophetic warnings.

"Beds of ivory" (Amos 6:4–7)

In a passage very similar to the "cows of Bashan" oracle, Amos here again condemns the wealthy of Samaria. They live in luxury, sleeping on beds inlaid with ivory and eating the choicest meats. Amos seems to wax sarcastic as he caricatures their idleness. They imagine themselves to be great musicians of David's legendary caliber. They drink wine in bowls. The Hebrew word used here might better be translated "basins," referring to large vessels used in worship settings. Those who use these basins for drinking wine not only overindulge but also profane the sacred. They also use the finest oils to anoint themselves. The anointing again calls up the image of David. It indicates the selfishness of the wealthy of Samaria and their overestimation of their self-worth.

The problem with the Samarian nobility is not their luxurious lifestyle per se, but their misplaced priorities. They live like kings but are not troubled (lit. "sickened") by the "ruin of Joseph." The nation is deteriorating all around them and yet they remain apathetic. Therefore, Amos says that they will be the first to go

into exile. Again, there is no prediction here, no detailing of time or circumstances, since it was common practice to take the nobility captive and to leave
the poor of the land behind. Amos merely refers to a common cultural practice
in voicing God's threat against the Samarian upper class.

"Neither a prophet nor a prophet's son" (Amos 7:10–17)

A priest named Amaziah at the royal shrine of Bethel accused Amos of treason,
citing his threats that Israel would be taken into exile.[8] Amaziah told Amos to
return to Judah and to ply his prophetic trade there, away from Israel's royal
sanctuary. Amos replied, "I am neither a prophet nor a prophet's son" (7:14),
meaning that he was not a prophet by profession or training; he had not learned
the trade of prophecy as the disciple or "son" of a prophet. Rather, he had been
called by Yahweh to prophesy. Amos quoted Amaziah as forbidding him to prophesy against Israel: "You must not prophesy against Israel. You must not preach
against the house of Isaac" (7:16). The quotation, and indeed the entire scene,
illustrates the understanding of prophecy shared by Amos and Amaziah; it is
preaching, usually preaching against or threatening. Amaziah found Amos's
threats against Israel to be dangerous and seditious.

Nevertheless, Amos goes on to prophesy against Amaziah. His wife will become a prostitute; his children will die by the sword; his land will be divided; and
he will die outside of Israel. Once more, these are threats based on the period
and culture rather than predictions. They all derive from the premise that Amaziah
would be taken captive by an invading army. His children would be killed in the
war. His land would be seized and parceled out to others. With no other means
of support, his wife would be forced to turn to prostitution. Amaziah would die
in the country to which he had been taken captive. All of these disasters are the
natural results of the military defeat that Amos threatens for Israel.

"Making the ephah small and the shekel great" (Amos 8:4–10)

In this text, Amos assails the oppressive business practices of those in Samaria
who take advantage of the poor. The ephah was a measure of capacity, so Amos
complains that the prosperous merchants of Samaria cheat buyers by selling less
for more, even vending the refuse, for their only concern is for profit. They keep
the religious holidays without genuine piety, for they only want to return to the
business of making profit. They even traffic in human life. The disaster Amos
threatens in this instance differs from that of previous oracles. It is not military
defeat but earthquake, eclipse, and mourning. Again, these are not specifics.
The precise cause of the mourning is not even explained; it is simply a vision of
doom and gloom.

The foregoing texts from Amos well illustrate the nature of Hebrew prophecy as characterized previously. Hebrew prophecy was always intimately tied to the prophet's own time and place. It referred to the future only in very general terms that were usually negative and hence better characterized as threat. Amos's message dealt originally with eighth-century Israel. He threatened destruction from Yahweh at the hands of an invading army. And, in fact, the Assyrians devastated the kingdom of Israel just a few decades later. That Amos did not pinpoint this invasion indicates that his oracles were not detailed predictions but general threats, which drew on a common source of disaster in the ancient Near East. Amos's threats, moreover, were understood to be conditional, even if their conditionality was rarely made explicit. The objective of prophecy was to effect change ("turn or burn") in the religious and social practices of its hearers or readers.

The Reinterpretation of Prophecy

Despite its connection to specific times and circumstances, Hebrew prophecy was not static. Subsequent generations, especially after the Babylonian exile, reinterpreted older prophetic writings and applied them to their later settings.

"The booth of David" (Amos 9:11–15)

The final oracle of the book of Amos differs markedly from the foregoing material in at least three ways. First, this oracle is optimistic. Rather than depicting destruction, these verses refer to raising, repairing, rebuilding, and restoring. They look forward to fertility rather than famine, security rather than captivity and exile.

Second, the subject of this oracle is no longer Israel but Judah. The "booth of David" (9:11) is an alternate expression for the "house of David," a way of referring to the Davidic dynasty, which ruled Judah for its entire history. The royal house of Judah is not a concern in any of the previous material in Amos.

Third, the setting of this oracle is no longer the eighth century in which the prophet Amos lived. The "booth of David" is fallen, an allusion to the destruction of Jerusalem and the Babylonian exile of 587 BCE when the kingdom of Judah and its dynasty effectively came to an end.

This final oracle is not part of Amos's original prophecies. Its vision of renewal following destruction is a common feature of the prophetic books. The destruction that follows, however, is that of Judah, not of Israel. This indicates that Amos's original words against Israel were reinterpreted as applying to Judah. Two factors likely contributed to this reinterpretation. First, the destruction of Israel by Assyria in 721 BCE enhanced Amos's reputation as a prophet whose threats had come true and might therefore have implications for other settings. The principles behind Amos's message might apply equally to Judah as to Israel, even if their circumstances were not identical. Second, with the demise of the Northern kingdom, Judah was essentially all that was left of Israel. The name "Israel" itself became ambiguous and could now be used for Judah. Hence, Amos's oracles originally directed toward Israel seemed perfectly appropriate for Judah.

"Comfort, comfort my people" (Isa 40–55)

The best example of the reinterpretation of prophetic works in the Hebrew Bible may be the book of Isaiah. Scholars have long recognized that Isaiah is composite and actually incorporates three distinct books. Isaiah 1–39 contains oracles of the eighth-century prophet from Judah after whom the book takes its name. Isaiah 40–55, often called Second or Deutero-Isaiah, was written in 539/ 538 BCE as the people of Judah who had been in Babylonian exile were preparing to return to their homeland. Isaiah 56–66, or Third Isaiah, comes from somewhat later, though its precise setting is hard to determine.

The opening of Second Isaiah makes its distinctive setting clear. The Babylonian exile, which began in 587 BCE with the destruction of Jerusalem, is described as a prison sentence that has been served by the city for its sin and is now at its end (40:1–2). Then, the command is issued to build a highway in the wilderness for Yahweh's return to the city (40:3–5). Later in the book, the same imagery is used. Jerusalem again appears as a captive woman, who is roused and told to change her clothes and remove her bonds in preparation for the return of her residents (52:1–2). Afterward, Yahweh leads the returnees out of Babylon back to Jerusalem (52:11–12).

Second Isaiah presupposes the accession of the Persian king Cyrus, who came to power in 539 BCE, after conquering Babylon, and issued the edict allowing the exiles to return home and rebuild Jerusalem and the temple (44:28–45:1). The first wave of returnees arrived in 538. Second Isaiah was written between these two events—after Cyrus's enthronement and the issuance of his edict but before the actual return. It describes the return in glorious terms that are idealized and visionary rather than realistic. Not only is the highway from Babylon depicted as straight and level, but springs and rivers break forth in the desert between the two sites, so that the returnees have plenty of water (43:19–20). The mountains and Jerusalem itself break into singing to greet them (49:13; 52:9). The actual return was laden with hardships, as detailed in other biblical books, especially Ezra and Nehemiah.

Isaiah 40–55, therefore, was written two hundred years after the original prophet Isaiah and deals with very different historical and social circumstances. Nevertheless, recent scholarship has pointed out themes that run through all parts of Isaiah. Such themes include the kingship of Yahweh and his relationship to his "anointed," the significance of Jerusalem, the survival of God's elect, Israel's place among nations, and the establishment of justice.[9] These themes bind the current book of Isaiah together: They begin with the eighth-century prophet, are developed in 2 Isaiah, and then furthered in 3 Isaiah. At each stage there is continuity as well as reinterpretation for a new setting.

The Book of Micah

The book of Micah is one of the best examples in the Hebrew Bible of the process of prophetic reinterpretation. It is also one of the most difficult when it comes to discerning the settings of the different reapplications of Micah's prophecies.[10]

There is widespread agreement among scholars that the oracles emanating from the eighth-century prophet, Micah of Moresheth, are confined to the first three chapters of the book.[11] One of the reasons for this judgment relates to the interpretation of Micah's prophecy in Jeremiah's day, which we discussed earlier. That episode shows that Micah was remembered at the time of Jeremiah as a prophet who confronted Hezekiah and denounced him and Judah, threatening the destruction of Jerusalem as punishment for sin. This recollection of the nature of Micah's prophetic career corresponds with the content of Micah 1 through 3. Micah characterizes his mission in these chapters precisely in these terms, as being "to declare to Jacob his transgression, to Israel his sin" (3:8).

The prophecies in these first three chapters are, like those in Amos, basically negative in orientation. They denounce the people of Judah and Jerusalem for social offenses—specifically, for the oppression of small land owners by stealing their land and property. Micah condemns the upper classes—rulers, priests, and prophets—for perverting legal decisions and religious teachings for bribes and profit. His statement that these people purport to trust in Yahweh and believe that no harm will come to them (3:11b) is similar to the point of Jeremiah's temple sermon that the people have come to trust in the temple building rather than in Yahweh. Hence, it is more than coincidence that Micah's threat of destruction for Jerusalem is quoted in the aftermath of Jeremiah's sermon.

The rest of the book of Micah (4–7) stems mostly, if not entirely, from the Babylonian exile or later. Chapters 4 and 5 are often considered a supplement to chapters 1 through 3 and are entirely positive. They refer to the "remnant," i.e., the survivors of Babylonian captivity. One verse (4:10) even mentions Babylon specifically. The passages about the remnant look forward to its redemption from captivity and its restoration as a nation. Thus, they all appear to have been written toward the end of the exilic period. Other passages envision this restoration as the establishment of an ideal kingdom of peace. This kingdom includes not just Judah and Israel but other nations, so that these chapters participate with

Jonah in the theological concept of universalism, which arose in the late exilic or postexilic period.

A subsequent addition to Micah (6:1–7:7) contains judgment oracles and seems designed to apply the condemnations of the original Micah to a later setting following the exile. The section begins with Yahweh suing Israel for the people's unfaithfulness from the time of the Exodus. Yahweh registers a complaint before the mountains and foundations of the earth and calls on them to judge the case. The following verses then make the point that Yahweh desires faithfulness and loyalty more than ritual sacrifice. They contain a very famous verse:

> He has told you, human, what is good.
> And what does Yahweh seek from you?
> Only to do justice, to love faithfulness,
> And to walk humbly with your God. (6:8, AT)

The thought and language of this section reflect the influence of Deuteronomy and the Deuteronomistic history and are therefore best dated in the seventh century BCE or later, a century or more after the prophet Micah. The threat against "the city" (6:9–16) is often taken by scholars to refer to Jerusalem shortly before its destruction in 587 BCE, again long after Micah's lifetime. One of the clearest differences of this entire section from the original part of Micah is that it is not just the upper class that comes under indictment. Rather, the entire society is depicted as corrupt and chaotic.

The final section of Micah (7:8–20) is liturgical or psalmlike. It begins with a lament of a person or entity (the city of Jerusalem?) that has suffered punishment for sin. This is followed by a poem that looks forward to restoration (7:11–13), when the walls of the city (Jerusalem) will be rebuilt and the nation's border extended, suggesting a date for the poem in the late exilic or early postexilic period. Next, there is a prayer asking Yahweh to "shepherd" his restored people as at the beginning of their history in the Exodus from Egypt (7:14–17). The book ends with a brief hymn of praise to God for his compassion and forgiveness.

The book of Micah, then, is an exercise in prophetic reinterpretation and reapplication. Less than half of the present book derives from Micah himself. His prophecies of destruction were reapplied to later situations. The Babylonian exile may have been seen in at least some circles as their eventual fulfillment. Other writers apparently perceived that the exile was not the final end and looked forward to restoration, which they articulated in hopeful oracles added to the expanding book. Despite this diversity of compositions, Micah retains a coherence of both literary organization and of themes. Its various parts all concern ideas relating to the interaction of the concepts of sin, justice, judgment, responsibility, hope, and forgiveness.[12]

We saw above the significance of understanding the historical setting of prophetic texts in order to grasp their original meaning. The interpretation in Jeremiah's day illustrated that the people of ancient Israel and Judah also understood the importance of historical setting. Nevertheless, further consideration of the process of composition behind the book of Micah shows how prophecy in the Hebrew Bible can take on a life of its own apart from its original setting. Prophetic texts could be isolated from their historical contexts and reapplied to other, often much later and much different situations. This process of reuse and reapplication, rather than one of prophecy and direct fulfillment, is at work in the New Testament's use of prophecies from the Hebrew Bible.

The Interpretation of Prophecy in the New Testament

Original Contexts

The genre of Hebrew prophecy in its original setting was unconcerned with the distant future. Therefore, the Hebrew Bible does not contain any prophecy intended as a prediction of Christ. All supposed prophecies of this nature initially addressed situations in the prophet's own day. This idea is not new to biblical scholars, but it may strike some readers as radical. Hence, I will demonstrate the point by analysis of some of the best-known prophetic texts quoted in the New Testament. For each of the following New Testament texts, I show how the prophecy addressed an issue or setting in ancient Israel that had nothing to do with Christ. The same point can be made for the enormous number of prophecy texts in the Hebrew Bible that supposedly refer to Christ.[13] That prophetic texts have their own original contexts does not necessarily mean that their citation by later, Christian authors is illegitimate. In the final section of this chapter, therefore, we deal with the issue of how the New Testament writers made use of Hebrew prophecy and what they meant by fulfillment.

Prime Example: Isaiah 7:14 (Quoted in Matt 1:23)

This verse from Isaiah is quoted in the Gospel of Matthew as referring to the virgin birth of Jesus. In its original context, however, Isaiah 7 recounts what is often called the "Syro-Ephraimitic Crisis," which took place in 734 BCE. (Other details can be filled in from the narrative in 2 Kings [15:29–16:20]). The following chart of the participants and names used in the chapter will facilitate understanding the description of this event and the surrounding circumstances.

King	Country	Capital
Ahaz ("house of David")	Judah	Jerusalem
Rezin	Aram (Syria)	Damascus
Pekah ("son of Remaliah")	Israel ("Ephraim")	Samaria
Tiglath-Pileser III	Assyria	Asshur

The event was a "crisis" for King Ahaz and Judah, who were attacked by the combined armies of Syria and Israel. The latter two countries had formed a coalition in an effort to resist the powerful Assyrian army of Tiglath-Pileser III. Ahaz refused to join the coalition. So Rezin and Pekah intended to remove him from the throne of Judah and replace him with a certain "son of Tabeel" who would join with them.[14] Isaiah the prophet was sent to quell Ahaz's fear. He told Ahaz to do nothing and not to be afraid. The plan of Rezin and Pekah would not succeed, so Ahaz should believe in Yahweh.

Apparently, Ahaz did not trust Isaiah or God. So Isaiah was sent back to try to persuade him. Isaiah offered Ahaz the chance to request a sign to prove to him that God would not allow Jerusalem to fall to Rezin and Pekah. But Ahaz, for unknown reasons, refused the opportunity. Isaiah, therefore, gave Ahaz a sign that Yahweh had chosen.

This sign concerned a certain "young woman," whose identity was not revealed.[15] One prominent interpretation is that she was Ahaz's wife; another is that she was Isaiah's wife. Whoever she was, she was evidently known to both Ahaz and Isaiah, for the text refers to her by using the definite article—*the* young woman. In any case, she was already pregnant when Isaiah delivered his oracle. He revealed that she would soon bear a son, whom she would name "Immanuel," meaning "God is with us."

All of this was background information for the real point of the sign, found in verses 15–16. These verses describe a certain stage in the development of the newborn son—the stage at which a child would learn to refuse what is bad and choose what is good. "Bad" and "good" here probably refer not to moral values but to food, since it was at this time that a child would eat curds and honey. As delicacies, these items would not have been available at the time of a siege like the one at the time of the Syro-Ephraimitic Crisis. The developmental stage, then, was probably that of weaning—when a child was taken off of breast milk and given solid food—usually at two to three years of age. The point of Isaiah's sign was that by the time the child, who was about to be born, reached this developmental stage, the countries of Syria and Israel would be deserted and no longer a threat to Judah.

This sign would not have brought much comfort to Ahaz, since its completion was probably at least two or three years away. The sign also called for him to believe that the attack of Rezin and Pekah would not succeed, something he had already failed to do. Ahaz had the chance to request a sign on his own and refused to do so. Hence, Isaiah's sign was not really meant to prove anything to him; it simply reaffirmed Isaiah's message. Ahaz still did not respond in faith after the sign. Elsewhere (2 Kings 16:7) we learn that he sent for help to Tiglath-Pileser III, thereby making Judah a vassal of Assyria's for years to come.

Isaiah's sign, then, was intimately related to the Syro-Ephraimitic Crisis. It bore the same message as his oracle to Ahaz, namely that Ahaz should trust in Yahweh to save Judah from its enemies. The sign was not a prediction of the far distant future and had nothing to do originally with the birth of Jesus eight hundred years later.

Other Examples from Isaiah

Isaiah 9:6–7 (Heb 9:5–6)

For a child has been born for us,
   a son given to us;
Authority rests upon his shoulders;
   and he is named
Wonderful Counselor, Mighty God,
   Everlasting Father, Prince of Peace.
His authority shall grow continually,
   and there shall be endless peace
for the throne of David and his kingdom.
   He will establish and uphold it
with justice and with righteousness
   from this time onward and forevermore. (NRSV)

This text is not quoted in the New Testament, although Matthew (4:15–16) quotes the beginning of the Isaiah oracle (9:1–2). The familiar passage is commonly cited by later Christian interpreters as a prediction of Christ. It is well known in this connection, mostly because George Friedrich Handel incorporated and set it to music in his oratorio *Messiah*.

This passage refers to the birth of a son in the line of David. But the boy's birth lies in the past rather than in the future. The verb forms in 9:5 (perfects and converted imperfects) are typically used in Hebrew for the past tense. As the NRSV translation indicates, the child, the subject of the poem, had been born already at the time the poem was written ("For a child has been born . . ."). Indeed, the poem celebrates the birth of a crown prince, the oldest son of one of the kings of Judah.

The names "Wonderful Counselor, Mighty God, Everlasting Father, Prince of Peace" are the reasons this poem has been interpreted traditionally as a reference to Christ. These names do not necessarily refer to the individual who bears them. Symbolic names are common in the prophets. The child Immanuel ("God is with us," Isa. 7:14), born in 734 BCE, was not divine. The names of Isaiah's other sons, Shearjashub ("a remnant will return," 7:3) and Maher-shalal-hash-baz ("spoil hurries, prey makes haste," 8:1), say nothing about those children. Hosea's children, Jezreel ("God sows"), Lo-ruhamah ("Not loved"), and Lo-ammi ("Not my people"), have names that symbolize the deteriorating relationship between Yahweh and Israel (Hosea 1). Later on in Hosea those names are changed to "Beloved" and "My People," indicating an improvement in the relationship. It is also possible, moreover, that the names in Isaiah 9 are not four phrases but two sentence names: "Mighty God is a Wonderful Counselor" and "Eternal Father is Prince of Peace."[16] Such sentence names were given as a way of praising and thanking the deity for the gift of the children who bore them.

Isaiah 11:1–9

This passage is also not quoted in the New Testament. The first line of the passage indicates its date and nature: "A shoot shall come out from the stump of Jesse (NRSV)." Jesse was the father of King David. The "shoot," therefore, is a new member of the Davidic dynasty, which ruled Judah. The fact that the new branch comes out of Jesse's "stump" indicates that the Davidic line has been cut off.[17] The passage, therefore, dates from after 587 BCE, when Jerusalem was destroyed, the Davidic king taken captive, and the Babylonian exile begun.

This passage can properly be called "messianic" since the word "messiah," meaning "anointed," was simply a title for a king. This text envisions the coming of a new king in David's line or the restoration of the royal line of David over Israel. The rest of the passage describes this new king and his reign, perhaps hyperbolically. The description, however, is hardly a prediction. It is highly idealized and envisions a perfect world of justice and universal peace. The new king will be filled with the divine spirit and will have complete knowledge, wisdom, and understanding. He will make decisions with unfailing righteousness and will faithfully execute the duty of the ancient Near Eastern king to ensure equity for the poor and disadvantaged. His reign will be one of absolute peace and harmony, not just between humans but among animals as well. This is a perfect world—an imagination of the world as it should be—rather than a prediction of the world as it ever will be.

A further indication that this passage is not a prediction is that the author does not seem to have a specific individual in mind. There is no mention of Jesus by name. There is no date or time frame. It is a utopian vision, an expression of hope intended to create hope and expectation within readers. At the same time, like all utopian visions, this one is distinctly earthly. Christians agree that Jesus's kingdom, contrary to the expectations of his disciples, was not of this world. The reign of the king imagined in Isaiah 11:1–9, on the other hand, is not a vision of heaven or the next world but the ideal in the present age—and actually in the past age of ancient Israel when the ideal form of government could still be viewed as monarchy.

Isaiah 52:13–53:12

According to the New Testament book of Acts, the evangelist Philip quoted this passage from Isaiah and taught the Ethiopian official about Jesus (Acts 8:32–33). The recent Mel Gibson movie, *The Passion of the Christ,* begins with a quotation from this text: "He was wounded for our transgressions" (Isa 53:5). Throughout the entire history of Christianity, this passage from Isaiah about the "Suffering Servant" has been interpreted as a description of Christ, especially in his passion and crucifixion. The passage, however, has its own original context and frame of reference within the book of Isaiah. Contrary to Gibson's *The Passion,* which gives "700 BC" as the date of this quotation, the passage lies within Second Isaiah and dates to 539/538 BCE, as we have seen. Isaiah 52:13–53:12 is one of a series of texts in Second Isaiah that biblical scholars typically treat together as the "Servant Songs."[18] The identity of this servant is very much debated. Within the context of Second Isaiah, the Servant Songs seem to refer to the nation or people of Israel since Israel is explicitly called Yahweh's servant several times here. These passages use the names "Israel" and "Jacob" synonymously, referring both to the nation and to the eponymous ancestor. Thus, they envision Israel both as the nation and as the individual. The second Servant Song also explicitly identifies the servant as Israel.[19]

Two other verses within the second Servant Song appear initially to contradict the identification of the servant with Israel. They seem instead to describe the servant's mission as "to bring Jacob back to him, and that Israel may be gathered to him" (49:5, NRSV) and "to raise up the tribes of Jacob and to restore the survivors of Israel" (49:6). But in both cases, the subject can probably be understood as God rather than the servant. Thus, 49:5a may be translated, "Now

Yahweh, who formed me from the womb as his servant in that he restores Jacob to himself and Israel is gathered to him, says." Similarly, 49:6a reads, "It is too light a thing, you being my servant, that I should raise up the tribes of Jacob and restore the survivors of Israel."[20]

The proper translation of the latter verse gets at the meaning of Israel as Yahweh's servant in Second Isaiah. The verse goes on to explain that Yahweh makes Israel a light to the nations, a conduit to bring salvation to all the earth. In the poem in Isaiah 53, the servant has suffered vicariously for the nations. In the context of Second Isaiah, this probably refers to the Babylonian exile. That is, the author says that Israel (= Judah) suffered not only for its own sins but also for those of the other nations. The images in the poem fit well with this interpretation: The nations were startled at Israel's appearance after its experience of suffering. There was nothing special about Israel, yet Yahweh chose it to be his servant to atone for other nations. Therein lies Israel's greatness.

This poem is a remarkable theological statement about Yahweh's plan to reach all people and Israel's role in that plan. In this way, the author of Second Isaiah seeks to come to grips with the reason for the trauma of the Babylonian exile. The author draws on eponymous imagery to describe Israel as an individual whose suffering is for the good of all people. Like all of the alleged prophecies of Christ in the Hebrew Bible, this poem had its own original context in ancient Israel that had nothing to do with Jesus. That context was literary as well as historical. The identity of the "Suffering Servant" in its original context can only be determined by comparison with the other references to the "servant" in Second Isaiah.

It is easy to see why this imagery has been so easily interpreted by Christians as referring to Jesus. Indeed, its language and images of vicarious suffering may well have influenced Jesus's sense of identity and mission. We will now turn to the question of how the New Testament writers made use of these prophetic texts and saw them fulfilled in Jesus.

New Testament Fulfillments

The New Testament's use of the Hebrew Bible is an extremely complicated matter that has generated a great deal of discussion among scholars.[21] The New Testament authors wrote from a perspective of faith. They were not historians trying to understand the context of the Hebrew Bible and in fact usually cited its Greek translation, the "Septuagint" (abbreviated LXX). Sometimes the point they wished to draw could only be made from the LXX and not from the Hebrew text.[22] Sometimes they paraphrase rather than quote because, after all, they had to depend on memory, books being not as readily available as they are today. Thus, the original contexts of the Hebrew prophecies were probably unknown and certainly irrelevant to them. The New Testament authors were concerned, rather, with trying to persuade their readers to accept belief in Christ. Their approach was rhetorical, not historical-critical, and they therefore related everything in the Hebrew Bible/LXX to Christ, often straining to find him there.

Nevertheless, the interpretive methods these New Testament writers employed were very similar to those used by contemporary Jewish interpreters.[23] This has become especially clear since the discoveries from Qumran, the community that copied the Dead Sea Scrolls. The Qumran authors related the Hebrew scriptures directly to the events of their own community in the same way that the New Testament authors related them to the early Christian community or church. This direct reapplication of ancient scripture was a continuation of the process of reinterpretation and reapplication to new situations already present in the prophetic books themselves.

Within this process of reapplication, the New Testament exhibits different kinds of "fulfillment" of Hebrew prophecy. The New Testament writers referred to the "fulfillment" of Hebrew prophecies for what we would categorize as different uses or reuses of those texts and in so doing, participated in a history of reinterpretation and reapplication going back to the prophets themselves and shared by contemporary Jewish authors. The Gospel of Matthew is an especially rich source of examples.

Inexhausted Meaning

In addition to being a renowned Bible scholar, Hugh Williamson is a confessing Christian believer. When he writes on 2 Isaiah, however, he labors to counter the idea that the servant in the text refers exclusively to Christ.[24] He contends that this is too narrow a construal of the idea of fulfillment. As examples, he cites sermons he has heard that refer to Jesus as the perfect fulfillment of love as described in 1 Corinthians 13. This does not mean, he points out, that Jesus exhausted the meaning of love for Christians; they should still aspire to such love in their own lives. In the same way, Williamson suggests, the meaning of the servant in its original context does not exhaust the potential of that image. It describes a role that remains to be fulfilled in Christ.

Isaiah 6:9

Williamson's explanation of more than one level of meaning refers to one kind of fulfillment used by New Testament writers. A good example of this kind of fulfillment may be that of Isaiah 6:9. The Gospels of Matthew, Mark, and Luke cite Isaiah 6:9 as the reason Jesus spoke in parables: "Keep hearing, but do not understand. Keep looking, but do not perceive."[25] Matthew calls it a fulfillment. In both cases—Isaiah's and Jesus's—the expression describes people who refuse to grasp the prophet's message and apply it to themselves. Isaiah was referring to his contemporaries, the people of Judah in the eighth century BCE. But the meaning of his words was not exhausted in the eighth century. They applied equally well to the heirs of his original audience in Jesus's day.

Micah 5:2

Another example of this category of fulfillment is Micah 5:2, cited in reference to Jesus's birth in Bethlehem (Matt 2:6).

Micah 5:2, 4 (Heb 5:1, 3)	Matthew 2:6
You, Bethlehem in Ephrathah, smallest among the clans of Judah, from you will come out one who will be ruler in Israel . . . He will stand and shepherd in the strength of Yahweh. (AT)	You, Bethlehem, in the land of Judah, are by no means least among the rulers of Judah; for from you shall come a ruler who is to shepherd my people Israel. (NRSV)

The passage in Micah looks forward to the birth of a new king in the line of David. It might be termed messianic, in that one of the titles of the king was "anointed one" ("messiah" in Hebrew). But the messiah described in Micah is an earthly king. This text was written in the exile and envisions the restoration of the Davidic monarchy. The new "anointed" king will rule Israel with the same kind of military strength as his ancestor, David. Foreign enemies will be vanquished (Micah 5:5–6), so that those under his aegis will live in peace and security. The author in Micah is not, therefore, predicting the birth of Jesus centuries later.

Nevertheless, the application of Micah's words to Jesus seemed appropriate for Matthew and other Christians, who came to see Jesus as the Messiah (Greek: "Christ") with a spiritual kingdom. Jesus's birth in the line of David and in David's hometown of Bethlehem suited perfectly the ultimate fulfillment of Micah's prophecy in Christian interpretation. The fit, however, may be too perfect. We have already seen that the genealogy for Jesus in Matthew is theological in orientation and may not represent Jesus's actual lineage. Similarly, the early Christians may have identified Jesus's birthplace as Bethlehem because of the affiliation with David. The Gospels uniformly recognize Jesus's home as Nazareth.[26] The change in Matthew's wording of the Micah text suggests the veneration of Bethlehem among early Christians. Rather than being the smallest of the clans of Judah, as in Micah, Matthew says it is by no means the least.

Reapplication

One of the texts quoted at the beginning of this chapter is from the Joseph story in the book of Genesis. Joseph is his father's favorite son, and this favoritism alienates his brothers. Their hatred for him is deepened by the dreams Joseph seems to delight in recounting about how he will one day rule over them. When he comes by himself to check up on them, they see it as an opportunity to kill him and be rid of him. They say, "Here comes the dreamer. Let us kill him and see what will become of his dreams."

These words are engraved on a plaque in front of the site where Dr. Martin Luther King Jr. was assassinated, now the National Civil Rights Museum, in Memphis. I doubt that there is anyone who believes that the words of Joseph's brothers in Genesis were originally spoken or written with Dr. King in mind. Yet, the use of this quotation in reference to him is highly appropriate because he was a minister who revered the Bible, because he gave a famous "dream" speech, and because he was assassinated. The same words take on new significance, even though they are reused for an entirely different setting unrelated to their original context.

New Testament writers often reuse words from the Hebrew prophets in the same way that the Civil Rights Museum plaque makes use of the quotation from Genesis. In this case, the reuse and reinterpretation may be triggered by one or more similarities in ideas or language. The original context of the prophecy and the new setting in which it is cited may otherwise have nothing in common. Jesus's reference to the "sign of Jonah" is somewhat akin to this kind of reuse: "Just as Jonah was three days and three nights in the belly of the sea monster, so for three days and three nights the Son of Man will be in the heart of the earth" (Matt. 12:38–40). Jesus was nothing like Jonah as a person nor were their respective attitudes toward other people or toward obeying God similar. The only reason for Jesus's allusion to the Jonah story was their respective three-day intervals buried in a kind of "tomb."[27]

Hosea 11:1

A particularly good example of reuse is in Matthew's account of the flight of Joseph, Mary, and Jesus to Egypt (Matt 2:13–15). Matthew says that this was to fulfill a prophecy from the book of Hosea (Hosea 11:1): "Out of Egypt I have called my son." This line is preceded in Hosea by the sentence "When Israel was a child I loved him." It is therefore clear that in its original context the "son" was a metaphor for the people of Israel and the calling from Egypt an allusion to the Exodus. Hosea was completely unaware of the birth of Jesus that would occur eight centuries later. Indeed, the text in Hosea is not future oriented but recalls one of Israel's historical traditions from the past. Matthew reapplies the Hosea text to the story of Jesus because of the word "son" and the mention of Egypt.[28]

Isaiah 40:3

Second Isaiah begins with a command to comfort Jerusalem now that it has served out its sentence in Babylonian captivity. Attention then turns toward the preparation of the return path from Babylon to Jerusalem: "A voice cries, 'Prepare a way for Yahweh in the wilderness; Make a straight highway for our God in the lowland" (40:3, AT). Toward the end of the book, Yahweh is envisioned as leading the former captives out of Babylon on their way back to Jerusalem, just as he led Israel out of Egypt in the exodus story.

Matthew cites Isaiah 40:3 as applying to the mission of John the Baptist. His reapplication is based on the reference to the wilderness, which was the location of John's ministry. Thus, instead of the wilderness being the place where preparations are to take place, Matthew locates the voice itself in the wilderness: "The voice of one crying in the wilderness" (Matt 3:3, NRSV). In addition, Matthew turns the straight path for easy return to Jerusalem in Isaiah into moral straightness as a way of encapsulating John's preaching.

Real Intent

In the famous "Sermon on the Mount" Matthew quotes Jesus as saying, "Do not think that I have come to abolish the law or the prophets; I have not come to abolish but to fulfill" (Matt 5:17, NRSV). The "prophets" here refers to the second major section of the Hebrew Bible, which incorporates the prophetic books we are discussing in this chapter. As becomes clear in the individual laws that Jesus expounds, "fulfill" here means to bring to full intent. Thus, when the law (specifically, the Ten Commandments) said, "You shall not kill," its real intent, according to Jesus in this sermon, was to prohibit not only murder but also hatred. The law's prohibition of adultery was really aimed at lust, and the commandment against swearing falsely applies to lying in general. "Fulfilling" in this sense does not mean closing out or ending but illuminating the original point behind the Hebrew Bible/Old Testament. While Jesus does not cite any specific Hebrew prophecies in this context, his stress on the original intent of the prophets highlights their role in calling for social and religious reforms in their own time periods rather than as predictors of distant events.

Conclusion

The proper understanding of the Hebrew prophets might help facilitate Jewish-Christian relations. Christians have sometimes adopted the attitude that Jews stubbornly refuse to accept the obvious fulfillments in Jesus of Old Testament predictions. As we have seen in this chapter, however, this attitude reflects a fundamental misunderstanding of the nature of biblical prophecy.

The messages of the prophets in the Bible were unfailingly tied to their individual social and historical settings. They did not really predict the future, certainly not the far distant future; that was not their concern. Their words about the future were primarily in the form of threats about the disasters that would occur if their contemporaries did not turn from their wickedness and become righteous. Occasionally, the prophets articulated hopeful, utopian visions about an ideal existence that waited on the other side of punishment. In short, the prophets in the Hebrew Bible had their own original contexts, and their prophecies had their own original meanings. The prophecies—at that time—were perfectly understandable as addressing those particular contexts. Thus, Jewish interpretation of those prophecies as unrelated to Jesus Christ hundreds of years later is entirely appropriate.

That prophetic texts from the Hebrew Bible had their own original contexts, however, does not rule out their fulfillment in the New Testament or render the New Testament use of such prophecies illegitimate. The prophetic texts were routinely reinterpreted and reapplied to later situations. This process of reinterpretation lies behind the very formation of the prophetic books in the Bible. The New Testament writers made use of the same methods of reuse and reinterpretation found among contemporary Jewish authors. The differences between Jewish and Christian interpretations stem not from different methods but from different religious convictions. Modern Christians should be careful to avoid too narrow a definition of "fulfillment" in their understanding of Christ's relationship to Old Testament prophecy. There is not a direct, exclusive relationship between such prophecies and the citation of them in the New Testament.

If Jews and Christians can recognize the validity of their respective methods of interpretation, perhaps their dialogue can progress to the consideration of the substance, both shared and different, of their faiths. Recognizing these similarities and differences validates both Jewish and Christian religious traditions.

Chapter Three

LIFE'S REAL QUESTIONS
Wisdom Literature in the Bible

The Misconception:
Wisdom literature is a divine guide for daily living in such matters as disciplining children and getting along with one's spouse; it also supplies the answers to such "mega" issues as the meaning of life and why bad things happen to good people.

> Do not be too righteous, and do not act too wise. Why should you destroy yourself?
>
> —Ecclesiastes (Qoheleth) 7:16, NRSV.

This chapter is different from the others in this book. It is different because its topic, wisdom literature, is unlike other kinds of literature in the Bible. Wisdom literature does not claim to be revelation from God—at least not in the same way as the other biblical genres we are exploring—nor does it describe God's revelation in history. Hence, Israel's historical traditions, such as the promises to the patriarchs, the exodus from Egypt, the law of Moses, the conquest of Canaan, the period of the judges, the monarchy, and so on, are not even mentioned in wisdom literature as they are in other genres of the Bible. And unlike the prophetic books, apocalyptic literature, and the New Testament letters, wisdom writings do not purport to convey direct revelation from God. They focus instead on the search through reason for meaning and happiness in this life.

This understanding of the wisdom genre contrasts with the way in which the wisdom books in the Bible are often understood and interpreted by modern readers. For instance, there is a biblical proverb that reads "The one who spares his rod hates his child" (Prov 13:24, AT), paraphrased in the familiar adage, "Spare the rod, spoil the child." It has been cited as a divine directive for the use of spanking by parents or to support the position of those who favor corporal punishment in the form of paddling in public schools. Another familiar adage drawn from wisdom literature is "so-and-so has the patience of Job." Careful reading of the book of Job shows that Job was not particularly patient. The attempt to characterize him as such springs from the assumption that the book's intent is to reveal how God wants people to respond to troubles and suffering in their lives. This is a misunderstanding of the genre of wisdom, and of the book of Job, the essence of which is debate rather than definitive answers.

In this chapter, we explore the three wisdom books in the Bible: Proverbs, Job, and Ecclesiastes, otherwise known by its Hebrew name, Qoheleth. We will continue to make use of the tools of form criticism by analyzing the structure, setting, and intent unique to each of these books. Our main focus will be on showing how each book exemplifies the genre of biblical wisdom literature by presenting divergent viewpoints on a topic or set of topics of significance to human beings.

Introduction to Wisdom Literature

Wisdom, as the name suggests, is about reasoned thinking. Its use as the name of a genre comes from the word "wisdom," which occurs frequently in these three biblical books as well as in other such nonbiblical writings. Still, it is a modern genre designation rather than an ancient one.

The wisdom books contain different kinds of literary forms, but these fall into two basic categories.[1] The first is brief aphorisms or "proverbs." These typically consist of two lines and offer advice or insight about life, the workings of the world, and human relationships. They are based on observation and experience; they can be religious or theological in orientation but are not necessarily so; they cover a wide range of topics such as marriage, prosperity and poverty, industry and sloth, and so on. They are, therefore, very similar to modern aphorisms such as, "Early to bed and early to rise, makes one healthy, wealthy, and wise."

The other basic form in wisdom literature consists of more extensive reflections on issues related to the meaning of life, its brevity, the causes for suffering and hardship during life, and the like. These reflections may be narratives, poems, dialogues, or various other literary types.[2] What makes these different types of literature similar is their themes and function rather than their form.

> What distinguishes these books (Proverbs, Ecclesiastes, Job) is a set of related genres and themes, defined primarily by a common educative function of fostering discernment, reflection, and action concerning life in general ("existence" or the human condition) and for a wide spectrum of specific situations.[3]

Wisdom literature reflects a discrete outlook and worldview from all the other kinds of literature in the Hebrew Bible. It is a perspective based on and informed by reason and personal experience rather than history or tradition. Unlike the other genres treated in this book, wisdom writings exhibit no real interest in Israel's historical traditions. Ideologically, wisdom is grounded in creation. The basic concept behind it is that God has placed the secrets to success and human happiness in the created order, and it is up to humans to discover these secrets by means of observation and intuition. Wisdom thought explores what is good for human beings, and wisdom literature attempts to articulate it.

> Wisdom is the reasoned search for specific ways to assure well-being and the implementation of those discoveries in daily existence. Wisdom addresses natural, human, and theological dimensions of reality, and constitutes an attitude toward life, a living tradition, and a literary corpus.[4]

There are four main thematic categories of wisdom.[5] They are: juridical, experiential, theological, and natural. *Juridical* wisdom is the employment of wise judgment in a legal setting. It is best exemplified in the Bible in the story of Solomon's discovery of the true mother of the disputed baby (1 Kings 3:16–28). *Experiential* wisdom arose out of real experiences of daily life and can be found in the majority of biblical proverbs or aphorisms. An essential principle of *theological* wisdom is the "fear of God." The deliberations about human suffering in the book of Job and about the meaning of life in Qoheleth also illustrate theological wisdom. *Natural* wisdom is not represented in the Bible. It consists primarily of encyclopedic lists of items and phenomena found in the natural world and was, therefore, a kind of ancient natural science.

Wisdom was based on observation of the world—what might be called "natural revelation"—and on reason. There is nothing distinctively Yahwistic or Israelite about it. Wisdom was a widespread phenomenon in the ancient Near East, particularly in Egypt and Mesopotamia. Its primary function or intent was education. Wisdom writing sought not only to move its audience to act sensibly but also to promote reasoned thought and reflection. In Egypt, wisdom occurred almost exclusively at the royal court for educational purposes. Egyptian wisdom texts are mostly in the form of "instructions"—lists of practical dos and don'ts in the form of proverbs.

In Israel, wisdom seems to have developed in three stages: family, court, and school.[6] That is, it began at home in the context of parental instruction, then became associated primarily with the royal court and the instruction of young nobles, and finally it became the property primarily of the scribal class, who were charged with educating the elite. That is why some biblical texts refer to "the wise" as a professional group in parallel with priests and prophets (cf. Jer 18:18).

This does not mean that all scribes or sages were in agreement about all matters. Quite the contrary. Wisdom was based on reason, experience, and observation, and since these things vary from person to person, the sages reached different conclusions about such questions as the meaning of life. "Experience was sometimes ambiguous, forcing the wise to question their own hardened dogmas."[7] Dialogue and debate were essential components of wisdom. The debate took different forms, as we will see in our treatment of the biblical wisdom books. Wisdom literature does not provide a "road map" to daily living or clear answers to the mega issues of life, but what it does do is sketch the parameters for debate and give approval to reasoning and contemplation, dialogue and disagreement.

Prime Example: The Book of Proverbs

The book of Proverbs is an anthology comprised of several distinct collections of wisdom materials. Perusal of the book reveals that it is structured according to four major collections: "The Proverbs of Solomon, Son of David, King of Israel" (Prov 1–9), "The Proverbs of Solomon" (Prov 10:1–22:16), "The Words of the Wise" (Prov 22:17–24:22), and "The Proverbs of Solomon that the Officials of King Hezekiah of Judah Copied" (Prov 25–29). In addition, there are other, smaller collections or independent documents included in the book: "The Sayings of the Wise" (24:23–34), "The Words of Agur son of Jakeh" (30), "The Words of King Lemuel" (31:1–9), and the acrostic description of the capable wife (31:10–31).

The attribution of Proverbs to Solomon is pseudonymous—the work is attributed to Solomon, although he was not its real author. Some portions of the book may have originated before the Babylonian exile of 587 BCE, but scholars generally date the book as a whole to the postexilic period (after 538 BCE), some four hundred years after Solomon. Still, the names of Solomon and other kings in the headings of these different collections indicate the association of wisdom with the royal court.

The book of Proverbs well illustrates the features of wisdom noted earlier. The book is all poetry except for the introductions to the collections it incorporates. It consists largely of brief aphorisms of two or four lines. But there are also extended poems, such as the hymn to wisdom (Prov. 8) and the poem in praise of the capable wife (31:10–31). (The latter is an acrostic, with each line beginning with a different letter of the Hebrew alphabet.)

The aphorisms draw on experience and observation of the world. They sometimes extract moral lessons from the workings of nature. Thus, a famous passage calls the attention of lazy persons to the industry of the ant (all translations here are the author's):

Go to the ant, oh sluggard;
Watch its ways and be wise.
It has no chief;
No officer or ruler.
Yet it prepares its food in the summer;
It gathers its edibles at harvest time.
How long, oh sluggard, will you lie about?
When will you arise from your sleep?
A little sleep, a little slumber,
A little hand clasping to lie down
Then poverty will come upon you like a highwayman,
And need like an armed bandit. (6:6–11)

Another proverb makes a similar point more subtly:

Where there are no oxen, there is no grain;[8]
Abundant yields come by the strength of the ox. (14:4)

The proverbs especially draw on observation of human activities and relationships.

On pride:

Pride goes before destruction;
And conceit before stumbling. (16:18)

On anger:

A soft response turns away wrath;
But a hurtful word arouses anger. (15:1)

On prudent speech:

Pleasant words are like a honeycomb;
Sweetness to the soul and healing to the bones. (16:24)

On aging:

Gray hair is a crown of glory;
It is found in righteous living. (16:31)

On marriage:

A noble wife is her husband's crown,
But the wife who shames him is like rottenness in his bones. (12:4)

On raising children:

> Discipline your child, and s/he will give you rest;
> They will give delight to your being. (29:17)

On family life in general:

> A dry crust of bread in quiet
> Is better than a contentious household that is feasting. (17:1)

There are numerous similitudes offering colorful comparisons of human attitudes and activities with phenomena in nature:

> Good news from a distant land
> Is like cold water to a thirsty soul. (25:25)

> Meddling in someone else's quarrel
> Is like seizing a passing dog by the ears. (26:17)

Another common type of proverb is the numerical saying, which lists three or four items in which the author perceives a shared quality. Typically, the fourth item in the list is the one that is the true object of the author's interest.

> Three things are too wonderful for me,
> Four things are beyond my understanding:
> The way of an eagle in the sky,
> The way of a snake on a rock,
> The way of a ship in the heart of the sea
> The way of a man with a young woman. (30:18–19)

Most of these aphorisms can be understood and appreciated by modern readers. Some are comparable to proverbs in our own culture. For instance, Proverbs 27:1 conveys a message similar to our own saying, "Don't count your chickens before they hatch," when it warns, "Do not boast about tomorrow, For you do not know what a day may bring."

The proverbs in the Bible come out of ancient Israelite life and culture. They speak about such matters as the proper deportment of kings and slaves, which are not institutions in our present culture, but their meanings often transcend time and culture because they deal with issues that are common to all human beings. This ability to transcend cultures is one of the key features of wisdom.

The "Loose Woman" in Proverbs 1–9

The major theme of the first nine chapters of Proverbs is a contrast that the writer builds between "Lady Wisdom," i.e., wisdom personified as a woman, and the "loose woman," who is variously described as a prostitute and adulteress. The Hebrew expression is literally, "strange woman," implying that she is also conceived of as a non-Israelite.

These chapters contain constant warnings to avoid the loose woman. The original audience of these warnings is sometimes obscured in translation. The Hebrew text is consistently directed at "my son." (The NRSV in its effort to avoid sexist language translates, "my child.") The principle that both male and female children should heed their parents' instruction is well taken. But the advice to avoid the loose woman and remain faithful to one's own wife (chapter 5) is clearly directed toward young noblemen. The loose woman may be a metaphor for folly, but the sexual imagery and overtones remain. Perception of young noblemen as the original audience of at least this section of the book illustrates its educational setting and intent. At points, the book refers specifically to teachers and instructors (5:13). The primary instructors, however, are the parents—father and mother, suggesting wisdom's origins in the family.

The reasons for avoiding the loose woman are eminently practical rather than theological. The writer does not quote from the Ten Commandments, "Thou shalt not commit adultery." The closest that the author comes to invoking divine judgment is to point out that all human activities are under Yahweh's scrutiny (5:21). The loose woman is to be avoided, however, because consorting with her inevitably brings death (5:5). The writer mentions two potential causes of death. The first is disease: "you will groan at the end of your life, when your skin and flesh are consumed" (5:11, AT). The second is jealousy: "For jealousy arouses a husband's fury, and he shows no restraint when he takes revenge" (6:34, NRSV). Thus, as is typical of wisdom literature, the advice regarding the loose woman is based on common sense rather than theological or moral considerations.

The poem in Proverbs 8 depicts Lady Wisdom inviting young men to herself just as the loose woman does. But there the similarity ends. Wisdom stands specifically beside the city gates, the place where justice was dispensed. Her summons appeals not to baser instincts but to the desire to learn, to the search for truth and personal refinement. Wisdom does not deceive but speaks honestly, and her product enriches more than material wealth, in part because wisdom and sober judgment are aids that lead to prosperity. The wisdom and prudence that she dispenses is essential even to kings and rulers.

Lady Wisdom, furthermore, is described as having an exalted place next to Yahweh at creation (8:22–31). Indeed, the language here depicts her as a consort or wife to Yahweh. It is only a slight exaggeration to say that wisdom is por-trayed here as the "mother" of creation, the means through which God created the universe and everything in it.[9] Other images in this passage are those of wisdom as the first creative act and wisdom as a master craft worker or archi-tect, again the agent of creation. Unlike the loose woman, who leads her victims to death, wisdom is the source of life and happiness. The benefits of wisdom and knowledge, accessible to young noblemen through education, are thus set in contrast to the foolishness of indulging youthful appetites without regard to the inevitable consequences.

The International Scope of Proverbs

The dangers associated with the loose woman are not distinctly Israelite or Yahwistic but apply equally in different cultures. There are even clearer examples of the international nature of wisdom elsewhere in Proverbs. We have already noted, for instance, that the final chapter of Proverbs contains a heading ascrib-ing at least its first nine verses to "King Lemuel." The word that follows may be translated either "an oracle" as in the NRSV or "of Massa," referring to a region of Arabia. The same holds for Proverbs 30:1, which is ascribed to a certain Agur son of Jakeh, who may also have been from Massa. It is interesting to note in this regard that chapter 30 refers to God but not specifically to the name of Israel's God, Yahweh. Even if the word "oracle" is correct in 31:1, it is still evi-dent that Lemuel was not an Israelite, since there was no king of Israel or Judah with that name. Thus, the book of Proverbs incorporates literature writ-ten by non-Israelites, and their wisdom and advice based on observation and experience was considered valuable and authoritative.

Another instance of wisdom with an international origin in the book of Prov-erbs is the section titled "The Words of the Wise" (22:17–24:34). Much of this section closely parallels an Egyptian document from approximately 1100 BCE known as the Instruction of Amenemope. The direction of borrowing is evident from the reference to "thirty sayings" in Proverbs 22:20. The Instruction of Amenemope has thirty paragraphs or "sayings," not all of which are paralleled in Proverbs 22:20.[10] Proverbs has borrowed from the Egyptian document, rather than the other way around. The biblical writer has adapted the Egyptian docu-ment to Israelite religion, as is clear from the various references to Yahweh in this section of Proverbs. Despite its foreign origin, then, the practical advice offered by the Egyptian sage remained pertinent in Israel. This is because it was based on experiences and observations common to all human beings rather than on revelation from Yahweh that was unique to Israel.

Proverbial Diversity

Since the various proverbs arise from experience, and experiences differ with individuals, it is not too surprising to find diversity and tensions among them. Modern proverbs can also be in tension with one another. We say, "Haste makes waste," suggesting that one should work slowly and deliberately so as to do a job correctly. But we also say, "A stitch in time saves nine," meaning that it is important to act with *haste* to resolve problems that arise before they grow larger. The two proverbs, while not directly contradictory, are in tension with one another. The same is true of biblical proverbs. One can find different ideas on any given topic within the book of Proverbs, and the ideas are sometimes in tension and may even contradict each other.

By way of illustration, let's consider the topic of poverty.[11] In the passage commending the industry of ants (Prov 6:6–11), poverty is blamed on laziness. That lesson is reinforced and restated in another, similar proverb (again, the translations here are those of the author):

> I passed by the field of a lazy person,
> By the vineyard of an individual lacking in sense,
> And found it overgrown with thistles,
> Its surface covered with weeds,
> Its stone wall was broken down.
> Then I perceived and took it to heart;
> I saw and took instruction.
> A little sleep, a little slumber,
> A little hand clasping to lie down
> Then poverty will come upon you like a highwayman,
> And need like an armed bandit. (24:30–34)

Other proverbs are even more explicit in attributing poverty to laziness and wealth to industry:

> A slack hand brings poverty;
> But the hand of the industrious enriches. (10:4)

As Crenshaw observes, "By this reasoning, the poor only get what they deserve, the just fruits of their own laziness."[12] Following this reasoning a step further, charity toward the poor makes no sense, and is even counterproductive, because it merely rewards the lazy.

Other texts in Proverbs, however, reflect quite a different attitude toward the poor. Far from suggesting that the poor deserve their state, some of these texts indicate that the poor are people of honor and integrity and that it is better to be poor than rich under certain conditions. The following two texts are clear in this regard.

> It is better to be a poor person who walks in integrity
> Than someone whose speech is perverted and who is a fool. (19:1)

Again,

> It is better to be a poor person who walks in integrity
> Than a rich person whose ways are perverted. (28:6)

Some texts go even further and suggest that the poor are favored by God.

> A person who oppresses the poor reproaches his Maker,
> But the one who honors him is kind to the needy. (14:31)

Similarly,

> A person who mocks the poor reproaches his Maker,
> And the one who rejoices at calamity will not be judged innocent. (17:5)

In this light, it is not surprising to find that a number of proverbs commend generosity toward the poor:

> One who hates his neighbor sins,
> But one who is gracious to the poor is blessed. (14:21)

> One who is generous will be blessed,
> Because he gives some of his food to the poor. (22:9)

> One who gives to the poor lacks nothing,
> But one who averts his eyes will be full of curses. (28:27)

One of the admirable traits of the ideal wife described in the last chapter of Proverbs is that

> She reaches her hand out to the poor;
> She extends her arms to the needy. (31:20)

The theme of poverty is only one of the topics that could be used to illustrate Proverbs' diversity. The same could be shown for pretty much every issue that it treats. The teachings that Proverbs offers on these issues is not monolithic. It is not a set of commands or divinely ordained rules. It is, rather, a collection of the advice gained by ancient Israelites, especially the sages, the wise teachers among them. There was no single "right" way of looking at things. There was disagreement, because life was and is complex, and circumstances fluctuate. What may be true for one person or a given situation is not necessarily universally so.

Proverbs as Wisdom Literature

Proverbs is a good illustration of the nature of the genre of biblical wisdom. Its sayings arose out of experience and observation of the world. Its setting was that of ancient Israelite education within the family and the nobility, and its intent was to educate, especially the upper-class youth of ancient Israel. The tradition of wisdom and some of its content were shared with other cultures because its concerns were basic to the human experience and not limited to any specific religious outlook. It is, thus, universal in its subject matter as well as particular in offering advice based on individual experience.

Although Proverbs, and wisdom in general, provide few if any final answers, they do afford the reader the freedom to make one's own observations based on personal experience and to come up with individual answers about what makes for a good life. To the extent that Proverbs reflects disagreement about the topics it covers, it may be said to incorporate dialogue or even debate. Such debate is even more pronounced in the books of Job and Qoheleth.

The Book of Job

Just as Proverbs shows the diversity of opinion inherent in wisdom literature, so the book of Job furnishes a wonderful example of wisdom as debate. The proposition under debate in Job is well articulated by one of the aphorisms in Proverbs:

> Misfortune pursues sinners,
> But prosperity rewards the righteous. (Prov 13:21, NRSV)

Most of Job is a discussion or debate between Job and his friends about the reason for Job's suffering and how he should respond to it. Their debate raises the larger question of the relationship between sin and suffering. It is a question that the book of Job never really resolves, not because the book offers no answer but because it offers two different answers. Then, just when it appears to favor one of them, the structure of the book reopens the issue so that the debate continues forever.

Outline of Job

Prologue (1:1–2:10)

Dialogues (2:11–42:9)
    Introduction of the parties (2:11–13)
    Job's lament (3:1–26)
    First cycle (4–14)
        Eliphaz's speech (4:1–5:27)
        Job's response (6:1–7:21)
        Bildad's speech (8:1–22)
        Job's response (9:1–10:22)
        Zophar's speech (11:1–20)
        Job's response (12:1–14:22)
    Second cycle (15–21)
        Eliphaz's speech (15:1–35)
        Job's response (16:1–17:16)
        Bildad's speech (18:1–21)
        Job's response (19:1–29)
        Zophar's speech (20:1–29)
        Job's response (21:1–34)
    Third cycle (22–27)
        Eliphaz's speech (22:1–30)
        Job's response (23:1–24:25)
        Bildad's speech (25:1–6)
        Job's response (26:1–27:23)[13]
    Interlude: A hymn to wisdom (28:1–28)
    Job's speech (29:1–31:40)
    Elihu's speech (32:1–37:24)
    Yahweh's response (38:1–41:34)
        Yahweh's first speech (38:1–39:30)
        Yahweh's challenge and Job's response (40:1–5)
        Yahweh's second speech (40:6–41:34)
    Job relents (42:1–6)
    Conclusion: Yahweh admonishes Job's friends (42:7–9)

Epilogue (42:10–17)

Job is a complex and rich book. It consists of two main parts. The prologue plus the epilogue are in prose and together constitute one part. The poetic dialogues in between, including their brief introduction and conclusion, make up the other part.[14] The prologue and epilogue draw on an old folktale; and the author of Job used it as the setting for the dialogues between Job and his friends. The dialogues changed the original focus of the folktale and as a result, the two main parts of the book deal with two different questions or issues.[15]

The Original Folktale

The question of the prologue and epilogue is: Why does a person serve God? Job is a test case. At the beginning of the book, he is described as the most blameless and upright of people, someone who fears God and turns away from evil. (In view of our discussion of the international nature of wisdom it is interesting to note that Job is not an Israelite. He is from the land of Uz, which probably refers to Edom, the area south and east of the Dead Sea.) He is pious and offers sacrifices on behalf of his children—just in case they may have sinned. Eliphaz's later words of praise for Job (4:3–4) suggest that Job's righteousness was positive as well as negative. That is, he not only turned from sin but he also undertook positive deeds of strengthening the weak and helping those in need.

Job is also portrayed as extremely blessed. He is very wealthy; he has ten children, seven of whom are sons, a sign of his blessedness. It is the suspected connection between the righteousness and the blessedness of Job that occasions his testing. The scene shifts to a meeting of the heavenly court or divine council, called literally "the sons of God." Among these beings is one who bears the title, "the adversary" or "accuser." This title is often mistranslated as a proper name, "Satan." The Hebrew word śāṭā simply means "enemy" or "adversary" and typically refers in the Hebrew Bible to a human foe.[16] The idea of a Devil or Satan, as a representative or personification of evil and a counterpart to God, did not yet exist when the book of Job was written.[17] The word occurs in Hebrew with the definite article, "the satan," showing that it is a title rather than a proper name. In this context, it refers to a kind of prosecuting attorney, or "accuser," whose job it is to patrol the earth in search of persons to accuse before God. This is indicated by Yahweh's questions to the Accuser in Job 1:7; 2:2.

Yahweh directs the Accuser's attention to Job. Yahweh is apparently confident in Job's righteousness, as he boasts that there is no one as blameless and upright as he. The Accuser, though, believes that Job is righteous only because Yahweh has surrounded him with blessing and protection. The Accuser makes a wager of sorts with Yahweh: Take away Job's possessions and he will curse God. Yahweh accepts the wager, granting the Accuser permission to take away all Job owns but with the provision that he may not harm Job. As a result, in one very bad day Job loses everything—livestock and servants, as well as his children. Job naturally mourns and laments. But the story says explicitly says that he does not sin by cursing God or accusing God of wrong (1:22). Yahweh wins the bet.

The second episode (2:1–10) of the prologue involves the same wager with higher stakes, at least for Job. Again there is a meeting of the heavenly court, and again the Accuser is present among them. Again Yahweh asks the Accuser where he has come from, and again the Accuser replies that he has been wandering the earth evidently looking for persons to accuse before God. Again Yahweh calls the Accuser's attention to Job, whom he again describes as incomparable in right-eousness, pointing out that Job has persisted in his integrity even though all he had was taken from him. The Accuser answers by proposing another, more rig-orous test for Job. Job will curse God, he claims, if his health is harmed and his life threatened. Again, Yahweh grants the Accuser permission to harm Job, with the provision that his life be spared.

The next scene finds Job suffering with horrible sores, such that he sits in ashes and scrapes himself with a piece of broken pottery. The sight of him is so appalling that his wife encourages him to curse God and end his suffering. Yet Job again retains his integrity. He speaks only good of God. The text says that he did not sin with his lips (2:10), and since the wager was that Job would curse God, Yahweh again wins the bet.

The issue raised in this original tale is human integrity. Does Job serve God because of the blessings and rewards he receives or does he serve God out of a true sense of what is right? The test proves that Job's faith is genuine. He serves God out of loyalty, integrity, and love, not because of the rewards. The Job of the folktale is a model for religious faithfulness.

At this point the original folktale moved appropriately to its conclusion. That conclusion is preserved, for the most part, in the epilogue.[18] Job has proven why he serves God, so it is appropriate for Yahweh to reward him. Yahweh does so, giving Job twice as much as he had before. Job's renewed prosperity and health are rewards for his genuine faithfulness and integrity rather than reasons for a false piety and feigned righteousness. The folktale thus can stand alone and makes perfect sense.

The Dialogues

The insertion of the dialogues between Job and his friends radically changed the main question of the story and thus the book's topic and direction. They also caused a tension in the book's ending. The dialogues no longer deal with why a person serves or should serve God but focus on the *reason* for Job's suffering. Again, Job represents all people, and the dialogues are a debate about the cause of human suffering.

The technical term for this issue of the cause behind suffering is "theodicy." The word literally means the justice or fairness of God and is used in reference to the question of how a beneficent and omniscient God can allow evil to exist. It applies to moral evil (sin) as well as natural disasters and physical suffering. If God is all-good and all-powerful, why does evil exist, and why do disasters happen? If God is all-good, then God cannot desire bad things to happen or evil to exist. If God is all-powerful, then God can do away with evil and disaster. The question of theodicy is one of the most vexing theological questions in the study of religion.

The dialogues in the book of Job are essentially a debate over this question. An overview of the first cycle will highlight the main points. There are two principal positions in the debate, represented by Job on the one hand and his three friends (Eliphaz, Bildad, and Zophar) on the other.

Job's friends claim that he is suffering because he has sinned. The view that they represent holds that suffering is punishment for sin and, conversely, that sin inevitably results in suffering. Eliphaz, therefore, asks, "Who that was innocent ever perished?" (4:7, NRSV). His point is that Job is "perishing" and cannot therefore be innocent but must be guilty of sin. Later in the same speech Eliphaz asks another rhetorical question: "Can a person be considered righteous before God? Can a human be clean before his/her Maker?"[19] (4:17, AT). Eliphaz's point is that everyone sins; no one is perfect. Therefore, even Job must have sinned—as proven by the fact that he is suffering. The claim begs the question as to why Job's suffering at the moment is particularly intense. As if in response to this objection, Eliphaz later advises, "How happy is the one whom God reproves; therefore do not despise the discipline of the Almighty" (5:17, NRSV). Job is suffering because Yahweh is disciplining him for sins that he has committed, and Eliphaz's advice to Job is that he repent.

Job represents the second position on the question of the reason for human suffering. His argument is more complicated and more difficult to synthesize. Job remains resolute in his conviction that he has not sinned. He does not claim to understand why he is suffering, but he is convinced that it is not as simple as his friends argue. Thus, in his response to Eliphaz, he challenges him and the other friends: "Teach me, and I will be silent; make me understand how I have gone wrong" (6:24, NRSV). In the next chapter, he seems to say that even if he has sinned, his suffering far outweighs any evil he may have done. He thus implies that God is being unfair to him. He asks why God doesn't just forgive whatever sin he might have committed. "Why have you made me your target?" he asks (7:20, NRSV), suggesting that the sufferings God has imposed upon him are sadistic and cruel. At first, then, Job wrestles with the assumption that suffering is the result of sin. He seems to have been indoctrinated with the idea and to have accepted it in principle—except he knows that he has not sinned. He therefore struggles to find some reason for his suffering.

The other speeches in the first cycle further illustrate these two basic positions on the question of theodicy. Bildad, the second friend, presumptuously rises to God's defense, asking, "Does God pervert justice?" (8:3, NRSV). He continues callously, "If your children sinned against him, he delivered them into the power of their transgression." Bildad here suggests that Job's children got what they deserved. He adds that Job will be restored by God if he will repent of his wrongdoing, seek God's forgiveness, and live uprightly. He claims, "Behold, God will not reject an upright person or strengthen evildoers" (8:20, AT). Job's suffering, he implies once more, is justified.

Job replies to Bildad in chapter 9 by confessing his inferiority to God in the areas of strength and power, but he still alleges that God is unjust and sadistic in making the innocent suffer and then mocking them. Job expresses the wish that there could be a mediator or umpire between God and him, and then Job could feel free to express his true feelings about what God is doing to him. His wish for an impartial umpire suggests that he thinks God really does have a grudge against him. In the next chapter, Job seems to say that he will speak freely anyway because his life has become so bitter with suffering. He demands to know why God is oppressing him.

Zophar's speech adds little to the arguments of his friends. He points out God's inscrutable nature and gives a series of platitudes claiming that if Job lives righteously he will prosper:

If iniquity is in your hand, remove it far away;
Do not let evil stay in your tents.
Then you can raise your face free of defect;
You will be established and will not fear.
For you will forget your trouble;
You will remember it like water that has passed.
Your life will be brighter than noon day;
Gloom will become like morning. (11:14–17, AT)

Zophar's statement that Job will forget his current trouble and live a happy life ("brighter than noon day") seems especially hollow in the face of Job's tremendous suffering. In his response to Zophar in chapters 12 through 13, Job recognizes, as he has admitted before, that God is more powerful than he. But this does not answer his complaint against God. He wants to meet God face to face so that God can explain why he is making Job suffer. He accuses his friends of speaking falsely for God. They have simply voiced standard, pat answers that fail to probe the depths of the matter. Job seems to think that God has listened to false testimony and false accusations against him. He wants to plead his case before God in order to set matters straight—to convince God that he has not sinned. Basically, Job thinks that God has made a mistake in punishing him for sins he hasn't committed and won't commit.

Thus, the first cycle of dialogues in Job shows that it presents two basic views of the reason for human suffering. The view of Job's friends might be called the orthodox position. It is expressed in part with maxims and aphorisms, indicating its widespread acceptance that suffering is the inevitable consequence of sin, and sin always yields suffering as punishment. But Job's position is more complex. At the beginning of the dialogues, Job appears to accept this orthodox view advocated by his friends; but Job *knows* he has not sinned. His knowledge of his innocence leads him to call the orthodox view into question, and he comes to the conclusion that God is treating him unfairly. He longs for a face-to-face encounter with God that would allow him to make the case for his own innocence and compel God to justify Job's suffering.

Job's Continuing Debate

What is surprising is that Job's position is upheld, with some revisions, as the right one. At the end of the dialogues, Yahweh speaks.[20] Yahweh does not really answer Job's queries about why he is suffering. What Yahweh does is to show Job that as a mortal he cannot comprehend the reasons for the deity's actions. Yahweh also overpowers Job (especially in his second speech, 40:6–41:34), saying, in effect, "Who are you to question or challenge God?" Job has already admitted that he is no match for God, but the speeches of Yahweh bring that lesson home to him in a personal way.

After instructing Job, Yahweh vents his anger against Job's friends. They have not spoken rightly of God as has Job (42:7) since Job's questioning of God reflects a truer understanding of the divine nature than do the platitudes voiced by Job's friends. Perhaps this is because their orthodox viewpoint actually places a restriction upon God. It makes the formula, suffering comes from sin and sin leads to suffering, a hard and fast rule that even God must follow. Job, in contrast, recognizes that things are indeed more complicated but even so, he never discovers the real reason for his own suffering. Only the readers of the book are privy to this information.

By concluding in this way, the dialogues counter the orthodox explanation of the reason for human suffering—the idea that it is punishment for sin. This orthodox viewpoint is represented within the Bible in the "turn or burn" theology typical of the Deuteronomistic history and of the prophets. As we have seen, the prophets threaten destruction for disobedience of Yahweh and the law. The Deuteronomistic history does the same and also explains the disastrous exiles of Israel and Judah as punishment for national sin. Some scholars have suggested that the real setting of Job was that of the Babylonian exile and that its intent was to counter the Deuteronomistic history's explanation of the exile. These scholars believe that the author of Job was trying to say that the exile was not necessarily punishment for Judah's sin but that the real reason lay in the mysterious will and working of God. Whether Job was actually written specifically to counter the Deuteronomistic history is impossible to know for certain; however, the main point of the book of Job in regard to theodicy does contrast with the cause-effect relationship between sin and suffering advocated by the prophets and the Deuteronomistic history.[21]

There remains one point about the book of Job left to explore—the tension between the book's main point about theodicy and its present ending. The current ending belongs to the old folktale, for which it is perfectly appropriate: Job proves that he serves God out of a sense of integrity rather than because of the benefits of wealth and health, so it is quite fitting for God to reward his faithfulness by giving him twice as much as he had before. As we saw, with the insertion of the dialogues, the focus of the book changes from the question of the proper reason for serving God to that of the reason for suffering. The message of the dialogues as a whole is that suffering is not necessarily punishment for sin but attributable to the mysterious will of God. The "flip side" of this conclusion is that prosperity and well-being are not necessarily rewards for righteousness. Here, we can clearly see that if suffering comes from sin and sin leads to suffering, then by the same reasoning, prosperity comes from righteousness and righteousness leads to prosperity.

The book of Job contends that the first of these equations is untrue. By extension, the second equation is also untrue. And yet, the present ending of the book seems to uphold the second equation: God rewards Job with prosperity because of his righteousness. Thus, the ending stands in tension with the book's main point. This tension is best viewed within the context of wisdom literature as a continuing debate. Just when the question seems to be resolved, the book's conclusion leaves it open.

Job as Wisdom Literature

Whatever the precise situation that the book of Job was written to address, its intent seems clear. It calls into question the idea that suffering is always punishment for sin, and it does so by presenting a debate about the reason for human suffering, especially the suffering of righteous or good people. The entire question that Job and his friends have been debating is left unresolved in the end.

This lack of clear resolution may be frustrating to modern readers, but it is characteristic of biblical wisdom literature, the essence of which is diversity of perspective. The book of Job compensates modern readers in another way. As is typical of wisdom, it deals with an issue common to all people—that of suffering. By not explaining its cause, Job legitimates the human struggle to understand the reason for suffering and calamity. The same features of debate and the legitimation of the human quest for understanding are also particularly prominent in book of Qoheleth.

The Book of Ecclesiastes (Qoheleth)

The third example of wisdom literature in the Bible is the book of Ecclesiastes, also known by its Hebrew name, Qoheleth. The word "Qoheleth," often translated "teacher" or "preacher," is the title of the book's author. Just as suffering is the main issue in the book of Job, so Qoheleth's primary concern is the question of the meaning of life. That is clear enough at the beginning. But then the book seems to turn into a strange mixture of texts dealing with life's meaning and of proverbs that are completely unrelated to that question. It can be a confusing read. Fortunately, recent work on Qoheleth's genre, or rather its subgenre, points a way out of the confusion.

The Subgenre of Qoheleth

As we saw in the introduction, genres can have subgenres. Just as Proverbs incorporates subgenres such as "instruction," and Job incorporates the subgenre of folktale, so Qoheleth represents a subgenre within wisdom, that of fictional autobiography.[22] Fictional autobiographies have three parts in common. They begin with a brief self-introduction claiming to be by the subject, followed by an extended narrative detailing that individual's exceptional deeds. The third section varies from work to work according to four varieties: a set of blessings and curses, a list of donations to a god's cult, a prophecy, or wisdom instruction. These texts, therefore, use the autobiographical format and a specific structure for different purposes. Qoheleth resembles the fourth variety. Its main section makes use of the structure of fictional autobiographies in order to present wisdom instruction focused especially on the question of the meaning of life.[23]

The understanding of Qoheleth as fictional autobiography accounts for its pseudonymous authorship. Qoheleth, like Proverbs, is attributed to King Solomon, although he was not its real author. The book of Qoheleth does not actually use Solomon's name, but its opening reference to "the son of David, king in Jerusalem" makes it clear that he is intended. There are also allusions, especially in chapter 2, to Solomon's wealth, power, and wisdom. Thus, Solomon is the subject of Qoheleth's fictional autobiography. The structure of a fictional autobiography allows Qoheleth to adopt the persona of Solomon as a way of exploring meaning in the wealth, power, and pleasure to which Solomon had unique access.

Qoheleth's Debate on the Meaning of Life

Like Proverbs and Job, the book of Qoheleth is not monolithic but is best understood as presenting a debate. A careful reading reveals significant theological and ideological inconsistencies relating to some of the leading topics covered in the book. Indeed, the tensions that we have seen within Proverbs pale by comparison with those in Qoheleth.[24] Let's look at the topics in which the inconsistencies are most apparent.

The main question of Qoheleth relates to the meaning of life. Its perspective is predominantly negative: Life is meaningless. This is the sense of the word "vanity" in the famous summary of its message, "Vanity of vanities, all is vanity." The Hebrew word here (*hebel*) means vanity in the sense of emptiness, meaninglessness. It is as fruitless as "striving after wind."[25] At the same time, this pessimistic attitude stands in tension with at least two other strains in the book. One of these is the *carpe diem* advice that one should enjoy life while it lasts. This advice occurs repeatedly in the book (the following translations are the author's):

There is nothing better for a person than to eat, drink, and find enjoyment in one's work. (2:24)

I know that there is nothing better for them than to be happy and enjoy life. Moreover, for everyone to eat, drink, and enjoy work is a gift from God. (3:12–13)

I saw that there is nothing better than that a person enjoy work, for that is a person's lot. (3:22a)

According to what I have seen, it is good for one to eat, drink, and enjoy all the work at which one toils beneath the sun the number of days of life that God gives to one, for that is one's lot. It is a gift from God when God gives a person wealth and treasures and enables that person to use them and to accept his/her lot enjoying his/her work. (5:16–17 [Heb 5:17–18])

I commend pleasure, because there is nothing better for a person beneath the sun than to eat, drink, and enjoy, and this will attend him/her at work all during the lifetime that God gives beneath the sun. (8:15)

The advice to enjoy life may not necessarily contradict the view that life is meaningless. The two could well be complementary: Life has no meaning, so one may as well enjoy it while it lasts. This seems to be the point of 9:7–10. After commending enjoyment of life, this text counsels: "Do everything your hand finds to do with all your strength, for there is no work or thought or knowledge or wisdom in Sheol where you are going" (AT). Sheol is the place of the dead—like Hades in Greek mythology. Hence, Qoheleth is saying, "Enjoy life before you die." Still, the tension between the ideas that life is meaningless and that one should enjoy it is sharp elsewhere. Near the beginning of the book, for instance (2:1–11), Qoheleth tests pleasure as a possible reason for living. He mentions various pleasures, including taking pleasure in one's work. Yet, Qoheleth still concludes that life is meaningless.

The second strain in tension with the view that life is meaningless is the pious idea that one should fear God. Again, this idea appears repeatedly in Qoheleth. Everyone should fear God because of what God has done (3:14). One verse (5:7b [Heb 5:6b]) simply commands, "Fear God." Fearing God allows one to walk the middle path between being too righteous and too wicked (7:16–18). On the other hand, those who fear God are contrasted with the wicked, and the God-fearers are promised well-being (8:12–13). The sharpest contrast of all occurs at the end of the book, where fearing God is commended as a person's whole duty. In other words, it is the meaning of life.[26]

It is also worth observing that the "enjoy life" and the "fear God" passages are in some tension with each other in certain texts. This is especially so in 11:9–12:7. While the expression "fear God" does not occur here, Qoheleth advises the youthful reader to "remember your creator" (12:1). The young man is told to enjoy life but at the same time warned that God will judge him for his youthful deeds (11:9). The two pieces of advice are incongruous.

There are similar tensions in Qoheleth regarding some of the things he tests as possibilities for the sources of meaning in life.

Pleasure

Pleasure and enjoyment are commended as the way to approach life, even as a gift from God. Nevertheless, Qoheleth's investigation determined that pleasure was useless: "I said of laughter, 'It is mad,' and of pleasure, 'What use is it?'" (2:2, NRSV). After indulging himself in every pleasure, he still found life empty and meaningless (2:10–11).

Wealth

The acquisition of possessions was part of the quest that Qoheleth undertook and that he eventually gave up as meaningless (2:1–11). He amassed all kinds of wealth to the point of becoming wealthier than any of his predecessors. Yet in the end he found wealth empty. Other texts agree: Those obsessed with increasing property are never satisfied (4:8), so it is ultimately an activity devoid of meaning (5:10–11 [Heb 5:9–10]). Besides, riches are easily lost with no lasting benefit for their owner (5:13–17 [Heb 5:12–16]). Still, one passage disagrees, referring to wealth as a gift from God, at least when accompanied by the ability to enjoy it (5:19 [Heb 5:18]).

Work

Work, like pleasure and wealth, is characterized in some texts as a gift from God and a source of enjoyment.[27] Elsewhere, though, Qoheleth describes all work as an "evil task" (1:13) and meaningless (1:14). The work, in particular, into which Qoheleth throws himself (2:4–6) turns out to be empty (2:11), so much so that he comes to hate his work (2:18–23). There is no profit in work, he suggests (3:10). It is motivated by envy (4:4), never-ending and ultimately unproductive (4:8).

Wisdom

Like wealth, pleasure, and work, wisdom is a gift from God—and a reward for the one who pleases God (2:26). Wisdom is advantageous to those who possess it (7:11); it brings them strength (7:19) more than physical might or weaponry (9:16–18). It is vastly superior to foolishness (10:2, 12). Despite all these advantageous, Qoheleth, who acquires great wisdom, determines that it is also meaningless and a source of frustration (1:17–18). While wisdom is better than folly, ultimately the wise and the fool meet the same fate—death—so that their respective wisdom or foolishness makes no difference in the end (2:13–16).

Meaning of Life and Retribution/Reward

Qoheleth's consideration of the value of wisdom in the face of death renews the focus on the question of the meaning of life. Is there any indication in this life or beyond it of reward for the righteous or pious and punishment for the wicked? Again, the views of this matter in Qoheleth are inconsistent. On the one hand, life seems patently unfair, with wickedness where justice and righteousness should be (3:16). The oppressed have no relief or comfort (4:1). The righteous die young, while the wicked live long lives (7:15). They enjoy fine reputations while they live; when they die, they are buried with honor (8:10). Hence, there seems to be no system of immediate punishment of the wicked in operation (8:11). Indeed, life as a whole is governed by "time and chance" rather than any rules of fairness or equity according to one's abilities (9:11). Otherwise, all are equal in the grave: "the same fate comes to all, to the righteous and the wicked, to the good and the evil, to the clean and the unclean, to those who sacrifice and those who do not sacrifice" (9:2, NRSV).

However, there is a series of texts in Qoheleth that reflect a very different view about divine retribution and reward. Some of these texts indicate the belief that God watches over human activities and rewards the faithful while punishing the wicked.

> For to the one who is good before him he gives wisdom, knowledge, and joy. But to the sinner he gives the task of reaping and gathering in order to give in turn to the one who is good before God. (2:26, AT)

Hence, failure to fulfill a vow to God may bring consequences (5:4 [Heb 5:5]), and pleasing God will keep one from being ensnared by a deceitful woman, who will trap a sinner (7:26). The "fear God" passages indicate success for those who revere and obey God (7:18). This is especially true of 8:12b–13 (the following translations are the author's):

> For I know that it will be well with those who fear God because they are in fear before him. But it will not be well with the wicked, and they will not lengthen their days like a shadow because they are in fear before God.

Some of these texts even betray the belief in a final judgment:

> I thought, "God will judge the righteous and the wicked," for he has set a time for every affair and every deed. (3:17)

We have already cited the warning to the youth that God will bring all his immature pursuits of pleasure into judgment (11:9). But the clearest statement of a belief in a final judgment is the last two verses of the book.

> The end of the matter; all has been heard. Fear God and keep his commandments, for this is a person's whole duty. For God will bring every deed into judgment over every secret thing, be it good or evil. (12:13–14)

These last two verses are an obvious addition, so that this raises the likelihood that the previous allusions to God's judgment in the book may have also been added by the author of the book's conclusion. Furthermore, some of the contradictory statements are in quite close proximity to each other. It is difficult to believe that the same author could have written them both, one after the other. For instance, 8:12a refers to sinners prolonging their lives, but then 8:13a denies that the wicked can prolong their lives. Similarly, immediately after 8:12b–13 states that it will be well with those who fear God but not with the wicked, 8:14 observes that righteous people are sometimes treated as though they were wicked and vice versa.

Death

We have seen that there is a skeptical perspective in Qoheleth, which holds that there is no meaning to life and no ultimate justice. For this outlook in particular the question arises as to whether life is at all worth living, or is death better than life? Death, after all, is inevitable for animals as well as humans, and there is no indication that humans have any advantage over animals in terms of life after death.

> For humans and animals have a common fate: As one dies, so dies the other. Everything has the same breath; humans have no superiority over animals, for everything is meaningless. Everything goes to one place. Everything came from dust, and everything returns to dust. Who knows whether the breath of humans goes up and the breath of animals goes down to the underworld? (3:19–21)

The dead go to Sheol, which is not life after death but simply the abode of the dead, where there is "no work or thought or knowledge or wisdom" (9:10).

Qoheleth comes to hate life because of its meaninglessness. "I hated life because the activity that was done beneath the sun was noxious to me. For everything is meaningless and striving after wind" (2:17). In a particularly gloomy passage, he expresses the view that death is better than life, but it is even better never to have lived in the first place.

> Again I saw all the oppressions that are practiced beneath the sun and the tears of the oppressed. They have no comforter. Their oppressors have power, but they have no comforter. I commended the dead, who were already dead, above the living who are still alive. But the one who has not yet lived, who has not seen the evil deeds that are practiced beneath the sun, is better than both of them. (4:1–3)

This thoroughly negative orientation toward life is directly contradicted in 9:4–6, which maintains that life is better than death.

> For the one who is tied to the living there is hope, since a live dog is better than a dead lion. For the living know that they will die, but the dead know nothing, and

they have no more reward, since the memory of them is forgotten. Also, their love, their hate, their jealousy are already lost, and they will never again have a part in anything that is done beneath the sun.

Moreover, despite many dark days, the person who lives many years should rejoice in them all (11:8). What is more, as we saw above, there is a theme in Qoheleth that affirms life and encourages the enjoyment of it. This theme runs alongside the deeply pessimistic one that values death over life.

The obvious inconsistencies within Qoheleth represent the book's greatest challenge for readers, and several different theories about the composition of the book have been proposed in an effort to explain this phenomenon. There are four such principal theories. (1) The inconsistencies are additions from one or more later editors of Qoheleth's words. (2) The inconsistencies arise from Qoheleth's citation and refutation of traditional wisdom. (3) The book is the work of a single author; the inconsistencies reflect the fact that Qoheleth wrote at different times in his life or tried to represent different points of view. (4) The inconsistencies represent a dialogue, real or imagined, between different positions and do not necessarily come from different writers.[28]

These four theories are not necessarily mutually exclusive. For instance, Qoheleth may have cited traditional wisdom in an effort to counter it (2), and then his own work may also have been supplemented by later editors (1). Biblical scholars used to focus almost exclusively on the first theory, attempting to isolate editorial strands within the book. The passages that advocate fearing God in the belief that God will reward the righteous and punish the wicked, especially in a final judgment, remain the best candidates for such a string of additions, since these two ideas are the focus of the final two verses of the book, which are widely recognized as editorial.

More recently scholars have tended to gravitate toward the idea that the book, or at least the main body of it apart from its framework, is the work of a single author. They prefer to explain the inconsistencies by means of one of the other three theories or a combination of them. There is a good illustration of this approach in the treatment of 8:11–14a found in a recent, leading commentary on Qoheleth.[29] This passage, as noted above, attests a series of apparent contradictions that might lead one to suspect editorial revision. To begin with, our commentator translates these verses as one long thought:[30]

Since sentence for evil work is not executed quickly, people dare to do evil; an offender does the evil of hundreds but lives long. Even though I know that good will come to those who fear God, who are fearful in his presence, and good will not come to the wicked and they will not prolong their shadowy days because they are not fearful before God, there is a vanity that is done on earth inasmuch as there are righteous ones who are treated as if they have acted wickedly, and there are wicked ones who are treated as if they have acted righteously. I said that this, too, is vanity.

The author's comments on this passage are indicative of the approach he and many other recent commentators take, and they are worth quoting at length.[31]

> The issue of delayed justice is raised in v 11. Significantly, the author never denies that there will be retribution. He is of the view that there will be "a time and a judgment" for every matter (see 7:6; 3:17), but he insists that no one knows when or how that will be (7:7). The inequities that exist in the world suggest to him that justice has been delayed, and a consequence of that delay is that more injustice is perpetrated because the wicked are emboldened to do even more. Already in vv 11–12a one senses the tension between what Qoheleth acknowledges to be true (that there must be just retribution somehow) and what he sees as reality (that there is no retribution that he can perceive). That tension is clarified in a long concession that reflects popular belief, but that the author himself also acknowledges to be true (vv 12a–13), and what he recognizes as a contradiction (v 14). He acknowledges with traditional wisdom that it will be well with those who fear God, but not with those who are wicked. Qoheleth tries to cope with that tension to some extent. He admits that the wicked may indeed live long (v 12), but he asserts that they will not finally be able to prolong the limited human life span (vv 13–14). They may live longer than they deserve, but they cannot change the ephemeral nature of human life. Nevertheless, something is amiss for him; there is *hebel* "vanity," something that simply makes no sense (v 14). What is done under the sun remains an utter mystery. Even if one rationalizes that death is a great equalizer in the end, the fact remains that there are inequities in the present. The righteous are treated as if they are wicked and the wicked as if they are righteous. This incomprehensible reality he calls *hebel* "vanity" (v 15). It is an enigma.

This commentator, thus, recognizes tensions and contradictions in 8:11–14. But he ascribes them to Qoheleth's citation of traditional wisdom and to Qoheleth's own struggle with reality as he has experienced it and which he finds enigmatic to the point of being beyond explanation.

Qoheleth as Wisdom Literature

Broadly speaking, it is fair to say that Qoheleth has at least two principal "voices" whose respective messages and points of view are in tension with each other. One voice maintains that there is no meaning to life or eternal reward and that at

best one may merely "eat, drink, and be merry." In this view, death marks the
end for everyone and everything, and no one knows what lies beyond the grave.
The other perspective holds that there will be a last judgment and that the meaning of life, therefore, lies in obedience to God. These voices have been ascribed
to different authors, different levels of tradition, different moods of the same
author, and attempts to represent different orientations on life.

The presence of different perspectives within Qoheleth should not be surprising for readers familiar with Proverbs and Job. Such internal diversity is characteristic of the genre of wisdom literature in the Bible. Whatever the origin of
the voices in Qoheleth, the point of the book lies in its presentation of the dialogue between very different perspectives that they represent Like Job, Qoheleth
does not ultimately answer the question that is its main topic. It is not the intent
of wisdom literature to provide such answers. Its intent, rather, is to present the
debate and thereby to license the reader to search for his or her own answers. In
line with its genre, therefore, Qoheleth does not explain the meaning of life or
supply a road map to find it. Qoheleth simply raises the question of whether life
has meaning and articulates conflicting responses to that question. It is up to the
reader to decide which response is correct using his or her own God-given insight, observation, and experience.

Chapter Four

NOT THE END OF THE WORLD
AS WE KNOW IT

Apocalyptic Literature in the Bible

The Misconception:

Apocalyptic literature in the Bible details future events leading to the end of the world.

Apocalyptic . . . was the mother of all Christian theology.

> —Ernst Käsemann, "The Beginnings of Christian Theology,"
> *Journal for Theology and the Church* 6 (1969): 40

Peter: "Or you could accept the fact that this city is headed for a disaster of biblical proportions."

Mayor: "What do you mean, 'biblical'?"

Ray: "What he means is Old Testament biblical, Mr. Mayor. Real wrath-of-God-type stuff. Fire and brimstone coming from the sky. Rivers and seas boiling."

Egon: "Forty years of darkness. Earthquakes. Volcanoes."

Winston: "The dead rising from the grave."

Peter: "Human sacrifice. Dogs and cats living together. Mass hysteria."

> —Scene from the 1984 Columbia Pictures movie *Ghostbusters*

In 1818, a New England farmer and self-educated Bible student named William Miller came to the conclusion that the world would end with the return of Christ some time between March 21, 1843, and March 21, 1844. He based his conclusion on Scripture: Determining that the 2,300 days in Daniel 8:14 were actually years, he calculated from 457 BCE, the year when Ezra was commissioned to return to Jerusalem (Ezra 7:1). The result was 1843, and the Jewish New Year began on March 21. Miller's following grew as 1843 approached. But when March 21, 1844, had passed without event, some of his followers determined that there had been an error in calculations. They set the new date at October 22, 1844; as that day grew nearer, they became aggressive in proclaiming the prediction and succeeded in convincing a large number of others. True believers closed their businesses, sold their homes, and sat waiting to greet their Lord. For most of them, October 22, 1844, became known as the "Great Disappointment," and they turned from following Miller's teachings. Some, however, were so convinced that they reasoned that Christ's return had indeed taken place on the heavenly plane, though not on earth.[1]

Miller was not the last person to make such a prediction. In 1970 Hal Lindsey's best-selling *Late Great Planet Earth* deduced that in answering questions about the time of his return (Matt 24), Jesus presumed the existence of the nation of Israel. Jesus had said that "this generation" would not pass before "all these things take place" (Matt 24:34). Since the modern state of Israel had been established in 1948 and a biblical generation was forty years, Lindsey thought it likely that Christ would return and the world end by 1988.[2]

At the end of July 2004 a colleague of mine passed on to me a CD he had received in the mail. It contained a book manuscript by a certain Zechariah Daniels (a pseudonym?) of Chicago titled *The Free Gift: Second Coming 2016.*[3] As the title suggests, the author is predicting that the second coming of Christ will occur in 2016 with the destruction of the world to follow a thousand years later. This conclusion is based on an interpretation of a verse in Daniel (9:25) that refers to a period of seven weeks between the announcement about rebuilding Jerusalem and the coming of an anointed prince. Zechariah Daniels interprets the latter as Christ's return. He equates the rebuilding of Jerusalem with Israel's capture of that city in the 1967 war. Taking "seven weeks" as 49 years (7 days x 7), he adds that figure to 1967 to reach 2016. I predict that 2016 will come and go much the same as did 1843 and 1988.

Most recent literature about the end of the world is more subtle. It does not try to pinpoint the date of Christ's return but simply provides vivid depictions of the events leading up to it, implying that the date is imminent. Such works sell well because they cater to the same mixture of curiosity and fear as science fiction and horror.[4] As examples of those genres, they may be appealing. As biblical interpretation, however, they reflect gross misunderstanding of apocalyptic literature.

Apocalyptic Literature

Origin

"Apocalypse" and "apocalyptic" are terms widely used in modern society but not well understood or defined. They are associated with the idea of the catastrophic end of the world brought about through either divine or human (e.g., nuclear explosion, biochemical warfare, or the like) activity. The root meanings of the words "apocalypse" and "apocalyptic," however, have nothing to do with the end of the world or with cataclysm.

There are two examples of apocalyptic literature in the Bible—the second half of the book of Daniel (Dan 7–12) in the Hebrew Bible and the book of Revelation in the New Testament. Note that the title of the latter is "Revelation" (singular) not "Revelations" (plural), as it is so often mispronounced—an important difference because it has to do with the origin of the term "apocalyptic." The Greek word meaning "revelation" is *apokalypsis*, from which the English "apocalypse" is derived; the definition of "revelation" being an act of revealing or communicating divine truth and not necessarily an end-of-the-world pronouncement. The book of Revelation begins with the words, "The revelation (apocalypse) of Jesus Christ." Even though the book contains many revelation*s*, its proper name is singular: Revelation, or Apocalypse.

It is not certain whether this word at the beginning of the book of Revelation was intended as a title or was simply a description of the book's contents, but it quickly became popular as the title for an entire genre of literature. Beginning from the late first or early second century CE, when the New Testament book of Revelation was written, many Christian works adopted the title "apocalypse" under its influence. But the genre of literature now known as "apocalyptic" is older than the New Testament. When Revelation was written, there were already several older Jewish apocalypses in existence, including the one in Daniel 7–12. The genre flourished from about 200 BCE to about 200 CE.[5]

Apocalyptic literature, therefore, has its primary roots in Hebrew prophecy. The book of Revelation also refers to itself as prophecy (Rev 1:3). We saw in a previous chapter that prophetic books like Isaiah and Micah include sections (esp. 2 Isa 40–55) that were added in the exile or later and that look forward to the restoration of the nation of Israel. We described these texts as "visionary" or utopian, in the sense that they painted an idealistic picture based on hopes for the future. We also hinted that the realities of the return from Babylonian exile provided a stark contrast to the utopian hopes voiced in the prophets. The books of Ezra and Nehemiah describe conflicts with the inhabitants of land, and 3 Isaiah (Isa 56–66) suggests bitter tensions between different factions within Judah:[6]

Who are you making fun of?
Against whom do you open your mouth wide
And stick out your tongue?
Are you not children of transgression,
Deceitful seed? (Isa 57:4, AT)

The utopian vision of universal peace and justice had not been realized:

> Therefore justice is far from us,
> And righteousness does not reach us.
> We wait for light, but there is only darkness;
> For brightness, but we walk in gloom. (Isa 59:9, AT)

This tension between "brilliant hopes and bleak realities" led to the development of apocalyptic literature, which is sometimes characterized as pessimistic because it reflected the view that there is no hope for resolution of present problems in the regular workings of the world. "Gradually God's final saving acts came to be conceived of not as the fulfillment of promises within political structures and historical events, but as deliverance out of the present order into a new transformed order."[7] Only a direct intervention from God could bring resolution.

> Yahweh saw and was displeased that there was no justice.
> He saw that there was no one; he was appalled that there was no one to
>   intervene.
> So his own arm won him victory;
> His righteousness sustained him.
> He put on righteousness like a breastplate,
> A helmet of salvation on his head.
> He dressed in clothes of vengeance;
> He wrapped himself in zeal as in a mantle. (Isa 59:15b–17, AT)

Third Isaiah borrowed ancient depictions of Yahweh as a warrior to describe this intervention. God's intervention would bring a complete transformation of the world: The world order and power structures would be reversed so that the oppressed would rule and their oppressors would be destroyed. The transformation was expressed in cosmic terms: "For I am about to create new heavens and a new earth" (Isa 65:17, NRSV).

Because of these features, 3 Isaiah is often described as "protoapocalyptic."[8] It is not "full blown" apocalyptic, like Daniel 7 through 12 or Revelation. It does not share all the traits of apocalyptic literature but represents a point in the development from prophecy to apocalyptic. Other prophetic writings also anticipate individual features of later apocalyptic literature, such as visions of the future that involve symbols, interpretation by an angel, and the destruction of the wicked in the present world order and the foundation of a new age.[9] But these texts remain within the realm of *prophecy* and do not cross over into *apocalyptic*. They lack the form of apocalyptic revelation through an interpreted, otherworldly vision or its content referring to the transformation of the cosmos as opposed to the transformation of the land of Israel alone.

The recognition that apocalyptic literature is rooted in prophecy is important because it indicates that apocalyptic is misunderstood for much the same reason and in much the same way as prophecy is misunderstood. Just as people commonly misconstrue prophecy as predicting the future far in advance, so they misconstrue apocalyptic as detailed predictions of the end of the world. Thus, each generation tends to interpret the Bible's apocalyptic visions as references to events of its time indicating that the end of the world is near. Meanwhile, world history marches on. This continuing tendency alone suggests that apocalyptic literature may really be about something else.

The word "apocalypse" by itself has nothing to do with the end of the world. As we have seen, it is simply the Greek word for "revelation." Another Greek word, *eschaton*, means "end," and "eschatology" describes thought and literature concerning the end of the world (or the present age) and theories associated with it, such as the final judgment and afterlife. The term "apocalyptic" comes into play in reference to writings that purport to "reveal" the events leading up to the "eschaton." The designation of this genre of literature as apocalyptic already suggests that its focus is on revelation rather than the specifics about the end of the world. Like prophecy, apocalyptic literature was more concerned with the time in which it was written than with the far distant future. As with prophecy, and perhaps even more than with prophecy, the key to understanding a particular apocalyptic work lies in discerning its original historical or social context.

Definition

Apocalyptic literature flourished in the period between 200 BCE and 200 CE. Christianity, which arose in this period, was and is essentially apocalyptic in orientation. It sees Christ as the ultimate revelation of God. It might also be considered eschatological, in that Christ inaugurates the final age of earthly existence. The focus of scholars studying apocalyptic literature, then, has been Jewish apocalyptic, which preceded and then gave birth to Christian apocalyptic. There is also a substantial body of Gnostic, Persian, and Greco-Roman literature from this period that shares the features of Jewish and Christian apocalyptic.[10]

One of the most important advances of biblical scholarship in recent decades has been the formulation of a definition of the genre of apocalyptic literature There were previous efforts at characterizing apocalyptic by listing the traits typical of such works.[11] As useful as these lists were and are, they provided only a sketch of the contours of the genre. Few apocalyptic works contained all of the items in these lists. So where was one to draw the line? How many items were necessary for a work to be considered apocalyptic? Which items were absolutely essential to the genre? There was a clear need for a definition of the genre itself.

That need was filled in 1979. The Society of Biblical Literature, the premiere organization in North America for the academic study of the Bible, initiated a project to define various genres in the Bible. In 1979 the "Apocalypse Group," those scholars who had collaborated to formulate a definition of apocalyptic literature, published its conclusion. It determined that

> Apocalypse is a genre of revelatory literature with a narrative framework, in which a revelation is mediated by an otherworldly being to a human recipient, disclosing a transcendent reality which is both temporal, insofar as it envisages eschatological salvation, and spatial insofar as it involves another, supernatural world.[12]

It may be helpful to "unpack" this definition by examining each of the three principal parts that relate to the content of apocalyptic.

"a revelation is mediated by an otherworldly being to a human recipient"

Behind the genre lies the assumption that there is a supernatural world of good and bad entities—God and the forces of good, including angels, on the one side, and the forces of evil, including demons, on the other. This supernatural world is normally hidden from humans and mysterious to them. Yet, it is actually the real world. The things that take place in it not only influence but determine events in the world of humans.

Because the supernatural world is usually hidden, access to it is granted only by special *revelation*. The revelation described in an apocalypse is typically conveyed through a vision, which usually occurs in the context of a trance or a dream. The experience is, nonetheless, portrayed as quite real to the person who receives the revelation. One of the major subgenres in apocalyptic is characterized by the description of transport of the visionary into otherworldly realms.[13] The experience can cause physical reactions such as fatigue, terror, and weeping.

The revelation to the visionary highlights the mysterious nature of the supernatural realm. It is full of symbols—monsters, such as dragons, and composite beasts, such as a leopard with bear's feet and a lion's mouth, often with exaggerated or multiple features, such as heads or horns (Rev 13:1–3). The same numbers occur repeatedly (3, 4, 7, 10, 12, 1000, and multiples), and they are all symbolic (e.g., 666). The names and titles are also symbols: the Beast, the Dragon, Gog and Magog, Ancient of Days, the great Whore, Babylon, the Lamb. These symbols are not simply the product of a wild imagination. While they seem arbitrary and unprecedented to modern readers, they draw from ancient mythology and from Israel's historical and literary traditions. Apocalyptic was the product of learned authors, who had engaged in intense study of biblical and other literature.[14] It is no coincidence that Daniel is depicted as a wise man and a scribe. Thus, one of the keys to understanding apocalyptic symbolism today is familiarity with the Hebrew Bible.

Familiarity with Hebrew scripture made the images of apocalyptic less foreign but did not automatically identify what each symbol was meant to represent. The vision had to be *mediated* or interpreted for the human recipient by a heavenly intermediary. This otherworldly interpreter was usually an angel, who could serve as guide to the visionary on the heavenly tour, and the interpretation usually took the form of a dialogue between the angel and the human visionary. It might also involve an extended speech by the interpreter or some other heavenly character or a written work, a scroll, or book.

The *human recipient* of the apocalyptic vision is usually pseudonymous. This means that the author of the apocalypse did not use his or her real name but chose instead to record the vision as that of a well-known character from the distant past, usually a highly regarded figure from the Bible. One of the best known and earliest examples of Jewish apocalyptic is ascribed to Enoch, who "walked with God" before the flood and was taken up into heaven (Gen. 5:21–24). Similarly, there are apocalypses ascribed to Adam, Seth, Moses, Abraham, and other ancient biblical characters. It is not generally recognized that Daniel may be a pseudonym borrowed from a legendary Canaanite character renowned for his wisdom (see the section on Daniel). Pseudonymous authorship was a widespread literary practice during the period 200 BCE–200 CE, which produced the apocalyptic literature we are discussing. The use of a pseudonym bolstered the author's credibility and added an aura of certainty to the visions in that the events they foresaw were determined from ages long past.

> *"disclosing a transcendent reality which is temporal,*
> *insofar as it envisages eschatological salvation"*

The revelation in an apocalyptic vision takes place along what scholars often refer to as two axes, one temporal, the other spatial. The temporal axis looks forward to the *eschaton* or "end." This is not necessarily the end of the world but rather the end of the present period of crisis in which the author and the audience of the apocalyptic work find themselves. As with prophecy, the real focus of apocalyptic is on the present context shared by author and audience rather than on the distant future.

In line with its focus on the present, apocalyptic describes the end as imminent. It details events leading up to the end; these events are usually disastrous
and catastrophic in nature—the raining of fire and hail from heaven and the like.
Whether it is the end of the world or the end of an age, it involves a great shift in
human history. It is, therefore, described in *cosmic* language—the same kind of
language used to tell about creation. Apocalyptic has even been defined as "the
use of ancient myth to express convictions about the end-time."[15]

Some apocalyptic writings provide a kind of historical review leading up to
the end. They trace history through various ages or dispensations that were *determined* from the beginning of time and cannot be altered. A technique for
emphasizing this determinism is *ex eventu* prophecy—prophecy "after the event."
That is, the pseudonymous visionary, who lived long ago, is portrayed as fore-
seeing human history leading up to the actual author's own time. The figure of
Daniel, for instance, foretells the coming of a series of kingdoms or world empires with the end coming in the latter days of the fourth kingdom (Dan 2; 7–8).
As we will see, this is an *ex eventu* prophecy, and the book of Daniel was actually
written during the time of the fourth kingdom that it purports to foresee. The
clues in the text that help to identify the fourth kingdom also tell when the book
was written and the circumstances it was intended to address.

The end envisioned by apocalyptic literature brings with it the judgment of
the wicked and the inauguration of a new age or new world. Apocalyptic is
often described as *dualistic*. As in the supernatural world, so in the world of
humans, there are two forces or powers—good or evil. The end of the age may
represent simply the overthrow of the ruling and oppressive power, be it political, social, or religious, and its replacement by the righteous who were formerly
oppressed. For apocalypses that envision the end of the world, the new age is
the afterlife. It is inaugurated with the destruction of the evil at the last judgment and the elevation or resurrection of the righteous to inhabit the newly
transformed cosmos now become paradise.

> *"and spatial insofar as it involves another,*
> *supernatural world."*

The second axis is spatial—it describes the divide between this world and the
supernatural one. With this element, the definition of apocalyptic literature
comes full circle. As we have seen, the existence of this supernatural world and
its influence on, indeed its control of, human history is a basic assumption behind apocalyptic literature. This supernatural world is not generally accessible
to humans. When access is granted through special revelation, its mysterious
symbols have to be interpreted by a supernatural agent. This focus on other-

worldly happenings diverts the attention of the righteous readers away from their present distress and assures them that the true powers of the universe are on their side. This observation raises the question of the function or intent of apocalyptic literature, to which we now turn.

Intent

The committee that formulated the 1979 definition of apocalyptic literature determined beforehand to deal *only* with the form and content of apocalyptic and to leave the question of its function or intent for further deliberation. Since we are concerned in this book especially with the intent behind the different genres in the Bible, this question is especially important.

The question of the function of apocalyptic was taken up in another *Semeia* volume seven years later, and several definitions were proposed. Perhaps the most widely recognized one characterized apocalyptic as "intended to interpret present, earthly circumstances in light of the supernatural world and of the future, and to influence both the understanding and the behavior of the audience by means of divine authority."[16] Another scholar in the same volume wrote, "In *function*, an apocalypse legitimates the transcendent authority of the message by mediation of a new revelatory experience for the audience to encourage them to modify their cognition and behavior in conformity with transcendent perspectives."[17]

John Collins, the author of the 1979 definition, later articulated much the same understanding of apocalyptic's intent: "The function of the apocalyptic literature is to shape one's imaginative perception of a situation and so lay the basis for whatever course of action it exhorts.[18]

These definitions have in common the recognition that apocalyptic literature has a rhetorical function, which is intended to persuade its audience of its author's authority and perspective so as to influence the audience's thinking and actions. The definitions above are all deliberately broad and vague because they are intended to include all apocalypses. Since our focus here is more narrowly on apocalypses in the Bible, i.e., Daniel and Revelation, we can be more specific.

Another contribution to the 1986 volume focused on Revelation and defined the function of apocalyptic as "intended for a group in crisis with the purpose of exhortation and/or consolation by means of divine authority."[19] The emphasis in this statement on crisis is true for the biblical apocalypses of Daniel 7–12 and Revelation, each of which were written during periods of opposition by foreign powers. In fact, it holds true for all apocalyptic works if one acknowledges that the crisis can take different forms.[20] In addition to governmental persecution, for instance, social struggles, culture shock, and religious disputes can bring distress to individuals and communities. Furthermore, it is not necessary that a crisis be "real" to outsiders as long as it is perceived as such by the author of an apocalyptic work or its audience. The point is that all apocalypses arise out of a sense of crisis, whether real or perceived. In the cases of the biblical apocalypses in Daniel and Revelation, the crises are largely political in nature and can be historically situated.

Those in crisis are suffering or feel themselves vicitimized, usually for their religious beliefs. They feel alienated from their societies, especially from their power structures. They lack hope for any change in their situation within the realities of their present world. Apocalyptic offers comfort and hope to people in despair—not from earthly sources but from heaven. "Empowerment to cope with such negative realities comes through denying them any ultimate validity."[21] It is the decisions and activities taking place in the heavenly realm that really count, and they insure the ultimate vindication of the righteous, whose suffering in the present is fleeting.

Parade Texts: Daniel 2; 7–8

The book of Daniel contains two distinct parts. Chapters 1 through 6 are stories about the figure of Daniel. These stories are set in the sixth century (actually beginning in 606 BCE according to Dan 1:1); they are stories about how Daniel and his friends maintain their faith and prosper in the courts of foreign rulers. As the following outline reveals, some of these stories are very well known.

Chapter	Story
1	Daniel & friends prove their diet of vegetables superior to the king's delicacies.
2	Daniel interprets Nebuchadnezzar's dream.
3	Daniel & friends thrown into the fiery furnace for not bowing to Nebuchadnezzar's statue.
4	Daniel interprets a second dream of Nebuchadnezzar's as predicting his temporary degradation as an animal.
5	Daniel interprets the handwriting on the wall.
6	Daniel thrown into the lion's den for worshipping Yahweh.

The second half of the book is an apocalypse consisting of three visions granted to Daniel, which are then interpreted for him by heavenly beings. The three visions are related in chapters 7, 8, and 10 through 12. Chapter 9 contains a prophecy covering essentially the same material as the visions and using similar imagery and is typical of apocalyptic literature.

The character of Daniel is based on a figure who was legendary in Canaan long before the Bible was written. The book of Ezekiel refers twice to this figure. In Ezekiel 14:14, Daniel is mentioned together with Noah and Job as men whose extraordinary righteousness would save only themselves and not the city of Jerusalem. The reference here is not to one of Ezekiel's contemporaries but, like Noah and Job, to a famous person of the distant past. Daniel is mentioned again in Ezekiel (28:3), in the context of an oracle against the king of the Phoenician city-state of Tyre: Ezekiel asks if the king is wiser than Daniel, suggesting that Daniel was a ruler renowned for his wisdom. Thanks to the discovery in the 1930s of texts from the city-state of Ugarit, which flourished 1400–1200 BCE, we now know that this was indeed the case (Daniel or Dan'el appears in the Ugaritic story of Aqhat as the king of a city-state). While that story does not showcase his wisdom, he is a pious ruler who pleads for and receives a son.[22]

The stories in the book of Daniel are very similar to the stories of other biblical characters, especially Joseph and Esther. All three exemplify the behavior of the righteous Jew in a foreign court. Joseph and Daniel, moreover, are both known for their interpretation of dreams, which leads them to positions of prominence in the royal administration. A major difference between the stories in Daniel 1–6 and the apocalypse in chapters 7–12 is their respective outlooks on foreign rulers. The stories depict such rulers as basically benevolent, though arrogant and sometimes foolish. The visions, however, reflect a bitter hatred of such rulers and portray them as beasts since the bitterness is occasioned by persecution suffered under such rulers. This different outlook suggests that the stories are of earlier origin than the visions.

As with other apocalypses, the Daniel who received the revelations in Daniel 7–12 is pseudonymous. That is, the name of the legendary figure from the ancient past was borrowed to serve as the human visionary. This name was then used as well for the stories in chapters 1 through 6. Although these stories are probably older than the visions in chapters 7–12, they have been adapted as the narrative introduction to those visions. Thus there is significant continuity between the contents of these two major sections. Chapters 1–6 present Daniel as an interpreter of dreams and revelations of other kinds, such as the handwriting on the wall. Then, in chapters 7–12 Daniel himself recounts revelations of various sorts that were given to him. The continuity is particularly strong between chapters 2 and 7–8, which trace past and present world empires and contain revelations about future ones.

The stories in Daniel 1 through 6 are not apocalyptic in nature, but they are part of the apocalyptic book of Daniel—they provide the narrative introduction to the apocalypse in chapters 7–12, and the definition of apocalyptic literature includes a narrative framework. The stories in Daniel 1 through 6 are probably best categorized as legends. Their purpose is not to recount exactly what happened in the past but to serve as a prelude to the revelations in the later chapters. The stories arouse a sense of wonder in the reader and also establish the reputation of the character of Daniel. Stories like these about wise individuals and the affairs of royal courts are also found outside of the Bible in literature from Greece and Egypt.[23] This indicates that the author or authors of Daniel were, like the character himself, part of the elite of the day—members of the upper class, well educated and well read.

The visions in Daniel concern both the temporal and spatial axes: spatial in their involvement of otherworldly regions and beings; temporal in that they are eschatological, with visions of the end of the age, judgment of the wicked, and even resurrection. Along its temporal axis, especially in chapters 7 and 8, the book traces the series of kingdoms or empires. It is this overview of world history that qualifies Daniel as an apocalypse of the "historical" type as opposed to the "otherworldly journey" type.[24]

Daniel 2

The story in Daniel 2 is in many ways typical of the court tales mentioned earlier. Daniel is among the wise advisors of King Nebuchadnezzar of Babylon. The king has a dream one night and demands that his advisors tell him both the dream and its meaning. The demand suggests that the king is skeptical of the advisor's abilities and motives. When no one can recount the dream, the king orders their execution. Daniel and his friends find out about the king's predicament only when the executioner comes for them. With characteristic "prudence and discretion" (2:14), Daniel reasons with the executioner and secures a postponement of the king's order, allowing him to consult God, who reveals the dream and its interpretation in an overnight vision.

Brought before the king, Daniel recounts the dream, giving God the credit for revealing it to him. The dream, he says, reveals "what will happen at the end of days." Nebuchadnezzar saw a statue composed of different metals—head and shoulders of gold, chest and arms of silver, torso and thighs of bronze, legs of iron, and feet of iron and clay mixed. A stone carved out of the mountain "not by human hands" struck the statue, pulverizing it. The stone then became a huge mountain that filled the earth.

Next, Daniel interprets the dream for the king. The statue represents a kind of timeline: Nebuchadnezzar himself and his kingdom are the head of gold.

After him will arise successive kingdoms, each inferior to its predecessor. In the days of the last kingdom, God will intervene, doing away with the previous kingdoms and setting up one that will endure in perpetuity.

Christian interpreters typically identify the four kingdoms of the dream as Babylon, (Media-)Persia, Greece, and Rome. The large boulder that decimates the statue would then be Christianity or the church, referred to as an eternal kingdom. This interpretation is supported by the historical fact that there was no independent kingdom of Media. The interpretation, however, has its problems. For instance, it is difficult in this interpretation to make sense of the reference to mixed marriages (2:43) within the context of the Roman empire. More seriously, the beginning of the Christian church did not take place in the latter, weakened days of the Roman empire as indicated by the feet of the statue being of mixed iron and clay. Hence, this interpretation does not really work.

Another interpretation more common among biblical scholars is that the four kingdoms can be identified as Babylon (gold), Media (silver), Persia (bronze), and Greece (iron and clay). The image of the statue combines two motifs common in ancient literature. One of these is the notion of ages of history represented by a series of metals declining in value. This motif is best known from the Greek historian Hesiod, who adapted the same basic scheme of gold, silver, bronze, and iron metals to his own purposes.[25] The second motif was the idea that the Near East was ruled by a sequence of four kingdoms or empires. This motif was widespread in the ancient world and in Greek and Roman documents.[26] The typical list of empires was: Assyria, the Medes, the Persians, and the Macedonians. The empire of the Medes was a traditional motif rather than historical fact. Macedonia was the home of Alexander the Great and so is equivalent to Greece in Daniel. However, the scheme in the book of Daniel begins with the Babylonians in order to adapt it to the setting of the figure of Daniel in the court of Nebuchadnezzar.

The feet in Daniel's vision—partly of iron, partly of clay—represent the "divided kingdom" of the Greek empire after Alexander's death. It was divided among four of his generals, each of whom established a dynasty in different parts of the empire. Judea was ruled successively by the Ptolemies (ca. 323–198 BCE) and the Seleucids (ca. 198–163 BCE). Instances of intermarriage between these two dynasties as alluded to in 2:43 are documented in 252 and 194/3 BCE.

Daniel 8

In addition to the considerations just mentioned, the content of Daniel 7 and 8 provides the best reason for interpreting the sequence of kingdoms as Babylon, Media, Persia, and Greece. Daniel 7–8 contain two visions. The two are related because the account of the second vision refers back to the first one (8:1), and both visions are narrated in first person. We begin with the second vision, the one in chapter 8, because it specifically identifies the countries to which both visions refer.

The vision in Daniel 8 describes a ram with two horns that is destroyed by a goat with a single horn. The goat's single horn is subsequently broken and re-placed by four other horns. From one of these springs a little horn, which grows toward heaven and even overthrows some heavenly bodies. It also overthrows the temple and halts its regular sacrifice. The "transgression that makes deso-late" and the trampling of the temple sanctuary are forecast to last 2,300 morn-ings and evenings or 1,150 full days.

The interpretation of the vision given to Daniel identifies it as a vision about the end (8:17). As we saw in the treatment of apocalyptic that began this chapter, this need not mean the end of the world but may simply refer to the end of an age. Horns are standard symbols for power and kingship in the Bible.[27] Thus, the three horns in this vision are identified, respectively, as representing the kings or empires of Media, Persia, and Greece (8:20–21). The goat's single horn, identi-fied as the first king of Greece, is obviously Alexander the Great. The four king-doms that subsequently arise from the broken horn of the goat (8:22) are Alexander's successors, the generals who divided up his empire after his death.

The little horn that became great and arrogant is the Seleucid ruler, Antiochus IV Epiphanes. In 167 BCE, he appalled the people of Judea by installing sacrifices to Zeus in place of the "regular burnt offering" in the temple in Jerusalem. This is the act alluded to in 8:11–13. The "transgression that makes desolate" elsewhere in Daniel is called the "abomination of desolation."[28] This "trans-gression" or "abomination" was the idol of Zeus that Antiochus had erected in the temple. The Hebrew word "desolation" or "desolating" (shōmēm) is a play on ba῾al shāmayim, "lord of heaven," one of the titles used for Zeus.

As is typical of apocalyptic literature, the reference to Antiochus's desecration of the temple is ex eventu, here meaning that the vision was composed some time after Antiochus's desecration of the temple in 167 BCE. While the vision itself does not describe Antiochus's downfall in detail, it does indicate the tem-porary nature of his desecration—1,150 days (8:14). Daniel is told that the horn will be broken "not by human hands" (8:25). Thus, the message of the vision is that the oppression currently being suffered at the hands of Antiochus will not last long because God is going to intervene to halt it. This makes clear that the intent of this vision—and indeed of the book of Daniel as a whole—is to com-fort, encourage, and console the faithful Jews who are suffering under Antiochus's persecution.

Daniel 7

The vision in chapter 8 mentions and presupposes the one in chapter 7. In chapter 7, Daniel describes four beasts that he saw come up from the sea, the fourth with ten horns. Then a "little horn" spouting "pompous words" replaced three of the earlier horns before the fourth beast was slain and burned in front of the "Ancient of Days." Afterward, "one like a son of man" appeared and was granted everlasting dominion by the Ancient of Days.

This vision is a good example of the reuse of images originally drawn from mythology. The beasts, like the sea god Yamm in Canaanite mythology, embody the "evil" force of primordial chaos. There is no reason other than their original association with Yamm for them to be coming out of the sea in this vision. The title "Ancient of Days" is similar to that of the chief Canaanite god El, "Father of Years." The "one like the son of man" is comparable to the god Baal. He comes with the clouds, as Baal is called the "rider on the clouds" in the Ugaritic texts. He approaches the "Ancient of Days" as Baal approaches El. Most important, he triumphs over the sea monster as Baal defeats Yamm.

In the interpretation of the vision given to Daniel, the four beasts, like the four metals in Daniel 2, represent four kingdoms, the fourth of which has ten kings (7:17, 23–24). An eleventh king, the "little horn," will subsequently arise and will persecute the "saints" or "holy ones" for "a time, two times, and half a time" (7:25)—probably three and one-half years—until dominion is taken from him and given to the saints forever. The main point of the vision, then, is the prediction that the "saints of the Most High" will receive and possess an eternal kingdom (7:17–18, 21–22).

The vision in chapter 8 specifically identifies the sequence of empires by naming Media, Persia, and Greece. This makes it clear that the sequence of four kingdoms in chapters 2 and 7 ends with Greece. The four kingdoms that the writer had in mind, therefore, were Babylon, Media, Persia, and Greece. The vision in chapter 8 also had clear allusions to the events of Antiochus's oppression in 167 BCE. The vision in chapter 7 also concerns the oppression of Antiochus IV. (Remember that it is typical of apocalyptic literature to place two visions about the same thing side by side.) Since the fourth beast is the kingdom of Greece, the troublesome little horn that arises from it is the same as the little horn on the goat in chapter 8, namely, Antiochus IV Epiphanes. The ten horns are rulers of the Seleucid dynasty who preceded him.[29]

As for the other features in the vision, the "Ancient of Days" is God. "One like a son of man" is a way of referring to a figure who looks human but is not. He is probably an angel; most scholars identify him with the angel Michael (Dan 10:13, 21). The "saints" or "holy ones," who, along with this figure receive an eternal kingdom, may refer to faithful Jews. Most scholars also identify them as angels, and indeed the term may encompass both groups. It illustrates the idea behind apocalyptic literature that earthly history is really determined by heavenly realities. Thus, Antiochus IV, by exalting himself and desecrating the temple, assaults the angels and oppresses them even as he oppresses faithful Jews.

As with the vision in chapter 8, so the point of the vision in chapter 7 is to encourage the earthly component of the saints. The vision assures them that the defeat of their oppressor is imminent and that the forces of good will triumph. When that happens, they will have a share of an eternal kingdom.

Date and Message of Daniel

The great fourth-century Christian scholar Jerome began his commentary on the book of Daniel by citing Porphyry, a third-century Neoplatonist philosopher:

> Porphyry wrote his twelfth book against the prophecy of Daniel, denying that it was composed by the person to whom it is ascribed in its title, but rather by some individual living in Judaea at the time of the Antiochus who was surnamed Epiphanes. He further alleged that "Daniel" did not foretell the future so much as he related the past, and lastly that whatever he spoke of up till the time of Antiochus contained authentic history, whereas anything he may have conjectured beyond that point was false, inasmuch as he would not have foreknown the future.[30]

Biblical scholarship has essentially confirmed Porphyry's view that Daniel is pseudonymous and was written substantially later than when it is set. However, contrary to Porphyry's negative view of Daniel as false and deceptive, it is best to understand these simply as typical features of the genre of apocalyptic literature.

The book of Daniel is the only example of "full-blown" apocalyptic literature in the Hebrew Bible. The three visions in chapters 2, 7, and 8 well illustrate its nature as apocalyptic. As noted, Daniel is an example of the "historical" type of apocalyptic, which contains an overview of history, rather than the type characterized by an otherworldly journey. This means that the book can be dated by the latest events alluded to in its *"ex eventu"* prophecy.

Daniel was written some time after December 167 BCE—the date of the latest event to which it alludes (Antiochus's halting of the burnt offering and desecration of the temple). The book of Daniel must also have been completed before 164 BCE, the year when Antiochus died and the temple in Jerusalem was reconsecrated, since there is no reference to the latter event in Daniel. Even more telling is that Daniel 11:45 seems to suggest that Antiochus would die while on campaign in the land of Israel, when he in fact died of illness in Persia. The hopeful anticipation of his death in such idealistic terms indicates that it had not yet become a real occurrence.

The late date of the book of Daniel accounts for other historical problems in it. These have long been noticed by scholars and are especially prominent in the book's first half.[31] Most famous among these is the claim that Darius the Mede succeeded Belshazzar, king of Babylon, and set up a new empire (Dan 5:31). There is no historical record of a Darius the Mede, nor, as we have observed, of a Median empire.[32] It is also now known that Belshazzar was the son of Nabonidus, the last Babylonian king, rather than of Nebuchadnezzar, and that Belshazzar never reigned as king.[33] These discrepancies reflect confusion about historical matters resulting from the book having been composed considerably later than the period in which chapters 1 through 6 are set. That is, the book was written not in the sixth century, as suggested by the tales in its first half, but in the second century, as indicated by the apocalyptic visions in its second half.

The purpose of Daniel, as is clear from the visions in chapters 7 and 8, is to encourage pious Jews who were suffering persecution under Antiochus IV to remain loyal to their faith. The book offers heavenly visions as a way of reassuring its readers that their suffering will not last long. The end—not of the world but of the age of persecution—is imminent and has been determined in heaven, where human affairs are ultimately decided. Thus, the arrogant persecutor will be broken "not by human hands" (8:25).[34]

As part of its encouragement to the persecuted, the book of Daniel introduces a new basis for hope—the resurrection of the dead (Dan 12:1–2). The idea was apparently in existence before Daniel, in apocalyptic works preserved in the book of 1 Enoch. It may also have precursors in other parts of the Bible.[35] But Daniel 12 contains the first *unambiguous* reference to a resurrection and final judgment in the Hebrew scriptures. It makes sense that the idea would have flourished during the persecution of Antiochus. The previous belief that all the dead go to Sheol, which was comparable to the Greek underworld Hades, would have offered little hope to Antiochus's victims. The promise of reward for the faithful, in contrast, in the form of resurrection and life after death could have been a source of courage and inspiration for those called upon to sacrifice their lives.

The idea of resurrection, which developed in Judaism around the time of the book of Daniel (second century BCE) and beyond, was obviously very influential in the New Testament and in Christianity. Other features of Daniel were also reused and reinterpreted in the New Testament. The way in which the New Testament writers reused and reinterpreted Daniel is similar to the use that they made of Hebrew prophecy.

A prominent example of this reapplication is Jesus's use of the title "Son of Man" in reference to himself in the New Testament Gospels (e.g., Mark 2:10). This does not mean, however, that Jesus was claiming to be the "one like a son of man" in Daniel's vision (esp. Dan 7:13). The title has a long history and simply means "human being."[36] Thus, the figure in Daniel is *like* a human being, in human form, even though he is actually an angel, an angel in the guise of a man. In a similar way, Jesus's use of the title in the Gospels invokes the image in Daniel and emphasizes both Jesus's humanity and his divinity. The "Son of Man," claim the Gospel writers, is a human being, but like the figure in Daniel, he is actually more, the Son of God.

Another example of an idea from Daniel that is reinterpreted in the Gospels is Jesus's reference to the "desolating sacrilege." In the context of what is sometimes called the "Synoptic apocalypse," Jesus tells his disciples that the imposing buildings of the temple in Jerusalem will be thrown down, and they inquire when this will occur. Matthew's version of Jesus's response incorporates the following warning:

> So when you see the desolating sacrilege standing in the holy place, as was spoken of by the prophet Daniel (let the reader understand), then those in Judea must flee to the mountains; the one on the housetop must not go down to take what is in the house; the one in the field must not turn back to get a coat. (Matt 24:15–18, NRSV)[37]

The expression "desolating sacrilege" is similar to the "abomination of desolation" in Daniel and refers to much the same thing. Just as it referred in Daniel to the statue and worship of Zeus erected in the temple by Antiochus in 167, so in the Gospels it alludes to idol worship within the temple (the "holy place") by foreigners. This in fact occurred when the Romans invaded Jerusalem in 70 CE. Since Matthew wrote his Gospel after this date, Jesus's words here are another example of *ex eventu* prophecy. In citing Daniel, Matthew is finding more than one level of meaning in the Daniel text and applying it to a later situation, just as was done with Hebrew prophecy.

Conclusion to Daniel

Jerome's quotation of Porphyry with which we began this section illustrates the role that proper understanding of genre can play for faith. Jerome wrote to counter Porphyry, who viewed the book of Daniel (because of its pseudonymity and *ex eventu* prophecy), as a pious fraud. (It is no accident that Jerome's defense was translated by Gleason Archer, who is a strong defender of the literalist way of reading of the Bible.)

The book of Daniel, like the book Jonah, has sometimes been used as a test case for faith in the literal meaning of the Bible. The nineteenth-century Christian author, E. B. Pusey, voiced these sentiments in an echo of Jerome:

> The book of Daniel is especially fitted to be a battlefield between faith and unbelief. It admits of no half-measures. It is either Divine or an imposture. To write any book under the name of another, and to give it out to be his, is, in any case, a forgery, dishonest in itself and destructive of all trustworthiness.[38]

While biblical scholarship has essentially confirmed Porphyry's view that Daniel is pseudonymous and was written substantially later than when it is set, these features do not undermine the book's credibility or theological value. In this respect Porphyry was wrong—Daniel is not a pious fraud. But the attempts by Jerome, Archer, and others to defend the historicity of the character of Daniel in the sixth century are also misguided. Both perspectives fail to recognize that the book of Daniel simply makes use of the conventions of the genre of apocalyptic literature, which were widely accepted at the time of its writing. Understanding this allows the reader clearly to see the book's message in its original setting and then to apply that message appropriately to other settings. The book of Daniel was designed to encourage Jews suffering persecution. The abiding message of hope that it offers is that God is in control of time and human affairs and that God has a long-range plan that will reward the faithful and righteous and guarantee the destruction of evil.

The Book of Revelation

Overview of Revelation

Apocalyptic literature takes its name from the New Testament book of Revelation (Greek: *apokalypsis*). Ancient books typically did not have titles but were known by the first few words in the book, so the name "Revelation" or "Apocalypse" may be more an overview or description of the book's contents than a title. The features of the genre of apocalyptic are succinctly represented in the beginning verses of the book:

> The revelation of Jesus Christ, which God gave him to show his servants what must soon take place; he made it known by sending his angel to his servant John, who testified to the word of God and to the testimony of Jesus Christ, even to all that he saw. (Rev 1:1–2, NRSV)

An apocalypse as a piece of literature records a revelation from God ("the revelation of Jesus Christ, which God gave") concerning the future ("what must soon take place"). It typically comes through a heavenly guide and interpreter ("he has made it known by sending his angel") to an earthly recipient ("to his servant John"). Further reading of the book reveals other typical features of the genre. The human recipient enters a visionary state ("in the spirit," 1:10) in which he is transported to heaven to view unusual images and events that determine what will take place on earth.

The content of the book of Revelation may be outlined as follows:

Preface in the third person (1:1–3)

Letter to the seven churches (1:4–22:21)

Greeting of letter (1:4–6)

Prophetic sayings (1:7–8)

Body of letter (1:9–22:5)

Christ's appearance to John (1:9–3:22)

Description of heavenly visions (4:1–22:5)

Vision of heavenly court (4:1–5:14)

  Other visions (6:1–22:5)
  Seven seals (6:1–8:2)
  Seven trumpets (8:3–11:19)
  Seven unnumbered visions (12:1–15:4)
  Seven bowls (15:5–16:20)
  Vision of Babylon (17:1–19:10)
  Seven unnumbered visions (19:11–21:8)
  Vision of new Jerusalem (21:9–22:5)
  Epilogue of warnings and exhortations (22:6–20)
  Postscript of letter (22:21)

There are a number of interesting characteristics in Revelation. First of all, it is a complex work, consisting of an apocalypse inside of a letter. [39] The letter provides a framework for the apocalypse and is, therefore, subordinate to it. In that sense, the letter is comparable to the first six chapters of Daniel.

The main organizing principle of the book is the number seven. There are seven churches with seven angels, seven seals, seven trumpets, seven bowls, and two sets of seven unnumbered visions. Scholars have discerned that each of the five visions of seven (seals, trumpets, bowls, and two unnumbered visions) follows a common pattern.[40] Each consists of a description of or allusion to persecution, a statement of judgment or punishment, and a declaration of victory. The book is not a sequential review of human history—not a foretelling of the future from John's time until the end of the world—but it is a series of visions with the same basic message about more or less the same thing or the same circumstances. The occurrence of different visions dealing with the same basic situation is identical to what we found in the book of Daniel.

Unlike Daniel, with its images of the four-part statue and the four beasts representing four kingdoms, the book of Revelation does not contain a historical summary. Its focus is on the historical and social situation of the seven churches of Asia Minor to whom it is addressed (1:4). The very fact that the book is addressed to such a specific setting suggests that it was never meant to predict all of history until the end of time. Its concern is with specific churches at a specific moment in time. Consideration of the address in 1:4 and then the specific messages to the angels of the seven churches (2:1–3:22) reveals other important information about the historical and social setting of the book.

To start, the identity of the author, John ("John to the seven churches that are in Asia" [1:4a]), is uncertain. There is no strong reason, either in Christian tradition or in the book's writing style, to identify him with the apostle John or the author of the Gospel of John.[41] At the same time, there is no good reason to regard this John as a pseudonym. As noted, the book does not present an overview of history leading up to the author's time and thus no need for the author to adopt the name of a revered figure from the distant past as a pseudonym. This means that the author was most likely named John and was a Christian living in exile on the island of Patmos because of his faith (1:9) around 95 CE.[42] The extensive use of images from the Hebrew Bible in the book indicates that he was Jewish in ethnicity and religious background. Unfortunately, as is the case for most of the authors of the books in the New Testament, we know very little else about him.

John wrote his apocalypse for the churches in Asia Minor (modern Western Turkey)—Ephesus, Smyrna, Pergamum, Thyatira, Sardis, Philadelphia, and Laodicea. The occasion for the apocalypse was the "tribulation" that John shared with the seven churches and his desire to encourage them to "patient endurance" in the midst of that tribulation (1:9, NRSV). This does not mean, however, that all of the churches to whom John wrote were suffering persecution. The church at Laodicea, for example, is described as being wealthy and complacent.

Overt persecution appears to be mentioned only at Pergamum, where an individual named Antipas was killed. Elsewhere, the opposition comes in other forms. The messages to Smyrna and Philadelphia refer to "the synagogue of Satan," indicating tensions with non-Christian Jews. The references to the Nicolaitans, the teaching of Balaam, and the prophet named "Jezebel" suggest conflicts with other Christian groups that John considered heretical. At least part of the issue with such groups was the extent to which Christians could accommodate themselves to the surrounding culture with regard to such practices as eating food sacrificed to idols (2:14, 20). There were also tensions felt with the worship of Roman gods, including the emperor, which was an integral part of the everyday life and culture of Asia Minor and indeed all of the Roman empire.

The crisis out of which the book of Revelation arose, then, was cultural in nature. The hatred of Rome expressed in the book emerges from a series of experiences, including Rome's destruction of Jerusalem in 70 CE, past persecution of Christians by the emperor Nero, and Rome's promotion, sometimes by force, of emperor worship. The conflict behind the book was ideological—that of exclusive monotheism of Christianity versus the power of Rome with its deified emperor on top. "The crisis addressed in Revelation is primarily an ideological conflict, arising from the author's utter rejection of the claims of the Roman Empire to power and authority."[43] Revelation's main purpose was "to discourage its audience from accepting the ideology of the provincial elite, which involved a pyramid of power and patronage with the emperor at the pinnacle, and from participating in any form of the imperial cult, which was the religious aspect of that system."[44]

As with Daniel, the book of Revelation was written to address a specific historical and social setting, and it is impossible to understand the book's message without being aware of that setting. To be sure, questions and uncertainties about the meaning of certain details in Revelation remain, but these generally arise because our information about the historical and social circumstances of the book is incomplete. The following analyses of specific texts in Revelation show the importance of understanding the book's setting for its interpretation along with the book's view of the end of the world and how it relates to its historical and social setting.

Revelation 13

Chapter 13 contains two visions (13:1–10 and 13:11–18), two in a series of seven visions reported in chapters 12 through 15. They typically begin with the statement, "Then I saw/looked." The visions are sequential and build upon one another. (The first vision in our chapter is the second vision in this sequence of seven, and it mentions the dragon, which is a main character in its predecessor.)

The Vision in 13:1–10

This vision begins with the description of a beast rising from the sea. The beast has seven heads with blasphemous names written on them. The heads also have ten horns bearing ten crowns. The beast is composite and contains features resembling those of a leopard, bear, and lion. (The imagery is adapted from Daniel 7 and by now is familiar to us: The beast(s) arise from the sea and take the forms of animals—a lion, a bear, and a leopard. The main difference is that there are not four beasts as in Daniel but only one.) The beast in Revelation is a composite of the imagery of the first three beasts from Daniel and may be intended as a representation of the fourth beast. Revelation thus reinterprets Daniel or at least reuses its imagery. Again, the source of that imagery was mythology. The beast and the dragon are images used for the sea god, Yamm, in Canaanite mythology, and they symbolize the forces of chaos opposed to the order of creation.

While the fourth beast in Daniel 7 represents Greece, the beast in Revelation 13 is Rome. The seven heads and ten horns are not interpreted at this point in the text, but in a later vision of another beast, the seven horns are the seven hills upon which the city of Rome was built as well as seven kings, and the ten horns are also ten kings which have yet to rule (17:9–10). The numbers "seven" and "ten" are typically symbols of completeness and probably stand for the Roman emperors as a whole. They may also be intended to draw a parallel with the dragon, which also has seven heads and ten horns with ten crowns (12:3).[45] The image is influenced by the fourth beast of Daniel 7, which also had ten horns. The blasphemous names are titles taken by various emperors implying or claiming divinity as part of the cult of emperor worship that was especially popular in Asia Minor.

The statement that the dragon gives its power and throne to the beast (13:2) illustrates the dualistic nature of apocalyptic literature and of Revelation in particular. In this view of the world there are two domains—good and evil—at war for the hearts and souls of human beings. Every person and every institution belongs to one or the other of these domains. The dragon is Satan. The Roman empire is seen as his instrument. In practical terms, this means that honoring the emperor was regarded by John as betraying God and the Christian faith. (The mention of the dragon's throne recalls the reference to Satan's throne being in Pergamum in Rev 2:12–13, and probably alludes to the Roman provincial seat with its imperial temple, which were located in that city.)

One of the beast's heads had received a mortal wound from which it had healed (13:3). This may be a reference to the emperor Nero, who died by suicide in 68 CE. There was a rumor in circulation at that time that Nero was still alive and even a legend arose that he would revive and return to power. The author

here makes use of these legends and rumors to present Nero as the evil counterpart to Christ, the Antichrist who is raised from the dead to renew his wicked
ways and his persecution of Christians. The duration of the Antichrist's rule is
forty-two months (13:5) or three and one-half years, in agreement with Daniel
7:25. As in Daniel, the point is that the period of oppression (described in Rev
13:6–10) will be temporary and relatively short.

Following this period, the faithful, whose names are written in the book of
life (13:8) will triumph. This vision, like the one in Daniel 7, "is a call for the
endurance and faith of the saints" (13:10, NRSV). These "saints" are the Christians in the churches in Asia Minor who were suffering under practices and conditions of the Roman government. Rome's persecution of Christians was sporadic
rather than systematic. But the ubiquitous imperial cult was in principle opposed to Christianity, and it generated social and cultural pressure that these
early Christians felt to be consistently oppressive. Encouragement toward "endurance and faith" is, indeed, reason for the composition of this book and much
other apocalyptic literature.

The Vision in 13:11–18

The next vision in the series begins with another beast, this one arising from the
earth. The ultimate source of this image is again mythology, according to which
a monster from the earth, called "Behemoth," allies itself with the sea monster
("Leviathan") in opposition to the Creator. The two monsters are mentioned by
name in other parts of the Bible (see Job 40–41). The land monster in Revelation
has the appearance of a lamb but speaks like a lion. It exercises all the authority
of the first beast and enforces worship of the first beast. It deceives with miracu-
lous signs and brings the image of the beast to life. It even orders the execution
of those who refuse to worship the beast.

The identification of this second beast is difficult. Many scholars believe that
it is meant to represent the priesthood of the imperial Roman cult. As priests,
these individuals may appear to be as harmless as lambs, but they are really agents
of the dragon, Satan, since they are, after all, representatives of the Roman empire. They perform magic, including the animation of cult statues, in part by
"interpreting" the oracles delivered through them. In any case, it is fairly apparent that this second beast is some local authority, individual, or group associated
with emperor worship.

The "mark of the beast" (13:14) is in direct contrast to the "seal of God" (7:3)
worn by the faithful. This again is dualistic, good vs. evil—everyone bears either
the mark or the seal. There is disagreement about how to interpret the mark. It
may simply be metaphorical; just as faithful Christians did not actually have a

secret seal on their foreheads, so those who worshipped the emperor did not really have marks on their right hands and foreheads. The idea of marking the head and right hand is unusual and may draw on the Jewish practice of wearing *tephillin* or "phylacteries." These are small boxes with scripture passages inside of them that are worn on the forehead and, usually, the left arm.

The mark of the beast is associated with commerce, so that those who do not have it cannot buy or sell (13:17). Because of this particular statement, some scholars have attempted to find a more concrete sense behind the mark.[46] One prominent suggestion is that the mark refers to use of Roman coins, which bore the images, names, and titles (often claiming divinity) of the emperors. Certain religious groups such as the Jewish Zealots (ca. 66–70 CE) refused to own or use such coins. Given the strong animosity toward all aspects of the imperial cult in the book of Revelation, this may have been John's stance as well and as such would obviously inhibit buying or selling anything in Asia Minor.

The mark of the beast is further identified as the number of its name. That number is 666 or, as some manuscripts have it, 616. This is an example of the practice of assigning numbers to the letters of the alphabet: A = 1, B = 2, etc. Of course, the alphabet in question was not English but Greek, Hebrew, Latin, or Aramaic. Indeed, in Hebrew the letters of the alphabet were actually used as numbers; there was not a set of distinct number signs. The first nine letters would represent 1–9, the next nine 10–90, and the remaining letters multiples of 100.

Admittedly, there are many possibilities for the identification of this figure, since many names and words can be made to have a numeric value of 666. This is one reason why such a large number of individuals and institutions have been identified over the centuries as the beast or Antichrist. The best explanation is probably that the number refers to Nero. His name and title in Hebrew was קסר (נרו(ן), "Nero" or "Neron" Caesar. The longer form of the name has the numeric value 666, and the shorter form has the value 616, thus satisfying both readings.[47] Nero was dead at the time of the writing of Revelation, but for John and his audience Nero represented all Roman emperors and all that was evil about them, especially the imperial cult. Since seven was the number representing completeness, 666 carried additional sense of inherent imperfection. The emperors as a whole were fatally flawed and unworthy to be objects of worship. Indeed, worship of them was an affront to God and in opposition to the life to which the faithful were summoned.

The two visions in Revelation 13 illustrate the nature of apocalyptic literature and the importance of recognizing the social and historical context for understanding it. The images in the visions and their overall point become clear only when one learns about the situation in Asia Minor under Roman rule in which

these visions were written and to which they were addressed. The question remains how Revelation's setting relates to its message about the end of the world,
and for that we turn to the book's final visions.

The Final Visions (17:1–22:5)

We have discussed the manner in which the main section of the book concludes
with visions concerning two cities, Babylon and Jerusalem, with a set of seven
unnumbered visions between them. The basic message of these visions is the
same as that presented earlier in the book—the final triumph of God and the
forces of good over Satan and the forces of evil, which include Rome. That message probably emerges most clearly and with its strongest eschatological emphasis in these final visions.

The city of Babylon is described as "the great whore" (17:1) and envisioned as
a richly clothed woman mounted on a beast with seven heads and ten horns
(17:4). The depiction of cities as women is common in the Hebrew prophets
(e.g., Ezek 16; 23). The identification of the city as a whore, especially a wealthy
one, implies prosperity derived from commerce. "Babylon" is a designation also
taken from the Hebrew Bible and the memory of Babylon as the empire that
destroyed Jerusalem (587 BCE) and took its residents captive. The identification
of the beast's seven heads as seven mountains (17:9) makes it clear that Babylon
is actually Rome, which was indeed built upon seven hills. Rome is denounced
for its persecution of the faithful, and its projected downfall is celebrated: "Fallen,
fallen is Babylon the great!" (18:2).

Following the destruction of Rome comes a series of visions of the final triumph of the heavenly forces of good over evil (19:11–21:8). The two beasts from
chapter 13 (the second one is now called the "false prophet") are thrown into the
lake of fire. Satan is confined for a thousand years and then ultimately defeated
and also thrown into the lake of fire. Christian martyrs reign with Christ during
the period of Satan's confinement. Then with his final defeat comes the general
resurrection and the last judgment. There is a "new heaven and new earth"—
cosmic transformation—for those judged righteous. They are rewarded with a
home with God in the "new Jerusalem" where there is no more death, sorrow,
suffering, or uncleanness. The final vision of the book (21:9–22:5) is a metaphorical description of this city as bejeweled, spacious, splendorous, and full of light.

The mention of a thousand-year reign of Christ while Satan is bound has
given rise to enormous controversy in Christianity. The controversy has produced heated divisions over whether Christ's second coming will take place before (premillennial) or after (postmillennial) the thousand years.[48] The widespread
and increasingly popular notion of a "rapture" or sudden taking up to heaven of

faithful Christians and a period of "great tribulation" preceding the millennium is part of a premillennial interpretation of this text. Once more, however, these ideas reflect a fundamental misunderstanding of Revelation and the genre of apocalyptic. The thousand-year period plays a relatively insignificant role in Revelation as a whole and hardly deserves all the attention it has received. It is not mentioned elsewhere in the book and thus has been blown out of proportion. The idea of a thousand-year period of messianic rule was a relatively common element of Jewish expectation and is attested in other examples of both Jewish and Christian apocalyptic.[49]

What is more interesting is the prophetic ideology behind John's use of this idea. Scholars have noticed that Revelation follows a pattern found in Ezekiel 36–48. The restoration of Israel under its Davidic king is followed by the ultimate battle and then by the vision of the new, idealized temple in a new Jerusalem. Similarly, Revelation describes the thousand-year reign of Christ before the final defeat of Satan and then the new heaven and new earth.

The millennium in Revelation represents a mixing of prophetic eschatology, like that found in Ezekiel, with apocalyptic eschatology. As we saw in our treatment of Hebrew prophecy, the prophets deal with problems in their own time and culture. They issue threats and warnings in the belief that their fellow Israelites are capable of change. Even if they do not improve their behavior, punishment from God, usually in the form of an invading army, will lead to repentance. For the prophets, improvement can come within the natural process of human history. The ideal envisioned, therefore, is the reign of another king like David who will rule in righteousness and execute justice and fairness. This ideal king might be called "messiah" purely in the sense of a royal title meaning "anointed."

In apocalyptic ideology, on the other hand, the crisis situation is too dire to be resolved within the course of normal history. Only a direct intervention by God can set things right. Indeed, the earthly persecutors are seen as agents of the forces of evil in the heavenly realm. The new ruler, the "one like the son of man" in Daniel, is not a human king but an otherworldly being. In Jewish apocalyptic he is an angel; in Christian apocalyptic he is Christ. "Christ" is the Greek translation of the Hebrew word "messiah" and in the context of Christian apocalyptic, "Christ" or "Messiah" is more than simply a royal title—it takes on the connotation of a spiritual savior.

Revelation combines these two ideologies by describing first a thousand-year period in which the Messiah will reign on earth followed by the intervention of God and the final defeat of Satan and the forces of evil. The millennium of messianic rule corresponds to the prophetic hope for an ideal age on earth ruled by a righteous Davidic king. Since only God can bring about the ultimate defeat of evil on a cosmic scale, this will follow the millennium. The vision of the final defeat of evil and the new heaven and earth furthers the hope in the resurrection and judgment expressed in Daniel. For it is only in the triumph of good in the afterlife that those who gave their lives for their faith have ultimate vindication.

Conclusion

While their eschatologies differ, apocalyptic literature and Hebrew prophecy have in common that they are both intimately connected with the historical and social contexts in which they were produced. Like prophecy, apocalyptic was not intended to predict the distant future. In the book of Revelation there are no specifics given about exactly when Rome's destruction will occur, nor does Revelation describe the historical circumstances immediately preceding the end of world. Indeed, the implication is that the world would end shortly after and in conjunction with the destruction of Rome, which was perceived imminent in the first century CE. Yet, the Roman empire did not end until the fourth or fifth century CE . . . and the world is still in existence. [50]

This is not a criticism of the book of Revelation. The problem is not with it but with the way in which it has been interpreted. To interpret Revelation as a prediction of the end of the world is to fail to understand the nature of apocalyptic literature.

> For the historically minded critical reader, the book of Revelation is not a cryptic summary of the history of the church or the world. It is not primarily a prediction of the timing of the end of the world. Rather, it is a work of religious poetry, inspired by the prophets of Israel and by the cosmic and political myths of the author's time. [51]

The point of Revelation, therefore, is not to summarize world or church history in cryptic terms, nor is it meant to predict the time and circumstances of the end of the world. Its purpose is to encourage Christians undergoing cultural and religious persecution to remain faithful by assuring them that God is in charge, that right will eventually triumph over evil, and that they will be rewarded for their perseverance.

Chapter Five

ISSUES IN THE CHURCHES
The Letters of the New Testament

The Misconception:
The letters of Paul and other writers in the New Testament provide a kind of rule book for Christian doctrine and practice.

I never receive a letter from you without being in your company forthwith. If the pictures of our absent friends are pleasing to us, though they only refresh the memory and lighten our longing by a solace that is unreal and unsubstantial, how much more pleasant is a letter, which brings us real traces, real evidences, of an absent friend! For that which is sweetest when we meet face to face is afforded by the impress of a friend's hand upon his letter—recognition.

—Seneca, *Moral Epistles* 40:1[1]

I am obliged to Alexis for so often adding his salutations, but why does he not do it in a letter of his own, as my Alexis [Tiro] does to you?

—Cicero, Letter to Atticus 5:20.9[2]

So also our beloved brother Paul wrote to you according to the wisdom given him, speaking of this as he does in all his letters. There are some things in them hard to understand, which the ignorant and unstable twist to their own destruction, as they do the other scriptures.

—2 Peter 3:15b–16[3]

As a capstone experience for its majors, the Department of Religious Studies at the college where I teach requires seniors to take a seminar in which they write a research paper on a topic of special interest or relevance to them. One particular year a student chose to write about the social and religious complexities involved in the adoption of Christianity into an Asian culture. She drew on her own experiences as a second-generation Christian in a traditionally Buddhist family. Her parents had been converted to Christianity in Korea and had immigrated to the United States, where her father had attended seminary and become a Baptist minister. Among the experiences from her upbringing that she related was her parents' prohibition against her dating anyone of other than Korean descent.

What surprised me was that the student's parents made this rule on religious, specifically Christian, grounds. They quoted from the Bible: "Do not be mismatched" (2 Cor 6:14), interpreting this verse as referring to race as a consideration in marriage. In fact, the context of the verse indicates that its author, Paul, was referring to business dealings. Moreover, the full quotation is "Do not be mismatched [literally, "misyoked"] with unbelievers," showing that Paul's concern had to do with the collaboration of Christians with non-Christians rather than with racial or ethnic differences.

The story illustrates the tendency of modern readers to take biblical passages out of context in order to support preconceived ideas, that is, views that they have already formed for other reasons. This young woman's parents were not the first or the only ones to interpret the Bible or the passage in 2 Corinthians racially.

This story also exhibits the tendency of Christians to attempt to read the letters in the New Testament, especially those of Paul, as a collection of rules for Christian living and definitions of Christian beliefs. My purpose here is to demonstrate the situational nature of the letters in the New Testament and their intended function of addressing specific issues and problems in the early church. Once their true nature as dealing with specific situations is perceived, the importance of understanding their historical and social context becomes clear. Armed with that understanding, one may properly approach the matter of appropriating their message for a modern setting.

Early Christian Letters

Ancient Letters

A letter is basically a substitute for oral communication. This was recognized by the first-century CE philosopher Seneca in the quotation at the beginning of this chapter. As Seneca's quote suggests, a letter is occasioned when oral communication is impossible, as when two people are separated by distance, or undesirable, as when a durable record of the communication is needed. The absence of telecommunications in antiquity made letters even more important than they are today.

Initially, letters were carried by messengers. The Greek word *epistolē*, a synonym for "letter," originally referred to oral communication sent by messengers (Herodotus, *Histories* 4.10.1). Messengers sometimes supplemented what was written in a letter with oral greetings or additional information. Before the establishment of postal service, the availability of a traveler who might serve as a messenger and letter bearer was often the occasion for the writing of a letter. As with so many other conveniences that we take for granted today, it was the Romans—specifically the emperor Augustus (27 BCE–14 CE)—who established the first postal system.[4] Postal systems continue to be an important part of our society, despite the invention of telecommunication, indicating the enduring significance and usefulness of letters.

In addition to the messenger, the sender of a letter in the ancient world would often use a scribe or professional letter writer. This was partly because many people, especially the commoners, were illiterate. In addition, in Greco-Roman culture letter writing was a skill and an art; it called for a degree of formality and expertise, which most people did not share and in which certain individuals were specially trained.

The genre of letters functioned in the ancient world much as it does today. Ancient letters, like modern ones, were written for a variety of reasons. Just as a modern personal letter differs in form from a business letter, so the specific forms of ancient letters varied according to their function. All letters can be divided into three general subgenres: private or documentary, official, and literary.[5]

Private or *documentary* letters served primarily as a way for friends and family members to maintain contact with one another. They were also a means of dealing with problems at home, making requests, giving instructions or advice, dealing with personal business concerns, and introducing or recommending a third party. Such letters were usually brief and dealt with specific matters. They were typically discarded soon after being read, although some authors kept copies of their letters for revision and preservation.

Official letters were typically those written from one government official to a constituted body or to (an)other official(s). They include imperial decrees and other forms of diplomatic correspondence. Official letters were often posted for purposes of public information and influence.

Literary letters are those intended primarily for a literary, philosophical, or educational purpose. Essays and treatises were sometimes couched in letter form. Letters of this kind were typically longer than private or official letters and were also often pseudepigraphic, that is, written under someone else's name, usually a person of prominence. Fictional letters could be embedded within a narrative. Some letters were even written to serve as models of letter writing or as the ideal of some letter form for educational purposes.

The typical Greco-Roman letter consisted of three parts. The *opening* or *pre-script* usually contained three parts as well. It identified the sender and the recipient of the letter and then offered a salutation, frequently the single word, "Greeting" (*charein* in Greek). The opening could be expanded in a variety of ways. One common expansion was the inclusion of a wish or prayer for the recipient's health or a statement that the sender prayed for or was thankful for the recipient.

The *main body* of the letter dealt with its principal agenda, the reason for writing it. It was not unusual for a sender to discuss travel plans near the end of the main body, particularly if those plans involved a visit to the recipient.

The *conclusion* might include a wish for the recipient's health or report of prayer, if these were not in the opening. It might also convey greetings to others not mentioned in the letter's main body. If the letter's sender employed someone else to do the actual writing of the letter, the sender might use the conclusion to add greetings in his or her own hand. Alternatively, the letter writer could identify himself and add a greeting if he were acquainted with the recipient. Letters then typically closed with the word "Farewell" (*erroso*).

Since letters were, in effect, substitutes for personal conversation, it is not surprising that their composition, especially in the Greco-Roman world, was strongly influenced by the conventions of rhetoric—the art of persuasion.[6] The study of rhetoric was a central component of education in that world. Anyone who was well-enough educated to write a letter, therefore, had likely received some training in rhetoric. As a result, the writing of a letter in the Greco-Roman world was not only an occasion for communication but also an opportunity to display one's skills at literary artistry and persuasion.

In a tradition going back to Aristotle, rhetoric was considered to be of three types. *Judicial* or *forensic* rhetoric was associated with the courts. It focused on the past and sought to convince hearers to adopt a particular understanding of what had happened in a given instance or event. Its tools were accusation and defense. *Epideictic* or *display* rhetoric dealt primarily with public gatherings in the present. It used praise or blame to induce hearers to honor or disdain a contemporary. *Deliberative* rhetoric was centered in politics and oriented toward the future. Its concern was to persuade hearers to adopt a particular course of action or direction.

Aristotle, followed by others, also delineated three components to deliberative rhetoric, which are regularly found in New Testament letters, especially those of Paul: the exordium, which set the mood of the hearers through praise; the proof (*probatio*), which appealed to the hearers' honor and self interest; and the peroration, which reviewed and expanded the appeal.

Other forms of oratory that helped to shape the New Testament letters were diatribes and sermons. The former was associated especially with an educational setting and often involved the Socratic method of question and answer with a hypothetical discussant or rival. The latter arose in both synagogues and churches and featured the explication of texts from the Hebrew Bible.[7]

The New Testament Letters

Letters were the most popular genre of writing in early Christianity. Letters are also the most common genre of literature in the New Testament. All of the New Testament books outside of the Gospels, Acts, and Revelation are commonly called letters. The full list, in their order in the New Testament, is:

Romans	Titus
1 Corinthians	Philemon
2 Corinthians	Hebrews
Galatians	James
Ephesians	1 Peter
Philippians	2 Peter
Colossians	1 John
1 Thessalonians	2 John
2 Thessalonians	3 John
1 Timothy	Jude
2 Timothy	

These letters can be classified in different ways. One way is according to their purported authors. The first thirteen of them (Romans through Philemon) are attributed by the books themselves to Paul and are known by the names of their addressees. Among these are the earliest books of the New Testament, with 1 Thessalonians, dated about 50 CE/AD usually considered the first. Hebrews has also been attributed to Paul but not by the book itself. The other books are known by the names of the authors named within them.

A second way of classifying these books is by their addressees. In this system, there are three groups. The first group consists of letters addressed to specific churches: Romans, 1 and 2 Corinthians, Galatians, Ephesians, Philippians, Colossians, 1 and 2 Thessalonians. Some of these are circular letters, designed to be circulated among several churches. Galatians, for example was written to the churches in the cities of the province of Galatia, rather than to a single city. The letter to the Ephesians may also have been circular.[8] Writing circular letters was borrowed from the Jewish practice of sending letters to synagogues in the Diaspora from the Jerusalem authorities.

The second group is letters addressed to individuals: 1 and 2 Timothy, Titus, Philemon, and 2 and 3 John. 1 and 2 Timothy and Titus are known as the Pastoral letters, because they concern the specific issues related to shepherding or pastoring a church.

The last group includes letters written to Christians at large: Hebrews, James, 1 and 2 Peter, and Jude. This group is often called the Catholic letters, using "catholic" in the sense of "universal." Among these, 1 Peter, and James are addressed to churches in the Diaspora, the term originally used for Jews scattered outside of Palestine. 1 Peter 1:1 also mentions the specific regions of Galatia, Cappadocia, Asia, and Bithynia. These regions covered such a large geographic area that it is unlikely that the letter was intended as a real circular letter.

Not all of these books are real letters. First John, for instance, neither begins nor ends as a letter; it has no opening address or prescript and no concluding wish or farewell. Other books are presented in the form of a letter but are really a different kind of document. Indeed, one of the reasons for the letter form being so popular in early Christianity was its flexibility. Almost any composition could be turned into a letter by framing it with a simple prescript and a concluding farewell. So, the book of Hebrews concludes like a letter but has no beginning prescript, and its contents appear to be a homily (sermon) or a tractate, i.e., an essay or pamphlet on a particular topic. Similarly, James, 2 Peter, and Jude all begin as letters but do not conclude as such; James has no real conclusion; 2 Peter and Jude end with doxologies. They are also addressed to broad audiences rather than to specific communities. All four of these books are presented in the dress of open letters to early Christians but are really documents of a different nature. James and Jude are tractates. 2 Peter appears to be a "testament," a work offering the last advice and warning before its author's death. Even Revelation, as we have seen, frames its message with the prescript and conclusion of a letter, though its genre is that of apocalyptic literature.

The New Testament has other examples of the literary use of letters. Two letters are embedded in the narrative of the book of Acts (15:23–29; 23:26–30), and the book of Revelation incorporates the seven letters to the churches of Asia Minor. The letters to the seven churches take the form of the official correspondence of a royal edict.

In 1895, a German scholar named Adolf Deissmann pioneered the study of letters in the New Testament by comparing them to ancient Greek papyri discovered in Egypt.[9] On the basis of his study, Deissmann drew a distinction between letters and epistles. A letter, he claimed, amounted to half of a private conversation. Letters, therefore, were informal, spontaneous, and personal with no concern for their literary form or writing style. Epistles, on the other hand, were public, intended for reading by a broad audience. An epistle was formal and mechanical, reflecting a conscious concern for literary artistry. Deissmann considered all of Paul's authentic letters and 2 and 3 John to be true letters, but he classified the Pastoral and Catholic letters as epistles.

Deissmann's distinction between letters and epistles was criticized and rejected almost immediately. There was no basis for such a distinction on the grounds of formality or artistry, since all of the New Testament letters use rhetoric and mix in other genres, such as hymns, prayers, or homilies. Deissmann's distinction was also not supported by considerations of audience. Paul, for instance, wrote to specific people for specific reasons—a letter; but he also intended his writings to be read publicly in the churches like an epistle.

Unfortunately, the attention given to Deissmann's differentiation between letters and epistles has sometimes obscured his main point, which was that the books of the New Testament did not appear out of nowhere, unconnected with human time and space, but that they were closely tied to the culture and issues of their day.

> The point of the distinction [between letters and epistles] as far as Deissmann was concerned, was to force those among his contemporaries, who thought of the New Testament writings as something apart and therefore timeless and rootless, to recognize that what Paul wrote were letters, a medium of genuine communication and part of real life in the mid-first century AD.[10]

This is an extremely important observation and one that, on the surface, is widely accepted today. Everyone recognizes, for instance, that Paul wrote to specific churches about their issues and problems. Yet, it is also the case that Deissmann's observation is better accepted in theory than it is in practice.

Like the student whose story I related at the beginning of this chapter, there has always been a tendency in the church to apply the instructions of the New Testament letters directly without regard to their specific contexts and settings. This tendency was evident already in the second century CE. "The second-century church preferred to understand apostolic letters in terms of their universal applicability rather than in terms of the particular situations in which they originated."[11] Thus, the second-century Latin church father Tertullian (ca. 160–230 CE), wrote that when the apostle [Paul] wrote to one church he wrote to all.[12] This desire to apply Paul's teachings more broadly may even have been part of the reason for the composition of some of the letters in the New Testament itself.[13] The author of 2 Peter, for instance, at the end of his letter, which is addressed to Christians at large, refers to the writings of "our beloved brother Paul."

This is not to suggest that the teachings in Paul's letters and the others in the New Testament have no application for the church in general. The question is how to apply them properly, and this can be done only if the historical, cultural, and literary contexts of the letters are taken fully into account. Granted, the general letters may not address a specific local community or circumstance, or their original audience may be unknown. But even they were written within a historical and cultural context in the first or second century CE, which was also the context of the audience for which they were intended. In the remainder of this chapter, we focus on Paul, the most prolific and important of the New Testament letter writers.

The Letters of Paul

Of the thirteen letters ascribed to Paul in the New Testament, scholars are agreed that seven were actually written by him: Romans, 1 and 2 Corinthians, Galatians, Philippians, 1 Thessalonians, and Philemon.[14] The others have all been suspected of being pseudonymous, mainly on the basis of style and vocabulary, but also sometimes because of content; and because this is a widely held viewpoint, we focus here on the seven letters listed for our synthesis of Paul's letter writing.

The seven letters of Paul are real letters, though most are substantially longer than ordinary private letters. With the possible exception of Romans they are all circumstantial. That is, they address concrete situations in the churches that were their recipients.

> In opposition to Cicero, who wrote regularly to his friend Atticus just for the sheer pleasure of communication, Paul never put pen to paper except when it was absolutely imperative. A letter for him always had a definite goal; he designed it to accomplish something.[15]

Thus Paul was not writing for literary purposes or to provide a model of the Christian letter. More important for our purposes, Paul was not writing to lay out a systematic explanation of Christian theology. He never instructed his readers to preserve his letters for posterity. Indeed, Paul apparently expected Christ to return during his lifetime (1 Thess 4:17), so he did not envision the issues that future generations of Christians would face.

Paul followed the conventions of letter writing, borrowing from both Greco-Roman and Jewish practice. There are good indications that he employed a secretary or professional letter writer. The book of Romans contains a greeting added by the secretary, Tertius: "I Tertius, the writer of this letter greet you in the Lord" (Rom 16:22). Paul's greetings in his own handwriting at the end of other letters suggest that the use of a secretary was his standard practice:

I, Paul, write this greeting with my own hand. (1 Cor 16:21)

See what large letters I make when I am writing in my own hand. (Gal 6:11)

I, Paul, am writing this with my own hand. (Philem 19)

Structure

Prescript

Paul's letters exhibit the three-part structure typical of Greco-Roman letters: an opening or prescript, the body of the letter, and a conclusion. In general, Paul seems to have followed the basic model of an official letter (as opposed to the personal or literary letter), and the prescripts are the best indicator of this.[16] Prescripts identified the sender and the recipients of a letter, accompanied with a greeting.

"Paul an apostle . . ."

Paul identifies himself by title, usually "apostle" or "servant of Christ," in all of his genuine letters except 1 Thessalonians, his earliest. The use of such titles was common in official Roman letters. The title is especially expansive in Romans, where he was not personally acquainted with the church and was introducing himself and his preaching, and in Galatians, where he was defending his authority. Paul used his titles to assert his authority as Christ's representative to the bodies of Christians in the churches to which he wrote.

"and Timothy our brother . . ."

In addition to himself, Paul frequently names companions, especially Timothy, as cosenders of all of his letters. They served as Paul's support base, similar to a court or governing body that stood behind an official's letter. They were also witnesses to Paul's messages. Some of those with Paul also served as letter carriers and dialogue partners. Though he does not mention them as cosenders, Paul's letters sometimes name the individuals who carried the letters. They were likely present at the reading of those letters and could elaborate on or interpret them for the addressees. Thus Paul mentions Titus, who has reported to him the Corinthians' reaction to his previous letter (2 Cor 7:6–12). He also names Epaphroditus as a messenger whom he entrusts with bringing joy to the Philippians (Phil 2:25–30).

"to the church in . . ."

The seven so-called genuine letters of Paul were all addressed to communities rather than individuals. The form of the official letter in which a government official addressed a group was well-suited to Paul's purposes, but Paul also incorporated elements of personal correspondence in this feature because he typically addressed his readers affectionately as "brothers."

"Grace to you and peace . . ."

Paul's greeting always consists of the words "grace" and "peace." Grace (*charis*) puns on and replaces the common Greco-Roman word "greeting" (*charein*); "peace" was a salutation common in Hebrew and Aramaic. Paul may have combined the two greetings consciously as a way representing the availability of the gospel to Jews as well as Gentiles or his ministry to both.

"I give thanks to my God always . . ."

The prescripts of Paul's letters are expanded by his expressions of thanksgiving for his readers. These thanksgivings preview the main themes of the letters. In 1 Thessalonians, for example, the thanksgiving highlights that church's faith, love, and hope (1 Thess 1:2–8, NRSV):

> We always give thanks to God for all of you and mention you in our prayers constantly remembering before our God and Father your work of faith and labor of love and steadfastness of hope in our Lord Jesus Christ. For we know, brothers and sisters, beloved by God, that he has chosen you, . . . And you became imitators of us and of the Lord, for in spite of persecution you received the word with joy inspired by the Holy Spirit, so that you became an example to all the believers in Macedonia and Achaia. For the word of the Lord has sounded forth from you not only in Macedonia and Achaia, but in every place your faith in God has become known, so that we have no need to speak about it.

The thanksgiving in this instance is especially long because of Paul's good relationship with the Thessalonians. In Galatians, by contrast, where Paul's message is largely one of reproof, he skips over the thanksgiving and instead launches into an expression of annoyed disappointment at the instability of their faith.

Body

In the bodies of his letters Paul dealt with the specific matters that had occasioned his writing in the first place. This is sometimes called the epistolary occasion or situation, and Paul often stated precisely what the epistolary situation or setting was in the course of his letter.

The bodies of official letters in the Greco-Roman world typically had two parts: background information and the message.[17] The background information often included an explanation of the basis for the decision leading to the letter's message. Similarly, the message sometimes incorporated a promise or threat.

Paul's letters also generally reflect this structure in their bodies. At the same time, they display a good deal of flexibility in the elements they incorporate and in their order.

Paul's letters have many of the same functions and elements of other Greco-Roman letters: autobiographical information, requests, responses to questions, and announcements of travel plans, to name a few. In addition, these letters incorporate a mix of other genres, including blessings ("Blessed be the God and Father of our Lord Jesus Christ, the Father of mercies and the God of all consolation" [2 Cor 1:3]); doxologies ("For from him and through him and to him are all things. To him be the glory forever. Amen" [Rom 11:36]); hymns ("Though he was in the form of God, did not regard equality with God as something to be exploited, but emptied himself, taking the form of a slave, being found in human likeness. And being found in human form, he humbled himself and became obedient to the point of death—even death on a cross. Therefore God also highly exalted him and gave him a name that is above every name, so that at the name of Jesus every knee should bend, in heaven and on earth and under the earth, and every tongue should confess that Jesus Christ is Lord, to the glory of God the Father" [Phil 2:6–11]); and confessions ("Jesus is Lord" [1 Cor 12:3]).

Above all, the letters record elements of Paul's teaching and preaching (or "paranesis"). They make use of different kinds of rhetoric—especially deliberative and forensic. They likely echo what he preached or taught in the past and certainly what he would have spoken in person. His frequent expositions on texts from the Hebrew Bible (cf. Rom 1:17–4:25) may reflect sermons delivered in synagogues or churches. Similarly his use of diatribe may draw on discussions he had with rivals. Thus, in 1 Corinthians 15:35, he raises a question, perhaps quoting opponents ("But someone will ask, 'How are the dead raised? With what kind of body do they come?'"), and then he proceeds to answer it.

It is important to keep in mind, however, that Paul did not write in the abstract. He tailored both his message and approach to the situations he faced. He mixed classes of rhetoric because the situations he faced were complex and demanded different approaches. When he sought to persuade, his approach was deliberative; when he defended himself or his ministry, he could switch to forensic rhetoric.

Conclusion

Paul usually leads into the conclusions to his letters by a discussion of his travel plans, followed by an exhortation. The conclusion proper may then include a doxology and personal greetings. It always includes his wish of grace (*charis*) for his readers. As with his prescript, Paul substitutes this word for the typical Greco-Roman "farewell." Otherwise, the conclusions vary and include other items such as a request for prayer:

I appeal to you, brothers and sisters, by our Lord Jesus Christ and by the love of the Spirit, to join me in earnest prayer to God on my behalf. (Rom 15:30)

Beloved, pray for us. (1 Thess 5:25)

a wish for peace:

May the God of peace himself sanctify you entirely; and may your spirit and soul and body be kept sound and blameless at the coming of our Lord Jesus Christ. (1 Thess 5:23)

or the conveyance of greetings from a third party, and/or the command to greet one another with a holy kiss:

Greet one another with a holy kiss. All the churches of Christ greet you. (Rom 16:16)

Timothy, my co-worker, greets you; so do Lucius and Jason and Sosipater, my relatives. I, Tertius, the writer of this letter, greet you in the Lord. Gaius, who is host to me and to the whole church, greets you. Erastus, the city treasurer, and our brother Quartus, greet you. (Rom 16:21–23)

All the brothers and sisters send greetings. Greet one another with a holy kiss. (1 Cor 16:20)

Greet one another with a holy kiss. All the saints greet you. (2 Cor 13:12)

Greet every saint in Christ Jesus. The friends who are with me greet you. All the saints greet you, especially those of the emperor's household. (Phil 4:21–22)

Greet all the brothers and sisters with a holy kiss. (1 Thess 5:26)

Epaphras, my fellow prisoner in Christ Jesus, sends greetings to you, and so do Mark, Aristarchus, Demas, and Luke, my fellow workers. (Philem 23)

Prime Example: Paul's Letter to Philemon

Structure

Of the letters of Paul preserved in the New Testament, it is Philemon, his short-est, that most closely follows the pattern of contemporary letters. Philemon is a letter of intercession and has a number of parallels from the Greco-Roman world.[18] It combines elements of personal and official letters and is addressed to Philemon concerning a matter involving just three persons: Philemon, Paul, and Philemon's slave Onesimus. But two other individuals, Apphia and Archippus, are named as addressees, and more to the point, so is the church meeting in Philemon's house. Paul goes public with the request he makes of Philemon in part, perhaps, as a way of pressuring Philemon to do what he wants. He also subtly asserts his apostolic authority for the same purpose. There is no mention of a secretary, and considering the letter's brevity, it was quite likely penned in its entirety by Paul himself.

The letter divides easily into the three parts typical of Greco-Roman letters:

Opening (1–7)   Body (8–22)   Conclusion (23–25)

The opening names the sender and the recipients with a greeting and then reports Paul's thanksgiving for Philemon. The body could be subdivided into background (8–16) and message (17–22). It articulates Paul's appeal for Onesimus, which is the purpose of the letter, and explains the reasons for it. As is typical of Paul's letters, the body ends with a mention of Paul's travel plans. He then concludes by conveying greetings from his companions and by wishing the recipients grace (*charis*).

Setting and Intent

Understanding the circumstances that led to Paul's letter to Philemon is essential for interpreting it. Yet, we are dependent on the letter itself for discerning that situation, and the letter is vague on several points. This situation has led to different interpretations. The questions raised by the book surround two main issues: (1) How and why did Onesimus come to be with Paul? (2) What does Paul want Philemon to do?

The traditional interpretation of the letter has been that Onesimus was a runaway slave and maybe a thief who somehow came into contact with Paul in prison. Under Paul's tutelage, he became a Christian. Paul, perhaps constrained by Roman law, returned Onesimus to Philemon but wrote to him trying to convince him not to punish Onesimus. He wanted Philemon to accept Onesimus as a fellow Christian and to set him free.

Recent research into Greco-Roman letters has called this interpretation into question and has allowed scholars to formulate a more likely setting for the letter. Contemporary Roman correspondence shows that it was not unusual for slaves who had trouble with their owners to seek the help of a third party as mediator in an effort to salve the owner's anger and improve the slave's working relationship and conditions.[19] Slaves in this situation were not runaways, in the strict sense of the word.

These letters indicate a likely context for Philemon. Onesimus did not run away from Philemon but sought Paul out in prison. Knowing that Philemon was a Christian and that Paul was a respected Christian leader, Onesimus solicited Paul's help as a mediator in some matter in which he had caused, or been accused of causing, a loss. This was probably not a theft, and Paul was not harboring a fugitive or a criminal. Even if Onesimus had been a runaway, Paul would not have been under any legal obligation to return him, since Philemon was probably not a Roman citizen.[20]

It is important to recognize that Greco-Roman slavery was not usually a permanent state but was often a transition to economic stability.[21] Slavery furnished job security and was economically preferable to having to search for work on a daily basis. Some people sold themselves into slavery in order to pay debts. Slaves in the first century were generally freed by the age of thirty and were granted Roman citizenship, a valuable commodity that could be a motive for selling oneself into slavery in the first place. Roman slaves could own property (including their own slaves), have savings, and receive wages or shares of profits. As a result, a high percentage of the population was comprised of slaves or ex-slaves.

Paul writes to Philemon as Onesimus's patron, focusing on the latter's conversion to Christianity. He wants Philemon to forgive Onesimus for any wrongdoing and to accept him as a fellow Christian. Moreover, he wants Philemon not to delay Onesimus's release on account of the trouble they have had but to release him as scheduled so that he can rejoin Paul.

Rhetoric and Argument

Philemon exhibits deliberative rhetoric in action. The thanksgiving (4–7) praises Philemon for his love and faith. All references to Philemon's emotions are positive, without reference to the anger he must have felt or to his need to forgive. There is special emphasis on his attention to the community ("all the saints") and a prayer that the sharing (lit. "fellowship") of Philemon's faith will be effective. Both items are pertinent as theological undergirding of Paul's appeal to Philemon to accept Onesimus as a brother.

In the appeal itself, Paul chooses not to command. He surrenders any authority he may have claimed and portrays himself more as an ambassador, a prisoner, and now Onesimus's patron. He makes the appeal on the basis of love and, less explicitly, appeals to Philemon's honor. He incorporates a word play on Onesimus's name, which means "profitable/useful," saying that he was formerly useless but is now useful as a Christian. He calls Onesimus his own heart, implying that Philemon should treat Onesimus as he would treat Paul.

The vagueness of Paul's appeal is part of his rhetorical strategy. He does not come right out and say that he wants Philemon to free Onesimus and return him. Rather, he says that he did not want to keep Onesimus without Philemon's consent, so that the latter's good deed would be voluntary. Philemon, thus, has an opportunity to display his magnanimous character, something Paul has already done in sending Onesimus back to his owner. Paul adds that Onesimus comes to him "no longer as a slave but more than a slave—a beloved brother," which begs the question, "How can one enslave a brother?"

The peroration (17–22) makes explicit what was hinted at earlier: Philemon should think of Onesimus as Paul and act accordingly. Paul anticipates a potential objection to his appeal by offering to repay any debt Onesimus owes Philemon. The clause in verse 19, "I say nothing about your owing me even your own self," is a rhetorical device for actually emphasizing a point, just as in modern English when someone says, "Not to mention . . . " The outright request is for spiritual refreshment, which can only be accomplished by Philemon's right handling of the matter, which Paul refers to in the following verse as "obedience." The announcement of his upcoming visit lets Philemon know that Paul will check on his compliance.

Other Examples from Paul's Letters

Structure in Galatians

Galatians has the three parts typical of Greco-Roman letters: a prescript or introduction (1:1–5), a body (1:6–6:10), and a conclusion (6:11–18). As usual, the prescript identifies the sender and recipients and greets them. The sender, of course, is Paul, though he also includes "all the brothers who are with me" as cosenders. Paul includes his title, "apostle," and is quick to add that his commission came through Jesus Christ rather than human authority. The title and defensive tone preview one of the major issues of this letter. The recipients are the members of the churches in Galatia, a region in central Anatolia (modern Turkey). Here it is obvious that this letter was meant to circulate. As mentioned previously, Galatians stands out among Paul's writings in that it lacks a section of thanksgiving for the recipients, launching instead into a rebuke (1:6–10), which anticipates the reproving nature of the letter as a whole.

Galatians also lacks any mention of Paul's travel plans. He apparently does not intend to visit Galatia, perhaps because of the tension between himself and the Christians there. The transition to the letter's conclusion is marked by Paul's reference to his own handwriting (6:11). Up to that point, he has been dictating to a secretary. He rehearses with his own pen the essential content of the letter: the irrelevance of circumcision for salvation and the hypocrisy of those who demand it of others. He blesses those who follow him in this matter, implying a curse upon those who do not. There are no personal greetings. The warning or plea that no one should cause him trouble because he bears the "marks of Jesus" on his body (6:17) serves to identify Paul as Christ's true representative, revisiting one of the main points of the letter. Paul's reference to the Galatians as his "brothers" in the context of his final wish of grace to his readers is unique among his letters and suggests that he hopes to repair the relationship he has with them.

Setting and Intent

As with all of Paul's letters, the setting behind Galatians must be inferred from the letter itself. Fortunately, the indications in the letter about the circumstances that occasioned it are generally clear. Paul writes to counter the "Judaizers," who taught that Gentiles had to accept Judaism and keep the law before they could be Christians. The controversy focused on the practice of male circumcision because it was an obvious physical mark of religious identity.

Paul refers to the teachings of the Judaizers as a "different gospel" and scolds the Galatians for being so quickly led astray by them (1:6–7). His rehearsal of his own Jewish background, conversion out of it, and conflicts with other Jewish Christian leaders (1:12–2:21) signal that the relationship between Judaism and incipient Christianity is at issue. His discussion of faith and the law (3:1–4:31) also points to this topic. He explicitly mentions circumcision in a series of verses:

> if you let yourselves be circumcised, Christ will be of no benefit to you. (5:2)

> For in Christ Jesus neither circumcision nor uncircumcision counts for anything. (5:6)

> It is those who want to make a good showing in the flesh that try to compel you to be circumcised. (6:12)

> For neither circumcision nor uncircumcision is anything; but a new creation is everything. (6:15)

At one point he bitterly alludes to circumcision as self-mutilation or castration and wishes it upon the Judaizers: "I wish that those who unsettle you would castrate themselves" (5:12).

For Paul, the teaching of the Judaizers was insidious because it advocated reliance on the law for salvation and thus effectively denied the grace of God. This is his main point in the body of the letter. Paul spent his mission activity among the Gentiles teaching that salvation in Christ was available to everyone who believed without respect to ethnic origin or adherence to the law. He therefore perceived the Judaizers' teaching as a personal attack upon him and his mission.

Rhetoric and Argument

Like Philemon, the body of the letter to the Galatians exhibits the three components of deliberative rhetoric. The exordium (1:6–11) prepares the recipients to hear the message of the letter. In the case of Galatians, Paul does not use praise but expresses disappointment, preparing his readers for what is largely a message of reproof. The proof (*probatio*, 1:12–5:1) begins with an autobiographical narrative sketching Paul's Jewish roots, his conversion to Christianity, and his dealings with other Jewish Christian leaders. It lays out Paul's basic position about justification by faith rather than by keeping the law and then proceeds to argue the case for this position in detail by means of exposition on texts from the Hebrew Bible/Old Testament. Much of this material is diatribe. That is, Paul carries on a kind of dialogue with his opponents according to what he anticipates they would say. Finally, the peroration (5:2–6:10) consists mainly of exhortations or paranesis to the Galatians to heed Paul's words and to configure their behavior accordingly. This material is not tacked on but is integral to Paul's argument. He makes the point that freedom from the law is not license for Christians to behave immorally. Rather, they are to lead ethical lives led by the Spirit.

Because of the defensive tone of Galatians, especially the autobiographical part, one prominent scholar has characterized it as an apologetic letter, whose rhetoric is forensic.[22] That is, Paul is essentially in the role of a defendant in a courtroom setting. The Judaizers are his accusers, and the Galatian Christians are the jury. Paul is trying to convince the Galatians of his innocence in the face of personal charges leveled against him by the Judaizers. Still, most scholars prefer to see the rhetoric of Galatians as deliberative rather than forensic.

The main difference between these rhetorical theories relates to the primary intent behind Galatians. As deliberative rhetoric, Paul's main intent is not simply to defend himself but to lead the Galatians through persuasion and instruction to a proper understanding of faith and its relationship to the law. The letter contains apologetic features, but these are designed to establish Paul's credentials in order to get the Galatians to heed his message. Paul's basic claim in this regard is that the gospel he proclaims comes from God, not from human beings. The questions and issues that Paul addresses in the letter do not necessarily all stem from accusations of the Judaizers but may indeed be rhetorical devices.[23] As part of his diatribe in the letter, Paul may have invented questions, allegations, and positions purely for the purpose of articulating a response to them.

Paul's use of rhetoric in Galatians is a significant consideration for interpretation. It is important to keep in mind that Paul is endeavoring to persuade his readers rather than to lay out facts. He is, therefore, prone to argumentation that modern readers may find odd or unconvincing. For instance, in Galatians 3:16 Paul makes a distinction between the singular and plural of the word "seed," (translated "offspring" in the NRSV) in the promise to Abraham in Genesis. He does this in order to argue that the word referred to Christ rather than to Abraham's descendants in general. The argument runs contrary to linguistic use in which the singular word "seed" in Hebrew, Greek, and English typically refers to all of one's children or descendants. Even Paul recognizes this in another letter where he interprets the same word as having a plural sense referring to Abraham's spiritual descendants, that is all who share Abraham's faith (Rom 4:12–17).

As with the prophecies we surveyed in a previous chapter, there is no prediction of Christ inherent in the Abraham story. Paul's interpretation in Galatians is a result of his rhetorical purpose in the letter rather than of close analysis of the story in Genesis.

In a similar move, Paul allegorizes the characters of Sarah and Hagar (4:21-5:1), saying that they represent two covenants, the one under the law (Hagar "bearing children for slavery") and the other under Christ (Sarah "she is free"). Allegory was widely used as an interpretive strategy in Paul's day. Accordingly, this reading is not the result of careful study of Genesis in its historical and literary context. It is, rather, a rhetorical argument intended to convince the Galatians of the correctness of Paul's perspective on the relationship of faith and law.

Structure in 1 Corinthians

The prescript (1:1–3) names Paul and Sosthenes as senders and the church in Corinth as the recipients of this letter. The mention of "all those who in every place call on the name of our Lord Jesus Christ" (1:2, NRSV) is somewhat confusing in English translation. Paul's point is that the Corinthians are fellow saints of those who are Christians everywhere, not that the letter was originally addressed to all Christians.

The thanksgiving (1:4–9) makes reference to speech and knowledge and spiritual gifts, all of which are topics that Paul discusses in detail in the body of the letter. Here Paul refers to these items as gifts from God, which have enriched the Corinthians spiritually. In the body he will critique the Corinthians' use of these gifts.

The body of the letter (1:10–16:12) is lengthy and deals with a variety of issues. It ends with a discussion of travel plans, Paul's and those of others.

The conclusion (16:13–24) includes closing exhortations, notes, and greetings. The greeting in Paul's own hand (16:21) indicates that he dictated the letter as a whole and then penned its final wish of grace himself.

Setting and Intent

Paul's association with the church in Corinth stemmed from when he resided there around 51–52 CE (Acts 18:1–18). This letter is at least the second one that Paul wrote to them, since he mentions an earlier letter (1 Cor 5:9), which is now lost to us. He wrote 1 Corinthians around 53–55 CE in answer to a letter from them (7:1) and in response to a report about them from "Chloe's people" (1:11). Scholars have noticed that Paul's tone seems sharper and more indignant when he appears to respond to oral reports, but calmer and more reasoned when he seems to be replying to their letter.[24] They have also observed that the language of 1 Corinthians differs from that of his other letters, at least in part because he quotes the Corinthians' own words and responds in kind (see 1 Cor 7:1 as an example).

This letter, then, deals with a variety of different subjects, mostly very practical matters, about which Paul is in dialogue with the Corinthian church. It is, in effect " . . . a personal communication addressed to a particular community, this letter contains arguments intended to persuade the hearers, not doctrinal treatises formulated to define Christian belief."[25] Following is a list of the topics treated in the letter.

> Divisions based on different leaders and claims of wisdom and spirituality (1:10–4:21)
> A man living with his stepmother (chapter 5)
> Lawsuits among Christians (6:1–8)
> Marriage and sexual relations (6:12–7:40)
> Meat sacrificed to idols (8:1–11:1)
> Head covering in prayer (11:2–16)
> Social division over the Lord's Supper (11:17–34)
> Spiritual gifts (12:1–14:40)
> Resurrection of the dead (15:1–58)
> Collection for the Christians in Jerusalem (16:1–4)

If there was a single problem common to all of the specific issues raised in 1 Corinthians it was that of divisions. Paul begins by addressing the matter of divisions, and it surfaces again explicitly in his discussions of the Lord's Supper and of spiritual gifts. The divisions may have been caused, at least in part, by a sense of conceit held by some of their own superior wisdom or spirituality. Paul begins the letter by addressing claims of greater wisdom and spirituality. Those who ate food sacrificed to idols believed they possessed superior knowledge, and those who spoke in tongues believed their gift to be superior. Paul wrote to try to resolve these controversies through the application of Christian moral teaching.

Some, if not all, of the problems in the Corinthian church resulted from tensions that arose when Christianity moved into Roman culture. The city of Corinth had been destroyed by the Romans in 146 BCE and then rebuilt by them in 44 BCE. The city quickly became a commercial center. Fashioned on a Roman model, it developed into the hub of Roman imperial culture in Greece. Initially, it was settled mainly with the poor and freed slaves from other cities, especially Rome.[26] Thus, Paul pointed out that the Corinthian Christians by and large did not come from the upper classes (1:27). The struggle for social improvement may have been one of the factors for claims of superiority on the part of some of the Corinthians. As they longed for or attained noble status socially, they also saw themselves as superior spiritually or in terms of wisdom or spiritual gifts.

In the context of a Roman city like Corinth there were questions and disagreements about whether it was right for Christians to eat meat that had been dedicated to a Roman deity before being sold in the market or served by a host (1 Cor 8; 10). The social divisions in conjunction with the Lord's Supper may also have been rooted in Roman social customs regarding dinner parties, which typically seated and served people according to social rank. Other problems dealt with in the letter confronted sexual mores and views of the afterlife that were prevalent in Roman culture.

A particularly good example of the situational nature of Paul's remarks is the passage about head covering (11:2–16). This is a confusing text and one that has occasioned a great deal of debate among interpreters; recent attention to archaeological evidence, however, has clarified its cultural background.[27] The issue with which Paul deals is the covering of the head by men and women in a worship setting, not hairstyles, as argued by some scholars.[28] The practice of men covering their heads in worship was common in Roman society. Given the dominance of Roman culture in Corinth, the practice had emerged there among at least some Christians. Paul argues against the practice and takes the opportunity further to contend for distinctiveness and modesty of dress on the part of Christian women. Paul's words on this subject again address a specific setting in the context and society of Roman Corinth.

... the Corinthian issue of whether a man may cover his head when he prays and prophesies emerged from a particular matrix of mores that were totally indigenous to Roman pietistic and devotional ethos, and had spread, as archaeology proves, to the urban centers of the Mediterranean basis, Corinth included, decades prior to the advent of Christianity.[29]

Rhetoric and Argument

The body of the letter evinces a three-part rhetorical division similar to what we saw in Philemon and Galatians. There is an exordium of sorts (1:10–17); it does not praise the Corinthians but prepares them for the letter's message by raising the issues of divisions and wisdom, which underlie its individual concerns. The *probatio* or proof does not really carry an argument throughout the letter. Rather, Paul proceeds one by one to discuss the problems and questions that have been reported to him orally or in writing. The third rhetorical component, the *peroratio*, is represented by 15.58. "Therefore, my beloved, be steadfast, immovable, always excelling in the work of the Lord, because you know that in the Lord your labor is not in vain." Compared to the perorations in Galatians and Romans, this one is quite brief. But this is due at least in part to the diversity of topics covered in 1 Corinthians. Still, this final exhortation of the letter's body does reiterate its overall message.

Deliberative rhetoric predominates in the letter, but there are also instances where Paul uses other kinds of rhetoric. For example, in chapter 4, he defends himself and his ministry in the face of criticism that he has evidently heard from the Corinthians. Here he employs forensic rhetoric, even using the metaphor of a court with himself as the defendant and God as the judge.

As noted previously, Paul sometimes quotes the Corinthians themselves in his responses to them. In the discussion of the issue of meat sacrificed to idols, for instance, he quotes them repeatedly, meaning that he is responding to concerns about which the Corinthians themselves have written to Paul. The heading, "Now concerning food sacrificed to idols" (8:1a), with which Paul begins his treatment of this matter, suggests that he is responding to another of the concerns about which they had written to him. His subsequent words appear to incorporate a quotation from their letter: "We all know that 'all of us possess knowledge'" (8:1b). In accord with the NRSV, Paul quotes the Corinthians own statement that "all of us possess knowledge." He then responds: "Knowledge puffs up, but love builds up" (8:1c).

Paul continues with more quotations, again presented as such by the NRSV: "We know that 'no idol in the world really exists,' and that 'there is no God but one'" (8:4). This is the substance of the position presented to him by an element of the Corinthian church: They *know* that there is only one God and that idols are meaningless. Paul agrees with this position, but points out that not everyone shares it. There are fellow Christians whose weak consciences will not allow them to eat food offered to an idol.

Paul moves the discussion along with another quotation, "Food will not bring us close to God. We are no better off if we do not eat, and no worse off if we do" (8:8). The NRSV renders only the first half of this verse as a quotation, though it is likely that the entire verse is such. Unfortunately, ancient Greek did not use quotation marks, so that the discernment of quotations is a matter of interpretation. The quotation in this case is once more from those Corinthian Christians who do not regard eating meat offered to idols as wrong. Again Paul agrees, but his concern is that their liberal perspective may lead others who do have scruples about eating sacrificed meat to violate their consciences and thus sin. Hence, Paul thinks it best not to eat such meat.

A particularly interesting example of Paul's rhetoric is again in the passage on head coverings (11:2–16). His point is that, contrary to Roman practice, men should not cover their heads in worship. Women, on the other hand, should cover their heads in worship. The reason for this distinction derives from the view of women in ancient Greco-Roman and Jewish cultures as imperfect males, sexually vulnerable and physically inferior to men.[30] Paul argues that women should be veiled in order to maintain social and religious order. He uses a play on the Greek word for "head" (*kephalē*) in laying out the religious and social hierarchy God, Christ, man, woman (11:3).

Paul further argues for this hierarchy from the order of creation in Genesis (1 Cor 11:8–9). Religious order is maintained when a woman speaks publicly in prophecy or prayer if her sexual attractiveness is veiled from the gaze of men so that their attention is not diverted away from God or the message conveyed through her. Another reason for veiling that is especially difficult for modern readers to understand is "because of the angels" (11:10b). This may be another argument drawn from Genesis—the story of the "sons of God" mating with human women in Genesis 6:1–4. If so, the point is to hide the women's sexual attractiveness from the angels. Alternatively, Paul may understand the angels as guardians of proper order in worship, who would be offended by women prophesying unveiled. The case for the latter interpretation has been made on the basis of writings found in the Dead Sea Scroll community.[31]

In addition to his exposition of the Hebrew Bible, Paul appeals to nature: "Does not nature teach you that if a man wears long hair it is degrading to him?" (11:14). This kind of rhetorical appeal to nature was popular in Paul's day.[32] By "nature" Paul apparently means "the way things are," the simple fact that men at that time typically had short hair and perhaps the prevalence of baldness among men as opposed to women. His contention is that this distinction between men and women is engrained in the nature of human begins. The two sexes, while interdependent, are distinct.

What is especially remarkable about this text is that at the end of it Paul seems to retreat somewhat: "But if anyone is disposed to be contentious—we have no such custom, nor do the churches of God." He appears to be saying that male veiling is after all a mere "practice" or "custom" and that those who resist his judgment on the matter should realize that they are out of step with the other churches. Thus, Paul has argued at length, employing his best rhetoric, along with theological considerations, against what is in the end a social custom rather than a theological or moral evil.

Structure in Romans

The book of Romans follows the letter structure typical of Paul's writings. Paul, the sender, addresses the letter to the Christians in Rome and greets them with grace and peace (1:1–7). Paul's self-description is longer than usual, because he includes a synthesis of the gospel as he proclaims it—Christ promised by the Hebrew scriptures now preached to Gentiles as well. The synthesis previews the primary concern of the letter.

The thanksgiving (1:8–15) also anticipates themes of the letter: Paul knows the Roman church by reputation. He wants to visit them in order to share with them the gospel that he proclaims. So far, however, he has been prevented from traveling to Rome.

The body of the letter contains two main sections. The main argument (1:16–11:36) lays out "the gospel . . . the power of God for salvation to everyone who has faith, to the Jew first and also to the Greek" (1:16). Then, based on that argument, the second section exhorts the Romans to righteous living (12:1 15:13). The division between these two sections is marked by a doxology: "For from him and through him and to him are all things. To him be the glory forever. Amen" (11:36). The body concludes with Paul's typical discussion of his travel plans (15:14–33), the end of which is also marked, this time with a benediction: "The God of peace be with all of you. Amen" (15:33). The conclusion (16:1–27) conveys greetings, including one from the secretary who wrote the letter, mixed with admonitions and the final "grace." The letter ends with a lengthy doxology:

> Now to God who is able to strengthen you according to my gospel and the proclamation of Jesus Christ, according to the revelation of the mystery that was kept secret for long ages but is now disclosed, and through the prophetic writings is

made known to all the Gentiles, according to the command of the eternal God, to bring about the obedience of faith—to the only wise God, through Jesus Christ, to whom be the glory forever! Amen. (Rom 16:25–27)

The doxology is an apt conclusion because it rehearses the main themes of the letter in terms similar to the opening salutation: Paul's gospel, revealed to the prophets of old, and now made known to the Gentiles.

Setting and Intent

Romans is typically perceived as the least occasional of Paul's writings. It was written to a church he had not founded or visited. He was not, therefore, addressing one or more specific problems in the church as he had in 1 Corinthians. His purpose was more general. This does not mean, however, that Romans is a treatise or systematic exposition of Paul's theology, though it is sometimes treated as such. It is still a letter, and there were specific circumstances in the Roman church and in Paul's own life that occasioned its writing.

Important for understanding the situation of the church in Rome is a piece of information supplied by the Roman historian Suetonius. He reports that in 49 CE the emperor Claudius expelled the Jews from the city because of trouble they stirred up over a certain "Chrestus."[33] "Chrestus" is probably a misspelling of "Christ." The trouble was caused by the growing influence of Christianity within Jewish circles. Some of those expelled were Jewish Christians, including Prisca and Aquila (Acts 18:2; Rom 16:3). The Jews returned after Claudius's death in 54 CE, just a few short years before Paul wrote his letter. By that time, however, the number of Gentile believers had probably grown substantially, so that the Jews found themselves to be a distinct minority.

While Paul had never visited Rome, he knew some of the Christians there and had obviously heard from them about others. He greets twenty-six by name (16:1–15) and is personally acquainted with at least the first seven of these. He thus was well aware of and interested in the situation of the church in Rome. Paul wanted to visit Rome and to use it as a "jumping off" point for his mission to Spain (15:24). He wrote his letter to introduce himself and the gospel he preached to this church, which did not know him well. He emphasized his mission "to the Jew first and also to the Greek."

But Paul wrote for more specific reasons than simply to introduce himself. As in Galatians, he frequently employs diatribe—one side of a debate against unnamed opponents.[34] The subject had to do with the question of the value and role of the Hebrew Bible law for Christians—the same basic issue as in Galatians. So much is clear from an overview of the content of the letter's body. Paul argues that Jews and Gentiles are equally sinful without Christ (1:16–3:20), that righteousness comes through faith in Christ not from obedience to the law (3:21–4:25), that Christians are not enslaved to sin any more than they are to the law (5:1–8:39), and that the Jews will be saved eventually through faith in Christ (9:1–11:36).

Unfortunately, it is difficult to be more specific about Paul's reasons for writing Romans because there are details about the setting of both the Roman Christians and Paul that remain uncertain. The book itself does not explicitly indicate that the church in Rome was divided along ethnic lines. One of the most recent treatments of Romans proposes that the earliest Christian community in Rome consisted of Jews and Gentiles who were drawn to Christianity through Judaism and that they continued to follow the ethical principles of the law even after the expulsion of the Jews by Claudius.[35] Paul wrote to them to correct suspicions they had about him and his ideas. These suspicions were caused by the rhetorical overstatements he had made in his letter to the Galatians. Specifically, Paul upheld the temporary value of the law and the importance of ethical behavior for Christians, but he also forcefully asserted that righteousness for Jews and Gentiles alike was available only in Christ.

Whether this proposal is correct or not, it illustrates the point that the book of Romans was written as a situational letter. Paul's intent in it was not to lay out a systematic explanation of Christian theology but to address a specific setting relating to the Christian community in Rome, their view of him, and his plans to use Rome as a launching pad for his further ministry in Spain.

Rhetoric and Argument

Perhaps more than Paul's other writings, Romans mixes different kinds of rhetoric. The body of the letter follows the three-part structure of deliberative rhetoric. The theme (1:16–17) serves as an exordium to the extent that it prepares the readers for the content of the letter, which focuses on Paul's understanding of the gospel. The praise function of the exordium is fulfilled in the thanksgiving (1:8). As in Galatians, the paranetic or exhortative section of the letter (Rom 12:1–15:13) functions as a rhetorical peroration by encouraging proper behavior based on salvation through God's grace that Paul has explained in the main section or proof (*probatio*) of the letter.

The proof (1:18–11:36) exemplifies epideictic rhetoric to the extent that it reflects Paul's position on various matters. At the same time, Paul makes extensive use of diatribe in this section. Here we see Paul the teacher at work. Because he was less familiar with the specifics of the Roman church, he relied on his teaching skills. In line with the "Socratic method," he frequently carries on a dialogue with a hypothetical conversation partner, raising and answering potential questions or objections and confronting erroneous conclusions.[36] These dialogues do not necessarily reflect the presence of real opponents in Rome or actual objections on the part of the Christians there. However, Paul had formulated his responses in actual situations with real opponents, such as those he faced at Galatia and Corinth.

The basic argument of the proof takes place in four segments.[37] The point of the first (1:18–3:20) is that "all have sinned and fall short of the glory of God" (3:23). The Gentiles chose to worship idols instead of the one true God whom they should have recognized in creation. As a result, God abandoned them and allowed them to be consumed by passion and to exchange "natural" sexual relations for "unnatural," leading them in turn to total depravity. Here Paul echoes the disdain of Hellenistic Jewish writers for Gentile morality. He also expresses the idea found among Greco-Roman moral philosophers that homosexual acts were the unnatural (nonprocreative) and self-indulgent overflow of heterosexual lust.[38] Paul adds that Jews had the advantage of the law but were condemned for failing to live up to its requirements.

The second segment (3:21–4:25) describes God's response: justification through divine grace by faith in Christ available to both Gentiles and Jews. Abraham is presented in chapter 4 as the prototype of justification by faith.

The third segment (5:1–8:39) further explores the interrelationships of faith, grace, law, and salvation. Christ is a new Adam; as the original Adam brought sin to humanity, the new Adam brings redemption. Grace increased in proportion to sin, but this means that believers are freed from enslavement to sin and should not allow it to control them any longer. Paul claims that the law multiplied sin by making sin apparent. But Christians are no more enslaved to the law than they are to sin. Christians have a new spiritual life in Christ, from whose love absolutely nothing can separate them.

The final segment (9:1–11:36) deals with God's plan for Israel, the chosen people. Paul's belief is that God's rejection of the Jews is partial and temporary, designed to allow the Gentiles to be grafted in, but that eventually "all Israel will be saved."

Appropriating the Letters (and the Rest of the Bible)

This chapter, like the ones before it, began with an example of how portions of the Bible are often misappropriated in modern interpretations. It seems fitting, therefore, to conclude the chapter—and this book—with some remarks about principles for using, understanding, and interpreting the Bible. The focus of these remarks will be the New Testament letters and hence the appropriation (or mis-appropriation) of them by Christians; they also may be applied more widely to the use of the Bible as a whole or its parts by modern readers of different faiths.

The discussions in these chapters have highlighted the importance of discerning (1) the settings of the author and (2) the original addressees of the New Testament letters for understanding them in their original contexts. There is yet another situation that must be taken into account in any attempt to appropriate the message of the New Testament letters for a modern setting—that of the interpreter(s), which is often quite different from those of the original correspondents. The differences between the two interpretations have not always been taken into consideration, often with harmful results.

The little book of Philemon is a perfect example. For example, it figured prominently in the debate over slavery in nineteenth-century America. Proponents of slavery argued for the biblical justification of slavery on the grounds that Paul accepted the institution and neither called for its obliteration nor commanded Philemon to free Onesimus. Indeed, Paul returned the slave to his owner. As we have seen, however, slavery in the Greco-Roman world was significantly different from the American version.[39] The two greatest differences had to do with the way in which a person became a slave and the length of enslavement. In the Greco-Roman world, unlike New World slavery, race was not a factor. Slaves shared the same cultural heritage as their owners. While most slaves in the first century CE were born as such, some sold themselves into slavery or were sold by their parents to pay a debt and for financial security. Slaves were often well educated, sometimes better so than their owners, and held important social offices as city officials, teachers, doctors, writers, ship captains, and the like. Slaves never comprised a distinct social class. Roman slavery was also not permanent but often functioned as a way of social mobility. Most slaves could expect to have their freedom by age thirty. Given these differences, Philemon should never have been used in support of American slavery. If anything, its emphasis on the brotherhood and equality of Christians regardless of social status would tend to undercut the practice of slavery in all forms.

The recognition of the interpreter's situation as a factor in appropriating the text is nothing new. Christians of all stripes have long recognized it. That is why few churches today practice foot washing or exchange the "holy kiss," despite direct commands to do so in the New Testament. Nor is the question of eating meat sacrificed to idols an issue in modern Western churches. These practices are all recognized as cultural, and modern culture has changed.

Still, the extent to which the New Testament letters are permeated by the culture that produced them does not always receive full consideration by modern interpreters trying to appropriate them. Thus, the text about head covering in 1 Corinthians 11 has a history of (ab)use and is still used today in some circles to argue for the subordination of women; yet the idea of the female body as an imperfect edition of the male body, upon which the text is based, was a product of an ancient culture and strikes a modern reader as ridiculous. Paul himself admits in the passage that he is dealing with a "custom," even though he presses theology into service for the sake of his rhetorical argument. This raises the question as to whether Paul's discussions of other issues (e.g., marriage, women's roles, homosexuality) also reflect his rhetoric and the culture surrounding him and may no longer be tenable for the modern understandings of such matters as gender roles, sexual orientation, and the like.

To return to the main point of this chapter—the misconceptions with which it deals—the New Testament letters do not provide a practical guide for modern Christian living because they address situations that belong to an entirely different time and culture.

> It is also incumbent upon us to *understand* what Paul said, why he said it in his own time and place, and whether and how it applies to contemporary Christians in the time and place that make up the latter days of the twentieth century. . . . Understanding necessitates an appropriation of the text for Christian living in the contemporary circumstance.[40]

How exactly do Christians go about the process of appropriating the New Testament letters for daily living? They have typically done so by searching for enduring or fundamental principles in them. All Christians recognize to some extent that the letters are situational and cannot be immediately applied to a modern situation. Hence, they attempt to filter out matters of time, culture, and specific situation in order to arrive at the fundamental principle that supercedes such issues.

Sometimes these principles are relatively easy to discern. The book of Philemon, for instance, teaches forgiveness and acceptance of fellow Christians regardless of social standing. Galatians presents the idea that God accepts people *just as they are* into the Christian faith, an idea that has implications for issues of race and sexual orientation faced by the modern church. It articulates principles of acceptance and unity:

> As many of you as were baptized into Christ have clothed yourselves with Christ. There is no longer Jew or Greek, there is no longer slave or free, there is no longer male and female; for all of you are one in Christ Jesus. (Gal 3:28)

There are, however, two problems with this approach. First, Christians do not agree—and never have—about what the fundamental principles of acceptance and unity are. Second, our treatment of the letters in this chapter has shown how thoroughly the historical and cultural situation permeates them. Not only does the situation determine the precise circumstances surrounding each letter, but the language, images, and even the form of argumentation are all embedded in the particular situation(s) of the author and the addressees. We saw, for example, that Paul's rhetorical arguments in Galatians about faith replacing the keeping of the Law were chosen for their persuasive value, not for their strict accuracy. Failure to recognize this has led Christians to regard the Hebrew Bible as irrelevant to their faith. Worse, it has fostered anti-Semitism. Even Paul's great "definition" of love in 1 Corinthians 13 is determined by the situation he addressed. He described love as patient and kind precisely because the Corinthians were being impatient and unkind in their disputes over spiritual gifts (chapters 12–14).

Dale Martin has cogently addressed this issue.[41] He notes that appeals to "what the Bible says" as foundational for Christian ethics without acknowledgement of the interpreter's situation constitute fundamentalism. "The only recourse in our radical contingency is to *accept* our contingency and look for guidance within the discourse that we occupy and that forms our very selves." In other words, Christians need to recognize that, like the writers and recipients of the New Testament letters, they stand within a given situation, cultural and otherwise. The way in which to appropriate those letters—and indeed the whole Bible—depends in part on that situation. The context for appropriation is the discourse or conversation between the Bible, Jewish and Christian tradition, and the modern situation. The single guiding principle is love. But that in itself does not render any easy solutions to ethical dilemmas. The precise attitude or course of action to be adopted will vary depending on what is the loving thing to do, because the very definition of what love entails may vary depending on the situation, as in 1 Corinthians 13.

In adopting this stance, Dale Martin cites the great Christian interpreter, St. Augustine: "Whoever, therefore, thinks that he understands the divine Scriptures or any part of them so that it does not build the double love of God and of our neighbor does not understand it at all" (*On Christian Doctrine* 1.35.40). Martin is no doubt aware that Augustine's ultimate source was the Hebrew Bible, and in that quote Augustine was recalling Matthew's Jesus:

> One of them, a lawyer, asked him a question to test him. "Teacher, which commandment in the law is the greatest?" He said to him, "'You shall love the Lord your God with all your heart, and with all your soul, and with all your mind.' This is the greatest and first commandment. And a second is like it: 'You shall love your neighbor as yourself.' On these two commandments hang all the law and the prophets." (Matt 22:36–40, NRSV)

Paul echoed the point when he wrote, "For the whole law is summed up in a single commandment, 'You shall love your neighbor as yourself'" (Gal 5:14, NRSV). Both were quoting the Hebrew Bible:

> You shall love the LORD your God with all your heart and with all your soul, and with all your might. (Deut 6:5)

> You shall love your neighbor as yourself. (Lev 19:18a)

In its original context, it is clear that by "neighbor" Leviticus 19:18 meant one's fellow Israelite. The complete verse reads:

> You shall not take vengeance or bear a grudge against any of your people, but you shall love your neighbor as yourself. I am the LORD.

By drawing a universal principle from a text aimed originally at Israelites, Jesus, Paul, and Augustine all appropriate a commandment that was initially situational.

Genres are by definition situational; as I hope this book has made clear, they are situated within specific human cultures and institutions. This is not to deny the divine inspiration of the Bible. It is, rather, to affirm that whatever the origin of biblical literature—whether divine or human—recognition of its different genres is an essential part of the process of communication and is therefore crucial to understanding it. And that has been the goal of the exploration of genres in this book—to contribute to a better understanding of the Bible.

NOTES

Introduction

1. "Yahweh" is the name of the God of Israel in the Hebrew Bible. It appeared as "Jehovah" in older English versions and is often rendered "the LORD" (in small caps) in modern editions such as the NRSV.

2. These notices are in 2:1 [Hebrew 2:2] and 4:2. The English and Hebrew verse numbers differ by one in chapter 2. For the sake of convenience, my verse citations follow the English numbers.

3. For a much more detailed study of Jonah's symmetry than is possible here see Phyllis Trible, *Rhetorical Criticism: Context, Method, and the Book of Jonah*, Guides to Biblical Scholarship (Minneapolis, MN: Fortress, 1994), esp. 110–17. See also the synthesis of observations about Jonah's structure in David Marcus, *From Balaam to Jonah: Anti-prophetic Satire in the Hebrew Bible*, Brown Judaic Studies 301 (Atlanta, GA: Scholars Press, 1995), 138–39.

4. I owe this observation to my colleague, Dr. Ryan Byrne.

5. Some scholars think the poem in chapter 2 is a later addition and not part of the original book of Jonah. They point to the change in the fish's gender as one piece of evidence supporting this possibility. The poem does appear to have been borrowed from a different setting, but it may have been incorporated by the book's author. The latter position was argued forcefully by George M. Landes, "The Kerygma of the Book of Jonah: The Contextual Interpretation of the Jonah Psalm," *Interp* 21 (1967): 3–31 and more recently by Kenneth M. Craig, Jr., *A Poetics of Jonah: Art in the Service of Ideology* (Columbia: University of South Carolina Press, 1993).

6. See A. Kirk Grayson, "Nineveh," *The Anchor Bible Dictionary*, vol. 4, 1118.

7. The Hebrew verb typically means to feel pity or compassion for.

8. DreamWorks, 1999, starring Tim Allen, Sigourney Weaver, Alan Rickman, and Tony Shaloub.

9. John J. Collins, "Introduction: Towards the Morphology of a Genre," *Semeia* 14 (1979): 1.

10. See for instance the treatments of Jonah in Harold Shank, *Minor Prophets,* The College Press NIV Commentary (Joplin, MO: Collegeville, 2001) and Douglas Stuart, *Hosea-Jonah,* Word Biblical Commentary 31 (Waco, TX: Word, 1987).

Chapter One

1. Christopher Shea, "Debunking Ancient Israel: Erasing History or Facing the Truth?" *The Chronicle of Higher Education* (Nov. 21, 1997): A12–14.

2. Michael Joseph Brown, *What They Don't Tell You: A Survivor's Guide to Biblical Studies* (Louisville: Westminster/John Knox, 2000), 39.

3. Brown (*What They Don't Tell You,* p. 5) helpfully defines "critical" in this sense as careful and deliberate study of the Bible "that engages the text and assumes the freedom to derive from the Bible meanings that may differ from those that traditional religion has seen in it."

4. John Van Seters, *In Search of History: Historiography in the Ancient World and the Origins of Biblical History* (New Haven: Yale University Press, 1983). Richard D. Nelson's *The Historical Books,* Interpreting Biblical Texts (Nashville: Abingdon, 1998) is a useful and readable introduction to the genre of history writing in the Bible.

5. Johan Huizinga, "A Definition of the Concept of History," in *Philosophy and History: Essays Presented to Ernst Cassirer,* ed. Raymond Klibansky and H. J. Paton, (Oxford: Clarendon, 1936), 9.

6. Herodotus, *Histories,* 1.5. Translation from Herodotus, *The History,* trans. David Grene (Chicago: University of Chicago Press, 1987), 35.

7. Herodotus, *Histories,* 2.123, 185.

8. Nelson, *The Historical Books,* 25. On Herodotus as a story teller, see James Romm, *Herodotus* (Hermes Books; New Haven: Yale University Press, 1998), 114–31.

9. Thucydides, *History of the Peloponnesian War,* I.22. See *Thucydides: History of the Peloponnesian War,* ed. and trans. Charles Forster Smith, Loeb Classical Library (Cambridge, MA: Harvard University Press, 1919).

10. Moses I. Finley, *Ancient History: Evidence and Models* (New York: Viking, 1986), 13.

11. Thus, Dionysius of Halicarnassus (first century BCE), called by Finley "the most acute and most learned of ancient critics and himself a prolific composer of speeches for his multi-volume *Roman Antiquities*" (Finley, *Ancient History,* 13), wrote a lengthy critique of the speeches composed by Thucydides (chapters 34–48 of "On Thucydides"). See *Dionysius of Halicarnassus: The Critical Essays in Two Volumes,* trans. Stephen Usher, Loeb Classical Library (Cambridge, MA: Harvard University Press, 1974) 1:563–613.

12. Finley, *Ancient History,* 9.

13. Van Seters (*In Search of History*, 44) points to Croesus's appeal to Athens and Sparta for a treaty against Persia (Herodotus, *Histories*, 1.56–70) as a case in point. It appears to be formulated from a later appeal (5.49–51) for the literary purpose of introducing information about the two city-states. The meeting between Solon and Croesus (1.29–33) is another possible invention, since it introduces the theme of human happiness that is so important for Herodotus.

14. Moses I. Finley, *The Use and Abuse of History* (New York: Viking, 1975), 29.

15. Finley, *Ancient History*, 4. On the way in which Herodotus's various ideologies shaped his history, see Romm, *Herodotus*, esp. 59–113.

16. For example, Herodotus includes the legend about Cyrus, the future king of Persia, surviving exposure as an infant by being suckled by a bitch (*Histories*, 1.22). But he explains it as a rumor begun by the boy's parents and drawn from the name of his foster mother. He also explains the channel between mountains through which the Peneus flows as the result of an earthquake—or of Poseidon, if Poseidon causes earthquakes (*Histories,* 7.129).

17. Van Seters, *In Search of History,* 4–5.

18. Rudyard Kipling, *Just So Stories: For Little Children* (London: Folio Society, 1991).

19. The Hebrew Bible contains a number of references to sea monsters or dragons— cf. Job 7:12; Pss 74:13; 148:7; Isa 27:1; 51:9; Jer 51:34; Ezek 29:3; 32:2. In Canaanite mythology the sea god, Yamm, was envisioned as a dragon and referred to as Leviathan. The same mythological background is apparent in the passages that refer to the sea as a dragon or use the name Leviathan (Job 7:12; Ps 74:13; Isa 27:1; Isa 51:9–10).

20. The division between chapters 1 and 2 is unfortunate and not an original part of the text of Genesis, since the Bible was first divided into chapters and verses in the thirteenth century CE.

21. NRSV's "Then" in 1:11 is interpretive.

22. Again, the NRSV in 1:26 has "Then," which is interpretive. The Hebrew text has "And."

23. The beginning of Genesis 1 is a highly technical matter that usually goes ignored. The Hebrew is ungrammatical and literally reads, "In the beginning of the God created the heavens and the earth." A slight change in vowels is required to make sense of the sentence. The usual solution is to read, "In the beginning, God created . . ." But this reading ignores the fact that v. 2 is subordinated to v. 1 in the Hebrew syntax. Reading v. 1 as a temporal clause is supported not only by Hebrew syntax but also by the fact that other creation accounts from the ancient Near East begin with a temporal clause. The famous Babylonian creation story, for instance, is named *Enuma elish* after its first two words, which mean "When above." The translation of Gen. 1:1 is theologically significant. The preferred interpretation indicates that the earth was already in existence as a formless, empty mass when God began to create. Creation in this sense means bringing order out of chaos rather than making something out of nothing (*creatio ex nihilo*).

24. *'ādām* occurs as a proper name in this story, i.e., without the definite article, only in 3:17, 21. The difference between definite and indefinite in those two instances is a single vowel that may very well have been accidentally miswritten. The rest of the time he is called "the *'ādām*," "the man." The genealogy in 5:1 is the first truly clear instance of *'ādām* as a proper name. Eve is named as such only near the end of the story (3:20).

25. See especially Phyllis Trible, *God and the Rhetoric of Sexuality,* Overtures to Biblical Theology (Philadelphia: Fortress, 1978). Trible contends that sexism and gender distinctions do not enter the story until the curse in 3:16. Her case falters on 2:23, where the man is already gendered and the woman taken out of him. However, Trible is certainly correct that subsequent tradition has introduced far more sexism into the story than is warranted by the text.

26. The word play here is with the Hebrew root *nḥm*. However, the name Noah actually comes from the root *nwḥ*, which still means "to rest, settle."

27. For an overview, see Stephen R. Haynes, *Noah's Curse: The Biblical Justification of American Slavery* (New York: Oxford University Press, 2002), esp. 23–40.

28. The descendants of Cush in Gen 10:8–12 appear to be out of place. Nimrod (= Nimrud), Babel (= Babylon), Erech (= Uruk), Akkad, Shinar, Nineveh, and Calah are all in Mesopotamia, particularly the southern part of the region, so that one would expect them to be listed as heirs of Shem rather than Ham. The misplacement is the result of confusion over the meaning of "Cush," which in addition to Nubia is sometimes used to refer to southern Mesopotamia because it was once ruled by people known as "Kassites," whose name in Hebrew resembles "Cush."

29. Again see Haynes, *Noah's Curse.* Unfortunately, Haynes dismisses the relevance of historical-critical scholarship of the Bible for countering this history of nefarious interpretation. His own response involves remythologizing Ham as victim (pp. 201–19), a strategy that is fanciful and uncompelling.

30. Abram and Abraham are variants of same name (like "Rob" and "Robert") with no real difference in meaning.. The author in Genesis 17 imputes meaning to the change in an etymological etiology.

31. The nature of the wickedness of Sodom and Gomorrah is controversial. The men of the city want to "know" the two newcomers, an idiom for sexual relations. This is not, however, the same as sexual orientation as understood today. If it were, Lot's offer of his daughters would have been meaningless. The view of homosexual intercourse, especially in the form of rape, is unquestionably negative. However, the story cannot be construed as a blanket condemnation of homosexuality.

32. See John Van Seters, "The Problem Childlessness in Near Eastern Law and the Patriarchs of Israel," *Journal of Biblical Literature* 87 (1968): 401–8.

33. Thus, Hagar carries the boy on the journey (21:14) and then casts him under a bush (21:15). This contrasts with some of the surrounding stories where he is at least thirteen years old. According to Gen. 16:16 Abraham is 86 years old when

Ishmael is born. In 17:1, he is 99, making Ishmael at least 13 at the time Isaac is born in chapter 21.

34. "Isaac" is probably an abbreviation of a longer theophoric sentence name, i.e., one that contained a divine element. Its original meaning was probably "God (El) smiles, is favorable" or "May God smile, be favorable."

35. The Hebrew text in 21:9 says that Sarah saw Ishmael "laughing" and determined on that score to send him away. Some English versions, like the NRSV, adopt the longer reading of the Septuagint (LXX) and render "playing with her son Isaac" or even "laughing at her son Isaac." The shorter Hebrew reading, however, is comprehensible. Ishmael's *laughter* reminds Sarah that he is the heir rather than her son Isaac, whose name means laughter, and that is why she insists on Ishmael going away.

36. See Ernst Axel Knauf, "Ishmaelites," *The Anchor Bible Dictionary*, vol. 3, 513–20.

37. An additional etiology is the one for Beer-lahai-roi in 16:13–14. Etiology may have shaped other details of the story. For instance, since the Wilderness of Paran, the home of the Ishmaelites according to Gen 21:21, lay between southern Palestine, where Abraham sojourned, and Egypt, the author may have deduced that Hagar was Egyptian.

38. Other texts referring to the nation as "Jacob" include Isa. 10:21; 17:4; 27:6, 9; Jer. 10:25; 30:7; and Ps 44:4 (Heb 44:5). It is especially common in what is known as 2 Isaiah (chapters 40–55), where it is frequently used in parallel to "Israel": 41:8, 14; 42:24; 43:1, 22, 28; 44:1, 21, 23; 48:12, 20; 49:5–6. "Esau" refers to the nation in Deut 2:5; Josh 24:4; Jer 49:10; Mal 1:13; and throughout the book of Obadiah.

39. "Jacob" is another abbreviated theophoric sentence-name originally meaning "God protects" or "May God protect."

40. The word "stuff" has to be supplied to make sense in English but is not actually there in Hebrew, which simply reads "red."

41. Gen. 32:28. The putative meaning of "Israel" in this passage is "he wrestles with God." Its actual meaning was probably "God (El) prevails, rules."

42. For the reconstruction of this poem, see Steven L. McKenzie, "The Jacob Tradition in Hosea 12:4–5," *Vetus Testamentum* 36 (1986): 311–22. The Jacob story in Genesis may be based on Hosea or the poem he cites. See Willam D. Whitt, "The Jacob Traditions in Hosea and Their Relation to Genesis," *Zeitschrift für die Alttestamentliche Wissenschaft* 103 (1991): 18–43.

43. The standard work on genealogies in the Bible is Robert R. Wilson, *Genealogy and History in the Biblical World*, Yale Near Eastern Researches 7 (New Haven: Yale University Press, 1977).

44. See Gary N. Knoppers, "Greek Historiography and the Chronicler's History: A Reexamination," *Journal of Biblical Literature* 122 (2003): 627–50.

45. There are no genealogies for the tribes of Dan and Zebulun in 1 Chron 1–9. However, their absence is probably due to accidental omission from the text or simply because the Chronicler had no real sources of information about the far northern

tribes. See the commentary on 1 Chron 7 in Steven L. McKenzie, *1–2 Chronicles,* Abingdon Old Testament Commentary (Nashville: Abingdon, 2004).

46. Compare 1 Chron 6:28 (Heb 6:13) with 1 Sam 1.

47. This is the explanation found in 1 Chron 22:8; 28:3.

48. The NRSV renders 1 Chron 21:1 as, "Satan stood up against Israel, and incited David to count the people of Israel." However, the noun *śāṭā* refers to an earthly "enemy, adversary" in a number of places (e.g., 1 Kings 11:14, 23), and that is its more likely sense here. The notion of a Satan or devil figure is a later development in late Israelite / early Jewish thought. See Peggy L. Day, *An Adversary in Heaven: śāṭā in the Hebrew Bible,* Harvard Semitic Monographs 43 (Atlanta: Scholars Press, 1988).

49. Compare 2 Chron. 2:11–16 (Heb 2:10–17) and 1 Kings 5:7 and 5:8–12 (Heb 5:21; 5:22–26).

50. There is an enormous amount of misinformation about the flood story, much of it generated by "ark seekers." A sober, well-documented resource is Lloyd R. Bailey, *Noah: The Person and the Story in History and Tradition,* Personalities of the Old Testament (Columbia, SC: University of South Carolina Press, 1989) and his older *Where Is Noah's Ark? Mystery on Mount Ararat* (Nashville: Abingdon, 1978). See also his article, "Noah and the Ark," in *The Anchor Bible Dictionary,* vol. 4, 1122–32.

51. The first version consists of 6:5–8; 7:1–5, 7–8, 10, 12, 16b–17, 23; 8:6, 20–22; 9:20–27; the second of 6:9–22; 7:6, 9, 11, 13–16a, 18–22, 24; 8:1–5, 7–19; 9:1–19, 28–29.

52. The theory presented here is basically that of Martin Noth, *The Deuteronomistic History,* Supplements to the *Journal for the Study of the Old Testament* 15 (Sheffield: JSOT Press, 1981), 42–46. Though a great deal has been written on Judges since Noth (original German, 1943) it is questionable whether there has been any real improvement on his model.

53. The beginning of the Deborah story in Judg 4:1 is set immediately after Ehud's death and lacks any mention of the intervening Shamgar. The Shamgar episode is anomalous in its brevity and lack of information about his tribal origin and the length of Israel's oppression or of his judgeship. His mother's name, Anat, is that of a Canaanite goddess, and has led to speculation that the story is a mythological or legendary fragment about a figure who was not even Israelite. Abimelech's story is added as an extension of that of Gideon (Jerubbaal). Abimelech is never called a judge, but declares himself king.

54. "The hammer-and-peg assault implied that Sisera must be lying, covered, in the tent. This posture meant that he was hiding, and hiding implied pursuit. But for there to be pursuit, Sisera must have fled on foot, with Baraq far enough behind to allow adequate leeway, but close enough to impel Sisera into her tent (4:22). Finally, Sisera's flight on foot implied that the rout was a mixed one of both cavalry and camp." Baruch Halpern, *The First Historians: The Hebrew Bible and History* (San Francisco: Harper & Row, 1988), 84–85.

55. The three stories are in 9:1–10:16; 10:17–27a; and 10:27b–11:15. The recognition of different sources behind 1 Sam 8–12 goes back at least to Julius Wellhausen, *Prolegomena to the History of Ancient Israel* (Gloucester, MA: Peter Smith, 1973; original German edition 1878). My observations on 1 Sam 9:1-10:16 owe a great deal to Ludwig Schmidt, *Jahwes Initiative: Studien zu Tradition, Interpretation und Historie in den Überlieferungen von Gideon, Saul und David*, Wissenschaftliche Monographien zum Alten und Neuen Testament 38 (Neukirchen-Vluyn: Neukirchener Verlag, 1970).

56. The original beginning of the story was lost from the Hebrew text but can be restored on the basis of a Dead Sea Scroll fragment, as has been done in the NRSV at 10:27b. The restored paragraph indicates that the source of the conflict was a border dispute between Nahash and the tribes of Gad and Reuben. Jabesh Gilead lay outside of the disputed area to the north but became involved because some of the Gadites and Reubenites fled there, and Nahash pursued them.

57. The expression is translated quite literally in the King James Version as "one who pisseth on a wall," using a verb that was accepted in its day but is considered vulgar by today's standards.

58. See Howard N. Wallace, "The Oracles Against the Israelite Dynasties in 1 and 2 Kings," *Biblica* 67 (1986): 21–40. See further Steven L. McKenzie, *The Trouble with Kings: The Composition of the Book of Kings in the Deuteronomistic History*, Supplements to *Vetus Testamentum* 42 (Leiden: Brill, 1991), 61–80.

59. See Donald B. Redford, *Egypt, Canaan, and Israel in Ancient Times* (Princeton: Princeton University Press, 1992), 408. Redford extrapolates a figure of 2.5 million Israelites from the biblical figures. Egypt's population at the time is estimated at 3–4.5 million.

60. For helpful and readable surveys of archaeological work relating to Israel's settlement in Canaan, including the problems with the "conquest" model and the evidence for Israel's indigenous origins, see William G. Dever, *Recent Archaeological Discoveries and Biblical Research* (Seattle: University of Washington Press, 1990), 37–84 and Israel Finkelstein and Neil Asher Silberman, *The Bible Unearthed: Archaeology's New Vision of Ancient Israel and the Origin of Its Sacred Texts* (New York: Free Press, 2001), esp. 72–122.

61. See Redford, *Egypt, Canaan, and Israel*, esp. 408–22. Redford thinks that the biblical story is a mythologized and elaborated faint memory composed in the Saite period (7–6th century BCE) of the expulsion of the Hyksos from Egypt, which took place a thousand years earlier.

62. See David E. Aune, *The New Testament in Its Literary Environment*, Library of Early Christianity (Philadelphia: Westminster, 1987), 17–76. For useful overviews, see Frans Neirynck, "Gospel, Genre of," *The Oxford Companion of the Bible*, ed. Bruce M. Metzger and Michael D. Coogan (New York: Oxford University Press, 1993), 258–59; and Willem S. Vorster, "Gospel Genre," *The Anchor Bible Dictionary*, vol. 2, 1077–79.

63. See Aune, *The New Testament in Its Literary Environment*, 77–157.

Chapter Two

1. Despite its proliferation in student papers and the popular press the verb "to prophesize" does not exist.

2. The Hebrew text in 7:4, 7 actually says "I will let you stay." However, a better reading, attested in the Latin Vulgate, is "I will stay with you." In the ideology of the ancient Near East, a temple is typically spoken of as the house of the deity to whom it is devoted. The word "place" in 7:3 is a common idiom in the ancient Near East and in the Bible for a shrine.

3. See 1 Samuel 1–4. Jeremiah was especially familiar with Shiloh because he belonged to the line of priests that had served in Shiloh and had trained Samuel. He was from Anathoth (Jer 1:1), where Abiathar of the priestly line of Eli had been banished by Solomon (1 Kings 2:26–27).

4. The books in the Hebrew Bible are not arranged in chronological order, so the book of Micah follows Jeremiah, even though the prophet Micah lived before Jeremiah.

5. There is debate among scholars about the originality of some of these oracles, that is, whether they come from Amos himself or from a later setting. Those against Tyre (1:9–10), Edom (1:11–12), and Judah (2:4–5) are often considered later additions. If they are later, they reflect the reinterpretation of Amos's words about Israel as applying to Judah. This kind of reinterpretation within the prophetic books themselves will be discussed later in this chapter.

6. For more on city gates see Philip J. King and Lawrence Stager, *Life in Biblical Israel,* Library of Ancient Israel (Louisville, KY: Westminster/John Knox, 2001), 234–36.

7. The classic work on treaty curses in the Hebrew prophets is Delbert R. Hillers, *Treaty Curses and the Old Testament Prophets,* Biblica et Orientalia 16 (Rome: Pontifical Biblical Institute, 1964). Amos's use of futility curses may indicate that he envisioned the relationship between Yahweh and Israel in terms of a covenant. However, covenant ideology does not play much of a role elsewhere in Amos and seems to be a later development under the influence of Deuteronomy. Amos was probably simply familiar with the language of curses, which were not limited to treaties. See Steven L. McKenzie, *Covenant* (St. Louis: Chalice, 2000).

8. Amaziah quoted Amos as saying that King Jeroboam would die by the sword (7:11). There is no such statement elsewhere in the book, though the threat in 7:9 that Yahweh would arise against the house of Jeroboam with a sword is close. Was Amaziah twisting Amos's words in order to sharpen his accusation? Was he paraphrasing? Or did Amos make such a pronouncement without its having been recorded in the book? Amos does not deny having threatened Jeroboam. According to 2 Kings 14:23–29; 15:8–12 the royal house of Jehu, to which Jeroboam belonged, fell during the reign of his son, Zechariah; Jeroboam himself apparently died peacefully.

9. See H. G. M. Williamson, *Variations on a Theme: King, Messiah and Servant in the Book of Isaiah* (Carlisle, UK: Paternoster, 1998). Williamson thinks that 2 Isaiah was responsible for the basic composition of Isaiah 1–39. See his *The Book Called Isaiah: Deutero-Isaiah's Role in Composition and Redaction* (Oxford: Clarendon, 1994).

10. Though they differ in certain details, the following commentaries offer helpful sketches of Micah's literary development: James L. Mays, *Micah: A Commentary,* Old Testament Library (Philadelphia: Westminster, 1976); William McCane, *The Book of Micah: Introduction and Commentary* (Edinburgh: T & T Clark, 1998); Hans Walter Wolff, *Micah: A Commentary,* trans. Gary Stansell (Minneapolis: Augsburg, 1990).

11. The reference in 1:6 to the fall of the Northern capital, Samaria, seems to place Micah in the last quarter of the eighth century, since Samaria fell to Assyria in 722 BCE. Some scholars find evidence of later editing in these chapters, especially in 2:12–13, which is positive in tone and looks forward to God gathering the exiles together again.

12. On the literary and thematic coherence of the book of Micah and the interplay of these themes see David Gerald Hagstrom, *The Coherence of the Book of Micah: A Literary Analysis,* Society of Biblical Literature Dissertation Series 89 (Atlanta: Scholars Press, 1988) and Mignon R. Jacobs, *The Conceptual Coherence of the Book of Micah,* supplements to *Journal for the Study for Old Testament* 322 (Sheffield: Sheffield Academic Press, 2001).

13. For such lists see Herbert Lockyer, *All the Messianic Prophecies of the Bible* (Grand Rapids: Zondervan, 1973) and J. Barton Payne, *Encyclopedia of Biblical Prophecy: The Complete Guide to Scriptural Predictions and Their Fulfillment* (San Francisco: Harper & Row, 1973).

14. We do not know anything more about this "son of Tabeel." The name Tabeel resembles the Aramaic for "no good" and may, therefore, be a pejorative imitation rather than a real name.

15. The Hebrew word ('almâh) referred to a young woman of marriageable age. It does not specifically mean "virgin," though young women of that age often were virgins. Similarly, the Greek translation of it (*parthenos*) could refer to a virgin, though it was not restricted to this meaning; it also meant "maiden."

16. H. G. M. Williamson, *Variations on a Theme,* 43.

17. The noun here is sometimes translated "stem" or "stock" as in the King James Version. But linguistic evidence indicates that the root meaning of the word is "to cut off," indicating that "stump" is the better translation of the noun.

18. The other "Servant Songs" are Isa. 42:1–4; 49:1–6; 50:4–9.

19. Isa 49:3. Some scholars regard this identification as secondary, because the name "Israel" is absent from some Hebrew manuscripts. At the very least, however, it shows that the servant was identified as Israel very early on in the textual transmission of Isaiah.

20. See the notes by J. J. M. Roberts on both of these passages in *The HarperCollins Study Bible* (San Francisco: Harper & Row, 1993).

21. For useful surveys of the topic and the questions involved see Hans Hübner, "New Testament, OT Quotations in the," *The Anchor Bible Dictionary*, vol. 4, 1096–104 and D. Moody Smith, "The Use of the Old Testament in the New," in *The Use of the Old Testament in the New and Other Essays: Studies in Honor of William Franklin Stinespring*, ed. James M. Efird (Durham, NC: Duke University Press, 1972), 3–65.

22. For instance, in Acts 15:17, James quotes from the LXX of Amos in support of the admission of Gentiles into Christianity: "in order that the rest of the peoples and all the nations over whom my name is called may seek the Lord." The Hebrew in Amos 9:12, however, has a very different sense, referring to Judah's rebuilding after the exile and its domination of the surrounding nations. It reads, "in order that [the people of Judah] may possess the remnant of Edom and all the nations which are called by my name."

23. Smith ("The Use of the Old Testament in the New," 20) writes that documents of contemporary Judaism "show that the ways in which the New Testament writers put the Old Testament to use are not at all unprecedented. While this usage may seem at places arbitrary enough, it is by and large neither more nor less arbitrary than the contemporary use of the Old Testament among Jews."

24. Williamson, *Variations on a Theme*, 143–44.

25. See Matt 13:14–15; Mark 4:12; Luke 8:10.

26. See Matt 2:23; Mark 1:9; Luke 1:26; 2:39; John 1:46.

27. Jesus's reference to the story of Jonah does not necessarily mean that the story actually happened any more than his telling of parables requires them to be actual occurrences. As we saw in the introduction, Jonah is satire, not history.

28. As in the case of Jesus's birthplace, it is possible that this detail was influenced by the prophecy in Hosea. In line with the techniques of history writing discussed earlier, the story of the flight to Egypt may have been invented as a way of presenting Jesus as embodying Israel. The citation of Hos 11:1 still exemplifies "fulfillment" that is in essence reinterpretation.

Chapter Three

1. James L. Crenshaw, *Urgent Advice and Probing Questions: Collected Writings on Old Testament Wisdom* (Macon, GA: Mercer, 1995), 2.

2. Ibid., 48–76.

3. Raymond C. Van Leeuwen, "Form Criticism, Wisdom, and Psalms 111–12," in *The Changing Face of Form Criticism for the Twenty-First Century*, ed. Marvin A. Sweeney and Ehud Ben-Zvi (Grand Rapids, MI: Eerdmans, 2003), 83.

4. James L. Crenshaw, *Old Testament Wisdom: An Introduction* (Atlanta: John Knox, 1981), 24–25.

5. Cf. Crenshaw, *Urgent Advice*, 2–3.

6. Ibid., 3.

7. Ibid., 4.

8. This reading is based on an emendation of the Hebrew text, which actually says, "Where there are no oxen, the crib is clean."

9. This is especially the case in 8:22, where the verb for "create" can also mean "engender."

10. John A. Wilson, trans., "The Instruction of Amen-em-Opet," in *Ancient Near Eastern Texts Relating to the Old Testament,* ed. James B. Pritchard (Princeton, NJ: Princeton University Press, 1969), 421–24.

11. See Crenshaw, *Urgent Advice*, 396–405.

12. Ibid., 399.

13. Some scholars think that 26:1–4 is an interruption by Job of Bildad's speech, which continues in 26:5–14, with Job then responding in chapter 27.

14. The Elihu speeches in chapters 32–37 are usually considered a later addition to the book. Elihu is the only character with an Israelite name. He is not mentioned elsewhere in the book or acknowledged by the other characters. The hymn to wisdom in chapter 28 is also typically considered an addition.

15. See James L. Crenshaw, "Job, Book of," *The Anchor Bible Dictionary*, vol. 3, 864–65.

16. As in Num. 22:22, 32; 1 Sam. 29:4; 2 Sam. 19:22 (Heb 19:23); 1 Kings 5:4 (Heb 5:18); 11:14, 23, 25; Ps. 109:6.

17. Job is difficult to date but most scholars place the book as it now stands in sixth century BCE or later, based on its language and thought. For a discussion of the date and other introductory matters of Job see Crenshaw, "Job," *The Anchor Bible Dictionary*, vol. 3, 858–68. On the meaning of the term *śāṭā* see Day, *An Adversary in Heaven*.

18. Specifically in 42:10–17. The prose section in 42:7–9 is dependent on the dialogues and cannot have been a part of the older folktale.

19. The NRSV rightly points out that the questions are ambiguous and might be translated as comparatives: "Can a person be considered more righteous than God? Can a human be purer than his/her maker?" The point about the sinfulness of humans remains in either case and is clarified by the following verses.

20. That is, after the speeches by Elihu, which are generally recognized as secondary.

21. For a detailed discussion of this matter see James L. Crenshaw, "Popular Questioning of the Justice of God in Ancient Israel," *Zeitschrift für die Alttestamentliche Wissenschaft* 83 (1970): 380–95.

22. In a series of studies beginning with his dissertation, Tremper Longman III has discussed the subgenre of Qoheleth. Longman focuses on a series of documents from ancient Mesopotamia that are fictional autobiographies. As the name implies, these works are all in the first person. Yet they were all written substantially later—sometimes by centuries—than the persons whose lives they purport to describe. They are, therefore, patently fictional.

23. Longman contends that Qoheleth exhibits the structure of a fictional autobiography in the first-person speech that comprises the book's main section. There is a brief introduction: "I, Qoheleth, was king over Israel in Jerusalem" (1:12). This is followed by a lengthy speech in which Qoheleth describes his search for meaning in various activities of life (1:13–6:9). After a brief transition (6:10–12), Qoheleth launches into wisdom advice and instruction comparable to portions of Proverbs (7:1–12:7). For other views of the structure of Qoheleth and a summary of this issues involved, see James L. Crenshaw, *Ecclesiastes: A Commentary* (Old Testament Library; Philadelphia: Westminster, 1987), 34–49.

24. Longman takes the material surrounding the main section of Qoheleth (1:1–11 and 12:8:12) as a frame added by a later author, because these passages refer to Qoheleth in the third person, and there is only one third-person reference to Qoheleth within the main body of the book (7:27). Longman views the composer of the framework as the book's real author, who quoted Qoheleth at length and then added his commentary and critique in the framework. Longman's real reason for adopting this position is theological. The main body of Qoheleth is largely skeptical, if not downright pessimistic, in outlook. Its message is that life is meaningless. This outlook on life in unacceptable to Longman, and he assigns the last theological word in the book to the much more positive framework author. In what follows, however, we will see far more inconsistency within the main body of Qoheleth than Longman admits.

25. Qoh 1:14; 2:11, 17; 3:19.

26. Qoh 12:13–14.

27. Qoh 2:24; 3:13; 5:18-19 [Heb 5:17–18]; 8:15; 9:9.

28. The list is that of Crenshaw, "Ecclesiastes, Book of," *The Anchor Bible Dictionary*, vol. 2, 272. For further discussion see his article, "Qoheleth in Recent Research," *Hebrew Annual Review* 7 (1984): 41–56.

29. Choon-Leong Seow, *Ecclesiastes: A New Translation with Introduction and Commentary,* Anchor Bible 18C (New York: Doubleday, 1997).

30. Ibid., 276.

31. Ibid., 294–95.

Chapter Four

1. For a more detailed recounting of the Millerite movement see Leon Festinger, Henry W. Riecken, and Stanley Schachter, *When Prophecy Fails* (Minneapolis: University of Minnesota Press, 1956), 12–23.

2. Hal Lindsey, *The Late Great Planet Earth* (Grand Rapids, MI: Zondervan, 1970), e.g., 42–54.

3. Zechariah Daniels, *The Free Gift: Second Coming 2016* (Chicago: JMB Productions, 2004).

4. Witness the "Left Behind" series of books and films by Tim LaHaye and Jerry B. Jenkins. For detailed discussions of apocalyptic movements throughout history, see *Apocalypticism in Western History and Culture*, ed. Bernard McGinn in *Encyclopedia of Apocalypticism*: vol. 2, and vol. 3, *Apocalypticism in the Modern Period and the Contemporary Age*, ed. Stephen J. Stein (New York: Continuum, 1998).

5. As demonstrated by Paul D. Hanson, *The Dawn of Apocalyptic* (Philadelphia: Fortress, 1975).

6. See Hanson, *Dawn*, 32–208.

7. Paul D. Hanson, "Apocalypticism," *The Interpreter's Dictionary of the Bible Supplementary Volume* (Nashville: Abingdon, 1976), 30.

8. Cf. Paul D. Hanson, *Old Testament Apocalyptic,* Interpreting Biblical Texts (Nashville: Abingdon, 1987), 35.

9. The book of Ezekiel (esp. chaps. 38–39) exemplifies symbolic visions of the future; Zechariah 1–6 illustrates interpretation by an angel; and examples of the destruction of the wicked in the present world order and the foundation of a new age may be found in Isa 24–27; Joel 2:28–3:21; Zech 12–14; Mal 3:13–4:6 (Heb 3:13–2).

10. See John J. Collins, *The Apocalyptic Imagination: An Introduction to Jewish Apocalyptic Literature,* 2nd ed. (Grand Rapids: Eerdmans, 1998).

11. The best known such lists were those compiled by Klaus Koch, *The Rediscovery of Apocalyptic,* Studies in Biblical Theology Second Series 22 (London: SCM, 1970), 24–33 and Philipp Vielhauer and Georg Strecker, "Apocalypses and Related Subjects," in Edgar Hennecke, Wilhelm Schneemelcher, and R. McL. Wilson, *New Testament Apocrypha,* rev. ed., vol. 2, (Louisville: Westminster/John Knox, 1992), 545–55. See also Greg Carey, "Introduction: Apocalyptic Discourse, Apocalyptic Rhetoric," in Greg Carey and L. Gregory Bloomquist, eds., *Vision and Persuasion: Rhetorical Dimensions of Apocalyptic Discourse* (St. Louis: Chalice, 1999), 4–5. For an overview of the phenomenon of apocalypticism and scholarly research on it see Mary Rose D'Angelo and E. Ann Matter, "Apocalypticism," in John H. Hayes, ed., *Dictionary of Biblical Interpretation* (Nashville: Abingdon, 1999), vol. 1, 40–44.

12. John J. Collins, "Introduction: Towards the Morphology of a Genre," *Semeia* 14 (1979): 9.

13. Collins (ibid., 13–15) identifies two main types of apocalypses based on whether they recount an otherworldly journey. Within each of these types he further identifies three subtypes according to the kind of eschatology and presence or absence of historical review.

14. Collins, *Apocalyptic Imagination*, 39.

15. Hanson, *Old Testament Apocalyptic*, 26.

16. Adela Yarbro Collins, "Introduction: Early Christian Apocalypticism," *Semeia* 36 (1986): 7.

17. David E. Aune, "The Apocalypse of John and the Problem of Genre, *Semeia* 36 (1986): 65–66.

18. Collins, *Apocalyptic Imagination*, 42.
19. David Hellholm, "The Problem of Apocalyptic Genre and the Apocalypse of John," *Semeia* 36 (1986): 27.
20. A point emphasized by Collins, *Apocalyptic Imagination*, 38.
21. Hanson, *Old Testament Apocalyptic*, 30.
22. Michael D. Coogan, *Stories from Ancient Canaan* (Philadelphia: Westminster, 1978), 27–47.
23. See John J. Collins, *Daniel with an Introduction to Apocalyptic Literature*, Forms of Old Testament Literature 20 (Grand Rapids: Eerdmans, 1984), 41.
24. An example of the "otherworldly" type is the apocryphal book of 1 Enoch, sections of which represent the earliest Jewish apocalyptic extant.
25. Hesiod, *Works and Days*, 1.109–201. See *Hesiod: The Homeric Hymns and Homerica*, trans. H. G. Evelyn-White, Loeb Classical Library 57 (Cambridge, MA: Harvard University Press, 1977). Hesiod actually includes five ages because he has inserted a non-metallic age between the bronze and iron ages as a way of incorporating Greek heroes, such as those of the Trojan war, into the scheme.
26. See the discussion and references in John J. Collins, *The Apocalyptic Vision of the Book of Daniel*, Harvard Semitic Monographs 16 (Missoula, MT: Scholars Press, 1977), 37–40. See also his "Daniel, Book of," *The Anchor Bible Dictionary*, vol. 2, 29–37.
27. See, for example, Pss 75:4, 5, 10; 89:23; 132:17.
28. Dan 9:27; 11:31; 12:11.
29. Scholars have come up with different possible lists of ten predecessors to Antiochus IV. However, the number 10 here is probably simply a round number intended to represent all those who ruled before him.
30. Gleason Archer, trans., *Jerome's Commentary on Daniel* (Grand Rapids: Baker, 1958), 15.
31. For more detail, see John J. Collins, *Daniel*, Hermeneia (Minneapolis: Fortress, 1993), 29–33.
32. There were several Persian kings named Darius. However, Darius I was the father of Xerxes I (Ahasuerus), not the reverse as claimed in Dan 9:1.
33. Other notorious problems are the claim of Dan 1:1 that Nebuchadnezzar laid siege to Jerusalem in the third year of King Jehoiakim (606 BCE) when both Babylonian records and other biblical texts (Jer 25:1) indicate that Nebuchadnezzar became king in 605 and that Jerusalem fell to the Babylonians in 587. See Collins, *Daniel*, 130–33. Also, the story about Nebuchadnezzar's madness (Dan 4) is based on traditions relating to Nabonidus (Collins, *Daniel*, 217–19).
34. The author here may be expressing a lack of confidence or support for the efforts of the Maccabees, who led a revolt against Antiochus. The story of the Maccabean revolt is narrated in the apocryphal book of 1 Maccabees.
35. See the discussion of Collins, *Daniel*, 394–98.
36. Ibid., 304–10.

37. Mark's version (Mark 13:14–16) is similar but lacks the reference to Daniel. Luke's version (Luke 21:20–21) differs more extensively and refers not to the "desolating sacrilege" but to armies surrounding Jerusalem.

38. E. B. Pusey, *Daniel the Prophet* (New York: Funk and Wagnalls, 1885), 75.

39. See Adela Yarbro Collins: *The Apocalypse* (Wilmington, DE: Michael Glazier, 1979), xii–xiii, and "The Book of Revelation," in *The Origins of Apocalypticism in Judaism and Christianity*, ed. John J. Collins, vol. 1 of *The Encyclopedia of Apocalypticism*, ed. Bernard McGinn, John J. Collins, and Stephen J. Stein (New York: Continuum, 1998), 384–414.

40. A. Yarbro Collins, *The Apocalypse*, xiii.

41. See A. Yarbro Collins, "Revelation, Book of," *The Anchor Bible Dictionary*, vol. 5, 702.

42. Ibid., 700–701.

43. J. J. Collins, *Apocalyptic Imagination*, 273.

44. Adela Yarbro Collins, "The Book of Revelation," in *The Origins of Apocalypticism in Judaism and Christianity*, ed. John J. Collins, vol. 1 of *The Encyclopedia of Apocalypticism* (New York: Continuum, 1998), 398.

45. Because they are not interpreted in the text, some scholars think that the references to the seven heads and ten horns with ten crowns both in 13:1 and in 12:3 are interpolations from 17:3. See David E. Aune, *Revelation 6–16*, Word Biblical Commentary 52B (Nashville: Thomas Nelson, 1998), 733.

46. See Aune, *Revelation 6–16*, 767–68.

47. The values of the letters in question are: $n = 50$, $r = 200$, $w = 6$, $q = 100$, $s = 60$. Thus, the longer form, נרון קסר = *nrwn qsr* has the value $50 + 200 + 6 + 50 + 100 + 60 + 200 = 666$. The shorter form lacks the second n and therefore has a value of 50 less or 616.

48. See John M. Court, "Millenarianism" in *A Dictionary of Biblical Interpretation*, eds. R. J. Coggins and J. L. Houlden (London: SCM, 1990), 459–61.

49. See the discussion and citations by G.-R. Beasley-Murray, *The Book of Revelation*, New Century Bible (London: Oliphants, 1974), 287–92.

50. Constantine moved the capital of the empire from Rome to Constantinople in 330 CE. Rome came under barbarian rule in 476 CE.

51. A. Yarbro Collins, "The Book of Revelation," *Encyclopedia of Apocalypticism* 1:412.

Chapter Five

1. See Richard M. Gummere, *Seneca: Epistles 1–65*, Loeb Classical Library (Cambridge, MA: Harvard, 1970).

2. See D. R. Shackleton Bailey, ed. and trans., *Cicero: Letters to Atticus*, 3 vols, Loeb Classical Library (Cambridge, MA: Harvard University Press, 1999).

3. All New Testament quotations in this chapter are taken from the NRSV.

4. Jerome Murphy-O'Connor, *Paul the Letter-Writer: His World, His Options, His Skills,* Good News Studies 41 (Collegeville, MN: Liturgical, 1995), 37.

5. There have been many attempts to classify ancient letters. The most recent and detailed study of this matter is Stanley K. Stowers, *Letter Writing in Greco-Roman Antiquity,* Library of Early Christianity (Philadelphia: Westminster, 1986), 49–173. Stowers has been criticized for failing to include many official and literary letters. The broad categorization followed here and much of the description of the categories is drawn from David E. Aune, *The New Testament in Its Literary Environment,* Library of Early Christianity (Philadelphia: Westminster, 1987), 161–62. Stowers's work remains especially useful for its categorization of types of private letters.

6. See George Kennedy, *New Testament Interpretation Through Rhetorical Criticism* (Chapel Hill, NC: University of North Carolina Press, 1984).

7. There was, of course, no New Testament yet. For a more detailed description of diatribes and homilies, see Aune, *The New Testament in Its Literary Environment,* 200–202.

8. Depending on whether the words "in Ephesus" in Eph 1:1 are original. They are missing in some of the best textual witnesses, leading to the suggestion that the letter was circular. It is important to recognize that the reference to churches at this point in time is somewhat anachronistic. These were loosely bound groups of believers, who did not yet have the organization usually associated with churches. I use the term "church," nevertheless, for the sake of convenience.

9. Adolf Deissmann, *Bible Studies,* trans. A. Grieve (Edinburgh: T & T Clark, 1901). See also his *Light from the Ancient East,* trans. L. R. M. Strachan, rev. ed. (London: Hodder & Stoughton, 1927).

10. Murphy-O'Connor, *Paul the Letter-Writer,* 44.

11. Aune, *The New Testament in Its Literary Environment,* 218. Aune cites the Muratonian Canon (ca. 170 CE) as alluding to the universal applicability of Paul's letters as well as Tertullian.

12. Tertullian, *Against Marcion,* 5.17.1. See *The Ante-Nicene Fathers,* vol. 3, ed. Alexander Roberts and James Donaldson, repr. (Grand Rapids, MI: Eerdmans, 1997).

13. A point also made by Aune, *The New Testament,* who states, "General letters (except Romans) tend to be both *late* and *pseudonymous.* . . . The tendency to understand Paul's letters in a general sense encouraged the production of pseudepigraphical letters (e.g., Ephesians, James, 1 Peter) in which past apostolic advice was understood as applicable to subsequent situations, and conditions."

14. Apparently, not all of Paul's letters survived, at least in their original form. 1 Cor 5:9 refers to a previous letter written by Paul to the Corinthians. Also, the "sorrowful letter" referred to in 2 Cor 2:4; 7:8 is considered lost by most New Testament scholars.

15. Murphy-O'Connor, *Paul the Letter-Writer,* 69.

16. See the recent book by M. Luther Stirewalt, Jr., *Paul, the Letter Writer* (Grand Rapids, MI: Eerdmans, 2003), esp. 25–55, which provides the basis for the following discussion.

17. Ibid., 46–47.

18. See Stowers, *Letter Writing in Greco-Roman Antiquity*, 153–65.

19. For details see S. Scott Bartchy, "Philemon, Epistle to," *The Anchor Bible Dictionary*, vol. 5, 305–10.

20. To judge from Col 4:17, which also mentions Archippus, Philemon was a resident of Colossae and probably a Phrygian.

21. See Bartchy, "Slavery (Greco-Roman)," *The Anchor Bible Dictionary*, vol. 6, 65–73. Also Dale B. Martin, *Slavery as Salvation: The Metaphor of Slavery in Pauline Christianity* (New Haven: Yale University Press, 1990), 1–49.

22. Hans Dieter Betz, *Galatians: A Commentary on Paul's Letter to the Churches in Galatia* (Hermeneia; Philadelphia: Fortress, 1979), 14, 24–25.

23. As Betz himself points out (Gal 6).

24. See esp. J. C. Hurd, *The Origin of 1 Corinthians* (London: SPCK, 1965), 61–82.

25. Richard A. Horsley, *1 Corinthians* (Abingdon New Testament Commentary; Nashville: Abingdon, 1998), 22.

26. But see the caveat of Richard E. Oster, "When Men Wore Veils to Worship: The Context of 1 Corinthians 11.4," *New Testament Studies* 34 (1988): 490–91. Oster points out that Crinagoras's complaint about Corinth's new inhabitants, from which New Testament scholars have drawn historical conclusions, comes from an angry Greek bemoaning the replacement of Greek culture with Roman.

27. Oster, "When Men Wore Veils" and "Use, Misuse and Neglect of Archaeological Evidence in Some Modern Works on 1 Cor (1 Cor 7:1–5; 8:10; 11:2-16; 12:14–26)," *Zeitschrift für die neutestamentliche Wissenschaft* 83 (1992): 52–73.

28. So Horsley, *1 Corinthians*, 152–57. Incidentally, the passage also has nothing to do with the Jewish practice of men covering their heads in prayer, which arose several centuries later.

29. Oster, "When Men Wore Veils," 505.

30. See Dale B. Martin, *The Corinthian Body* (New Haven: Yale University Press, 1995), esp. 229–49.

31. Cf. Joseph A. Fitzmyer, "A Feature of Qumrân Angelology and the Angels of 1 Cor. 11.10," *New Testament Studies* 4 (1957–58): 48–58.

32. Compare Epictetus, *Discourses*, 1.16.9–14. See *Epictetus: Discourses Book I*, trans., Robert F. Dobbin (Oxford: Clarendon, 1998).

33. Suetonius, *Lives of the Caesars, Claudius* 25.4.

34. See Thomas H. Tobin, SJ, *Paul's Rhetoric in its Contexts: The Argument of Romans* (Peabody, MA: Hendrickson, 2004), esp. 88–98, who contends that the genre of the body of letter is diatribe.

35. Ibid.

36. Cf. 2:1–4, 17; 3:1–4; 6:1–2; 7:7; 9:14, 19–24; 11:1, 19. As noted previously (n. 34), Tobin thinks that the genre of the entire letter body is diatribe.

37. The division is that of Charles D. Myers, Jr., "Romans, Epistle to the," *The Anchor Bible Dictionary*, vol. 5, 821–24.

38. Ibid., 827. See also Dale B. Martin, "Heterosexism and the Interpretation of Romans 1:18–32," *Biblical Interpretation* 3 (1995): 332–55.

39. Bartchy, "Slavery (Greco-Roman)," *The Anchor Bible Dictionary*, vol. 6, 65–73 and Martin, *Slavery as Salvation*, 1–49.

40. Brian K. Blount, "Reading and Understanding the New Testament on Homosexuality," in *Homosexuality and Christian Community*, ed. Choon-Leong Seow (Louisville: Westminster/John Knox, 1996), 29.

41. Dale B. Martin, "*Arsenokoitês* and *Malakos*: Meanings and Consequences," in *Biblical Ethics & Homosexuality: Listening to Scripture*, ed. Robert L. Brawley (Louisville: Westminster/John Knox, 1996), 130–31.

BIBLIOGRAPHY

Ackerman, James S. "Satire and Symbolism in the Song of Jonah." In *Traditions in Transformation: Turning Points in Biblical Faith,* Essays in honor of F. M. Cross edited by Baruch Halpern and Jon D. Levenson. Winona Lake: Eisenbrauns, 1981.

Allen, Leslie C. *The Books of Joel, Obadiah, Jonah, and Micah.* The New International Commentary, Old Testament. Grand Rapids: Eerdmans, 1958.

Archer, Gleason, trans. *Jerome's Commentary on Daniel.* Grand Rapids: Baker, 1958

Aune, David E. "The Apocalypse of John and the Problem of Genre." *Semeia* 36 (1986): 65–96.

———. *The New Testament in Its Literary Environment.* Library of Early Christianity. Philadelphia: Westminster, 1987.

———. *Revelation 1–5.* Word Biblical Commentary 52. Dallas: Word, 1987.

———. *Revelation 6–16.* Word Biblical Commentary 52B. Nashville: Thomas Nelson, 1998.

Bailey, Lloyd R. *Where Is Noah's Ark? Mystery on Mount Ararat.* Nashville: Abingdon, 1978.

———. *Noah: The Person and the Story in History and Tradition.* Personalities of the Old Testament. Columbia: University of South Carolina Press, 1989.

———. "Noah and the Ark." *The Anchor Bible Dictionary* 4. New York: Doubleday, 1992.

Bartchy, S. Scott. "Epistle to Philemon." *The Anchor Bible Dictionary* 5. New York: Doubleday, 1992.

———. "Slavery (Greco-Roman)." *The Anchor Bible Dictionary* 6. New York: Doubleday, 1992.

Beasley-Murray, G. R. *The Book of Revelation*. New Century Bible. London: Oliphants, 1974.

Betz, Hans Dieter. *Galatians: A Commentary on Paul's Letter to the Churches in Galatia*. Hermeneia. Philadelphia: Fortress, 1979.

Blount, Brian K. "Reading and Understanding the New Testament on Homosexuality." In *Homosexuality and Christian Community*, edited by Choon-Leong Seow. Louisville: Westminster/John Knox, 1996.

Bolin, Thomas M. *Freedom beyond Forgiveness: The Book of Jonah Re-Examined*. JSOT Supplements 236. Sheffield: Sheffield Academic Press, 1997.

Brettler, Marc Zvi. *The Creation of History in Ancient Israel*. London: Routledge, 1995.

Brown, Michael Joseph. *What They Don't Tell You: A Survivor's Guide to Biblical Studies*. Louisville: Westminster/John Knox, 2000.

Burrows, Millar. "The Literary Category of the Book of Jonah." In *Translating and Understanding the Old Testament: Essays in Honor of Herbert Gordon May*, edited by H. T. Frank and W. L. Reed. Nashville: Abingdon, 1970.

Buss, Martin. "Form Criticism, Hebrew Bible." *Dictionary of Biblical Interpretation* 1. Nashville: Abingdon, 1999.

Buttrick, George A., ed. *The Interpreter's Dictionary of the Bible*. 4 vols. Nashville: Abingdon, 1962.

Campbell, Antony F. S.J. "Form Criticism's Future." In *The Changing Face of Form Criticism for the Twenty-First Century*, edited by Marvin A. Sweeney and Ehud Ben-Zvi. Grand Rapids: Eerdmans, 2003.

Carey, Greg. "Introduction: Apocalyptic Discourse, Apocalyptic Rhetoric." In *Vision and Persuasion: Rhetorical Dimensions of Apocalyptic Discourse*, edited by Greg Carey and L. Gregory Bloomquist. St. Louis: Chalice, 1999.

Collins, John J. *The Apocalyptic Vision of the Book of Daniel*. Harvard Semitic Monographs 16. Missoula: Scholars Press, 1977

———. "Introduction: Towards the Morphology of a Genre." *Semeia* 14 (1979): 1–19.

———. "The Jewish Apocalypses." *Semeia* 14 (1979): 21–59.

———. *Daniel with an Introduction to Apocalyptic Literature*. Forms of Old Testament Literature 20. Grand Rapids: Eerdmans, 1984.

———. "Apocalypses and Apocalypticism: Early Jewish Apocalypticism." *The Anchor Bible Dictionary* 1. New York: Doubleday, 1992

———. "Daniel, Book of." *The Anchor Bible Dictionary* 2. New York: Doubleday, 1992, 29–37.

———. *Daniel*. Hermeneia. Minneapolis: Fortress, 1993.

———. *The Apocalyptic Imagination: An Introduction to Jewish Apocalyptic Literature*. 2nd ed. Grand Rapids: Eerdmans, 1998.

Coogan, Michael D. *Stories from Ancient Canaan*. Philadelphia: Westminster, 1978.

Court, John M. "Millenarianism." In *A Dictionary of Biblical Interpretation*, edited by R. J. Coggins and J. L. Houlden. London: SCM, 1990.

Craig, Kenneth M. *A Poetics of Jonah: Art in the Service of Ideology.* Columbia: University of South Carolina Press, 1993.

Crawford, Sidnie White. "Jonah." In *The Harper Collins Bible Commentary*, edited by James L. May, and others. San Francisco: HarperCollins, 1998.

Crenshaw, James L. "Popular Questioning of the Justice of God in Ancient Israel." *Zeitschrift für die Alttestamentliche Wissenschaft* 83 (1970): 380–95.

——. *Old Testament Wisdom: An Introduction*. Atlanta: John Knox, 1981.

——. *Qoheleth in Current Research. Hebrew Annual Review* 7 (1984): 41–56.

——. *Ecclesiastes: A Commentary.* Old Testament Library. Philadelphia: Westminster, 1987.

——. "Ecclesiastes." *The Anchor Bible Dictionary* 2. New York: Doubleday, 1992.

——. "Job." *The Anchor Bible Dictionary* 3. New York: Doubleday, 1992.

——. "Jonah." In *The Oxford Companion to the Bible*, edited by Bruce M. Metzger and Michael D. Coogan. New York: Oxford University Press, 1993.

——. *Urgent Advice and Probing Questions: Collected Writings on Old Testament Wisdom*. Macon, GA: Mercer, 1995.

D'Angelo, Mary Rose and E. Ann Matter. "Apocalypticism." *Dictionary of Biblical Interpretation*. 1:40–44. Nashville: Abingdon, 1999

Day, Peggy L. *An Adversary in Heaven: śāṭā in the Hebrew Bible*. Harvard Semitic Monographs 43. Atlanta: Scholars Press, 1988.

Deissmann, Adolf. *Bible Studies*. Trans. A. Grieve. Edinburgh: T & T Clark, 1901.

——. *Light from the Ancient East*. Trans. L. R. M. Strachan. Rev. ed. London: Hodder & Stoughton, 1927.

Dever, William G. *Recent Archaeological Discoveries and Biblical Research*. Seattle: University of Washington Press, 1990.

Dobbin, Robert F., trans. *Epictetus: Discourses Book I*. Oxford: Clarendon, 1998.

Evelyn-White, H. G., trans. *Hesiod: The Homeric Hymns and Homerica*. Loeb Classical Library. Cambridge: Harvard University Press, 1977.

Festinger, Leon, Henry W. Riecken, and Stanley Schachter. *When Prophecy Fails*. Minneapolis: University of Minnesota Press, 1956.

Feuillet, A. "Les sources du livre de Jonas." *Revue Biblique* 54 (1947): 161–86.

Finkelstein, Israel, and Neil Asher Silberman. *The Bible Unearthed: Archaeology's New Vision of Ancient Israel and the Origin of Its Sacred Texts*. New York: Free Press, 2001.

Finley, Moses I. *The Use and Abuse of History.* New York: Viking, 1975.

———. *Ancient History: Evidence and Models.* New York: Viking, 1986.

Fitzmyer, Joseph A. "A Feature of Qumrân Angelology and the Angels of 1 Cor. 11.10." *New Testament Studies* 4 (1957–58): 48–58.

Fox, Michael V. *Qoheleth and His Contradictions.* Bible and Literature Series 18. Sheffield: Sheffield Academic Press, 1989.

Fowler, Jeaneane D. *Theophoric Personal Names in Ancient Hebrew: A Comparative Study.* JSOT Supplements 49. Sheffield: JSOT, 1988.

Freedman, David Noel, ed. *The Anchor Bible Dictionary.* 6 vols. New York: Doubleday, 1992.

Good, Edwin M. *Irony in the Old Testament.* Sheffield: Almond, 1981.

Gowan, Donald E. *Daniel.* Abingdon Old Testament Commentary. Nashville: Abingdon, 2001.

Grayson, A. Kirk. "Nineveh." *The Anchor Bible Dictionary* 4. New York: Doubleday, 1992.

Grene, David, trans. *Herodotus: The History.* Chicago and London: University of Chicago Press, 1987.

Gummere, Richard M. *Seneca: Epistles 1–65.* Loeb Classical Library. Cambridge: Harvard University Press, 1970.

Hagstrom, David Gerald. *The Coherence of the Book of Micah: A Literary Analysis.* Society of Biblical Literature Dissertation Series 89. Atlanta: Scholars Press, 1988.

Halpern, Baruch. *The First Historians: The Hebrew Bible and History.* San Francisco: Harper & Row, 1988.

Halpern, Baruch, and Richard Elliott Friedman. "Composition and Paronomasia in the Book of Jonah." *Hebrew Annual Review* 4 (1998): 79–92.

Hanson, Paul D. *The Dawn of Apocalyptic.* Philadelphia: Fortress, 1975.

———. "Apocalypse, Genre." In *The Interpreter's Dictionary of the Bible Supplementary Volume*, edited by Keith Crim. Nashville: Abingdon, 1976.

———. "Apocalypticism." In *The Interpreter's Dictionary of the Bible Supplementary Volume*, edited by Keith Crim., Nashville: Abingdon, 1976

———. *Old Testament Apocalyptic.* Interpreting Biblical Texts. Nashville: Abingdon, 1987.

———. "Apocalypses and Apocalypticism: The Genre and Introductory Overview." *The Anchor Bible Dictionary* 1. New York: Doubleday, 1992

Hasel, Gerhard F. *Jonah: Messenger of the Eleventh Hour.* Mountain View, CA: Pacific Press, 1976.

Hayes, John H. *Dictionary of Biblical Interpretation.* 2 vols. Nashville: Abingdon, 1999.

Haynes, Stephen R. *Noah's Curse: The Biblical Justification of American Slavery*. New York: Oxford University Press, 2002.

Hellholm, David. "The Problem of Apocalyptic Genre and the Apocalypse of John." *Semeia* 36 (1986): 13–64.

Hillers, Delbert R. *Treaty Curses and the Old Testament Prophets*. Biblica et Orientalia 16. Rome: Pontifical Biblical Institute, 1964.

Horsley, Richard A. *1 Corinthians*. Abingdon New Testament Commentary. Nashville: Abingdon, 1998.

Hübner, Hans. "New Testament, OT Quotations in the." *The Anchor Bible Dictionary* 4. New York: Doubleday, 1992.

Huizinga, Johan. "A Definition of the Concept of History." In *Philosophy and History: Essays Presented to Ernst Cassirer,* edited by Raymond Klibansky and H. J. Paton. Oxford: Clarendon, 1936.

Hurd, J. C. *The Origin of 1 Corinthians*. London: SPCK, 1965.

Jacobs, Mignon R. *The Conceptual Coherence of the Book of Micah*. JSOT 322. Sheffield: Sheffield Academic Press, 1936.

Kennedy, George. *New Testament Interpretation Through Rhetorical Criticism*. Chapel Hill: University of North Carolina Press, 1984.

King, Philip J., and Lawrence Stager. *Life in Biblical Israel*. Library of Ancient Israel. Louisville: Westminster/John Knox, 2001.

King, Stephen. *On Writing: A Memoir of the Craft*. New York: Scribner, 2000.

Kipling, Rudyard. *Just So Stories: For Little Children*. London: Folio Society, 1991.

Knauf, Ernst Axel. "Ishmaelites." *The Anchor Bible Dictionary* 3. New York: Doubleday, 1992.

Knoppers, Gary N. "Greek Historiography and the Chronicler's History: A Reexamination." *Journal of Biblical Literature* 122 (2003): 627–50.

Koch, Klaus. *The Rediscovery of Apocalyptic*. Studies in Biblical Theology Second Series 22. London: SCM, 1970.

Lacoque, André, and Pierre-Emmanuel Lacoque. *Jonah: A Psycho-Religious Approach to the Prophet*. Columbia: University of South Carolina Press, 1990.

Landes, George M. "The Kerygma of the Book of Jonah: The Contextual Interpretation of the Jonah Psalm." *Interpretation* 21 (1967): 3–31.

———. "Jonah." In *The Interpreter's Dictionary of the Bible Supplementary Volume,* edited by Keith Crim. Nashville: Abingdon, 1976.

———. "Jonah: A *Māšāl*?" In *Israelite Wisdom: Theological and Literary Essays in Honor of Samuel Terrien,* edited by John G. Gammie and others. Missoula: Scholars Press, 1978.

Limburg, James. *Jonah: A Commentary*. Old Testament Library. Louisville: Westminster/John Knox, 1993.

Lockyer, Herbert. *All the Messianic Prophecies of the Bible.* Grand Rapids: Zondervan, 1973.

Long, V. Philips. *The Art of Biblical History.* Foundations of Contemporary Interpretation 5. Grand Rapids: Zondervan, 1994.

Longman, Tremper, III. *Fictional Akkadian Autobiography.* Winona Lake: Eisenbrauns, 1991.

———. *The Book of Ecclesiastes.* The New International Commentary, Old Testament. Grand Rapids: Eerdmans, 1998.

———. "Israelite Genres in Their Ancient Near Eastern Context." In *The Changing Face of Form Criticism for the Twenty-First Century,* edited by Marvin A. Sweeney and Ehud Ben-Zvi. Grand Rapids: Eerdmans, 2003.

Magonet, Jonathan. *Form and Meaning: Studies in Literary Techniques in the Book of Jonah.* Frankfurt: Peter Lang, 1976.

———. "Jonah." *The Anchor Bible Dictionary* 3. New York: Doubleday, 1992.

Marcus, David. *From Balaam to Jonah: Anti-prophetic Satire in the Hebrew Bible.* Brown Judaic Studies 301. Atlanta: Scholars Press, 1995.

Martin, Dale B. *Slavery as Salvation: The Metaphor of Slavery in Pauline Christianity.* New Haven: Yale University Press, 1990.

———. *The Corinthian Body.* New Haven: Yale University Press, 1995.

———. Heterosexism and the Interpretation of Romans 1:18–32. *Biblical Interpretation* 3 (1995): 332–55.

———. "*Arsenokoitês* and *Malakos*: Meanings and Consequences." In *Biblical Ethics & Homosexuality: Listening to Scripture,* edited by Robert L. Brawley. Louisville: Westminster/John Knox, 1996.

Mays, James L. *Micah: A Commentary.* Old Testament Library. Philadelphia: Westminster, 1976.

McCane, William. *The Book of Micah: Introduction and Commentary.* Edinburgh: T & T Clark, 1998.

McGinn, Bernard, John J. Collins, and Stephen J. Stein. *The Encyclopedia of Apocalypticism.* 3 vols. New York: Continuum, 1998.

McKenzie, Steven L. "The Jacob Tradition in Hosea 12.4–5." *Vetus Testamentum* 36 (1986): 311–22.

———. *The Trouble with Kings: The Composition of the Book of Kings in the Deuteronomistic History.* Supplements to *Vetus Testamentum* 42. Leiden: Brill, 1991.

———. *All God's Children: A Biblical Critique of Racism.* Louisville: Westminster/John Knox, 1997.

———. *Covenant.* Understanding Biblical Themes. St. Louis: Chalice, 2000.

———. *1–2 Chronicles.* Abingdon Old Testament Commentary. Nashville: Abingdon, 2004.

Meeks, Wayne, ed. *The HarperCollins Study Bible.* San Francisco: HarperCollins, 1993.

Murphy-O'Connor, Jerome. *Paul the Letter-Writer: His World, His Options, His Skills.* Good News Studies 41. Collegeville: Liturgical, 1995.

Myers, Charles D., Jr. "Romans." *The Anchor Bible Dictionary* 5. New York: Doubleday, 1992.

Neirynck, Frans. "Gospel, Genre of." In *The Oxford Companion of the Bible,* edited by Bruce M. Metzger and Michael D. Coogan. New York: Oxford University Press, 1993.

Nelson, Richard D. *The Historical Books.* Interpreting Biblical Texts. Nashville: Abingdon, 1998.

Noth, Martin. *Die israelitische Personennamen im Rahmen der gemeinsemitischen Namengebung.* Beiträge zur Wissenschaft vom Alten und Neuen Testament 3, 10. Stuttgart: Kohlhammer, 1928

———. *The Deuteronomistic History.* JSOT Supplements 15. Sheffield: JSOT Press, 1981.

Oster, Richard E. "When Men Wore Veils to Worship: The Context of 1 Corinthians 11.4." *New Testament Studies* 34 (1988): 481–505.

———. "Use, Misuse and Neglect of Archaeological Evidence in Some Modern Works on 1 Cor (1 Cor 7:1–5; 8:10; 11:2–16; 12:14–26)." *Zeitschrift für die Neutestamentliche Wissenschaft* 83 (1992): 52-73.

Payne, J. Barton. *Encyclopedia of Biblical Prophecy: The Complete Guide to Scriptural Predictions and Their Fulfillment.* San Francisco: Harper & Row, 1973.

Person, Raymond F., Jr. *Conversation with Jonah: Conversation Analysis, Literary Criticism, and the Book of Jonah.* JSOT Supplements 220. Sheffield: Sheffield Academic Press, 1996.

Pritchard, James B., ed. *Ancient Near Eastern Texts Relating to the Old Testament.* 3rd ed. Princeton, NJ: Princeton University Press, 1969.

Pusey, E. B. *Daniel the Prophet.* New York: Funk and Wagnalls, 1885.

Redford, Donald B. *Egypt, Canaan, and Israel in Ancient Times.* Princeton: Princeton University Press, 1992.

Roberts, Alexander, and James Donaldson, eds. *The Ante-Nicene Fathers.* vol. 3. Reprint. Grand Rapids: Eerdmans, 1997.

Romm, James. *Herodotus.* Hermes Books. New Haven: Yale University Press, 1998.

Sasson, Jack M. *Jonah.* Anchor Bible 24B. New York: Doubleday, 1990.

———. *Hebrew Origins: Historiography, History, Faith of Ancient Israel.* Chuen King Lecture Series. Theology Division, Chung Chi College, The Chinese University of Hong Kong. 2002.

Schmidt, Ludwig. *Jahwes Initiative: Studien zu Tradition, Interpretation und Historie in den Überlieferungen von Gideon, Saul und David.* Wissenschaftliche Monographien zum Alten und Neuen Testament 38. Neukirchen-Vluyn: Neukirchener Verlag, 1970.

Seow, Choon-Leong. *Ecclesiastes: A New Translation with Introduction and Commentary.* Anchor Bible 18C. New York: Doubleday, 1997.

Shackleton Bailey, D. R., ed. and trans. *Cicero: Letters to Atticus.* 3 vols. Loeb Classical Library. Cambridge: Harvard University Press, 1999.

Shank, Harold. *Minor Prophets.* The College Press NIV Commentary. Joplin: Collegeville, 2001.

Shea, Christopher. "Debunking Ancient Israel: Erasing History or Facing the Truth?" *The Chronicle of Higher Education* (Nov. 21, 1997): A12–14.

Simon, Uriel. *Jonah.* The JPS Bible Commentary. Philadelphia: JPS. 1999.

Smith, Charles Forster, ed. and trans. *Thucydides: History of the Peloponnesian War.* 4 vols. Loeb Classical Library. Cambridge: Harvard University Press, 1919.

Smith, D. Moody . "The Use of the Old Testament in the New." In *The Use of the Old Testament in the New and Other Essays: Studies in Honor of William Franklin Stinespring,* edited by James M. Efird. Durham, NC: Duke University Press, 1972.

Stirewalt, M. Luther, Jr. *Paul, the Letter Writer.* Grand Rapids: Eerdmans, 2003.

Stowers, Stanley K. *Letter Writing in Greco-Roman Antiquity.* Library of Early Christianity. Philadelphia: Westminster, 1986.

Stuart, Douglas. *Hosea-Jonah.* Word Biblical Commentary 31. Waco: Word, 1987.

Sweeney, Marvin A. *The Twelve Prophets I.* Berit Olam. Collegeville: Liturgical, 2000.

Sweeney, Marvin A., and Ehud Ben-Zvi, eds. *The Changing Face of Form Criticism for the Twenty-first Century.* Grand Rapids: Eerdmans, 2003.

Tigay, Jeffrey. *The Evolution of the Gilgamesh Epic.* Philadelphia: University of Pennsylvania Press, 1982.

Trible, Phyllis. *God and the Rhetoric of Sexuality.* Overtures to Biblical Theology. Philadelphia: Fortress, 1978.

———. *Rhetorical Criticism: Context, Method, and the Book of Jonah.* Guides to Biblical Scholarship. Minneapolis: Fortress, 1994.

Usher, Stephen, trans. *Dionysius of Halicarnassus: The Critical Essays in Two Volumes.* Loeb Classical Library. Cambridge: Harvard University Press, 1974.

Van Leeuwen, Raymond C. "Form Criticism, Wisdom, and Psalms 111–12." In *The Changing Face of Form Criticism for the Twenty-First Century,* edited by Marvin A. Sweeney and Ehud Ben-Zvi. Grand Rapids: Eerdmans, 2003.

Van Seters, John. "The Problem Childlessness in Near Eastern Law and the Patriarchs of Israel." *Journal of Biblical Literature* 87 (1968): 401–8.

————. *In Search of History: Historiography in the Ancient World and the Origins of Biblical History.* New Haven: Yale University Press, 1983.

Veyne, Paul. *Did the Greeks Believe in Their Myths? An Essay in the Constitutive Imagination.* Translated by Paula Wissing. Chicago: The University of Chicago Press, 1988.

Vielhauer, Philipp, and Georg Strecker. "Apocalypses and Related Subjects." In Edgar Hennecke, Wilhelm Schneemelcher, and R. McL. Wilson, *New Testament Apocrypha.* Rev. ed. Vol. 2. Louisville: Westminster/John Knox, 1992.

————. "Apocalyptic in Early Christianity: Introduction." In Edgar Hennecke, Wilhelm Schneemelcher, and R. McL. Wilson, *New Testament Apocrypha.* Rev. ed. Vol. 2. Louisville: Westminster/John Knox, 1992.

Vorster, Willem S. "Gospel Genre." *The Anchor Bible Dictionary* 2. New York: Doubleday, 1993.

Wall, Robert W. "Introduction to Epistolary Literature." In *The New Interpreter's Bible* 10. Nashville: Abingdon, 2002.

Wallace, Howard N. "The Oracles Against the Israelite Dynasties in 1 and 2 Kings." Biblica 67 (1986): 21–40.

Wellhausen, Julius. *Prolegomena to the History of Ancient Israel.* Gloucester: Peter Smith, 1973.

Whitt, William D. "The Jacob Traditions in Hosea and Their Relation to Genesis." *Zeitschrift für die alttestamentliche Wissenschaft* 103 (1991): 18–43.

Williamson, H. G. M. *The Book Called Isaiah: Deutero-Isaiah's Role in Composition and Redaction.* Oxford: Clarendon, 1994.

————. *Variations on a Theme: King, Messiah and Servant in the Book of Isaiah.* Carlisle, UK: Paternoster, 1998.

Wilson, Robert R. *Genealogy and History in the Biblical World.* Yale Near Eastern Researches 7. New Haven: Yale University Press, 1977.

Wolff, Hans Walter. *Obadiah and Jonah: A Commentary.* Translated by M. Kohl. Minneapolis: Augsburg, 1986.

————. *Micah: A Commentary.* Translated by Gary Stansell. Minneapolis: Augsburg, 1990.

Yarbro Collins, Adela. "The Early Christian Apocalypses." *Semeia* 14 (1979): 61–121.

————. "Introduction: Early Christian Apocalypticism." *Semeia* 36 (1986): 1–11.

————. "Apocalypses and Apocalypticism: Early Christian." *The Anchor Bible Dictionary.* New York: Doubleday, 1992.

————. "The Book of Revelation." In *The Origins of Apocalypticism in Judaism and Christianity,* edited by John J. Collins. *The Encyclopedia of Apocalypticism,* vol. 1. New York: Continuum, 1998.

INDEX